THE FAMILY AT HOME

THE
FAMILY AT HOME

OR

FAMILIAR ILLUSTRATIONS

OF

VARIOUS DOMESTIC DUTIES

GORHAM D. ABBOTT
Author of *Early Piety Illustrated*

Solid Ground Christian Books
Birmingham, Alabama USA

Solid Ground Christian Books
715 Oak Grove Road
Birmingham, AL 35209
205-443-0311
sgcb@charter.net
http://solid-ground-books.com

THE FAMILY AT HOME
Familiar Illustrations of Domestic Duties

Gorham Abbott (1807-1874)

Taken from 1834 edition by Crocker & Brewster, Boston

Solid Ground Classic Reprints

First printing of new edition March 2007

Cover work by Borgo Design, Tuscaloosa, AL
Contact them at borgogirl@bellsouth.net

Cover image is from the frontispiece of the original work.

ISBN: 1-59925-111-6

NOTICE.

The following volume was placed in my hands by one of the most active members of the Executive Committee of the London Religious Tract Society, with an earnest request, that I would introduce it to the American Christian community. And I do this the more readily, and with more pleasure, from the conviction which I have, that it is calculated to shed a most happy influence over the *relative duties* of domestic life.

It seems to me, so far as I am able to understand the *spirit* of the Bible, that more is implied in the religious obligations involved in the *family tie*, than is ordinarily recognized at the present day.

If we look back upon the history of the world, with a view to discover the principles of the government of God from his dealings with men, there is evidently no unimportant design in the arrangement, which he has constituted, for dividing the whole race into distinct and separate family circles. This is equally obvious, whether we regard the nature of the relations which are thus established, or whether we reflect upon the consequences, which have grown out of them, as they are developed in every page of history, sacred or profane.

Perhaps we have no certain assurance, that, even if our first parents had continued faithful and obedient, *their children* would have followed their example, and that all successive generations of parents and children, in their turn, down to the end of time, would have perpetuated the example and the imitation of parental and filial obedience to the divine commands, and consequently have secured the enjoyment of divine favor. But of this we are certain, that, among every nation, kindred, tongue and people, the example of *disobedience* has been, and certainly will be followed, except where Sovereign Mercy interposes and rescues the parent or the child from the deadly influence of the *examples of sin*, which they have witnessed and imitated.

It is perfectly evident, in the patriarchal days, that God regarded the head of the family as, in some measure at least, responsible for the religious character of the whole household. He was to be the representative of Jehovah himself, in making known to the *whole domestic circle* the moral duties and ceremonial observances, which the Almighty had enjoined. He was, in this capacity, to act as the family Prophet. In offering the sacrifices, and in leading the devotions of the social circle, the head of the family was obviously the family Priest. And every where, the authority of the master of the house is manifest to have been supreme. He was, to all intents and purposes, the *absolute King*. The movements of all that appertained to the Patriarch were directed by his will. And guilt in the family was guilt and shame upon his head. The consequences of disobedience and sin, not the offender alone, but the parent and all the family were to share.

In conformity with this view, the sin of Esau, in selling his birthright, appears in a stronger and clearer light. Not only did he alienate from himself the birthright of an earthly inheritance, conveyed by primogeniture, but he *lightly esteemed* the sacred and priestly prerogative of the head of the household. And for this it was, that his story stands so conspicuous in the oracles of God, as an instance of the guilt of *such sin* in the eyes of the Father of all, for future generations to ponder and avoid.

A most striking proof of the peculiar manner in which the family relation is regarded by the Lord appears in the promise to the Father of the Faithful—" In thee shall all the *families* of the earth be blessed."

Whatever may tend to turn the attention of God's people to this subject, must be considered as a token for good. The multiplied avocations of the religious world at the present day, which are calculated to divert the mind from the duties, responsibilities, and privileges, that lie appropriately " at home," need some restraining influence. There is danger of diverting our Christian sympathies, efforts and prayers, unduly away from our homes. This vineyard should be sacredly cultivated.

This book, we hope and believe, will be found a useful and interesting volume. And we commend it to the kind blessing of Him, who is the God of all the families of the earth.

On putting the present volume to press, it was ascertained, that another work was announced in Philadelphia, under the title of " The Family Book," which was the original title of this work. In order to prevent mistakes, the name of this was changed. Appropriate articles from different sources have been added, so that the work is nearly double the size of the original English copy.

GORHAM D. ABBOTT.

Boston, Dec. 22, 1833.

Contents

Introduction		9
Chapter I –	*My Family and Friends*	12
Chapter II –	*The Sutton Family*	15
Chapter III –	*Deference to Parents*	33
Chapter IV –	*Speculation and Suretiship*	41
Chapter V –	*Self-Conceit*	45
Chapter VI –	*Punctuality*	49
Chapter VII –	*Procrastination*	52
Chapter VIII –	*Decision of Character*	58
Chapter IX –	*Mutual Forbearance*	60
Chapter X –	*Maxims on Waste*	61
Chapter XI –	*Female Dress*	64
Chapter XII –	*Sobriety and Moderation*	68
Chapter XIII –	*Nursing the Sick*	75

CONTENTS

Chapter XIV –	*Health and Sickness*	80
Chapter XV –	*Accidents*	92
Chapter XVI –	*Looking for Things in Wrong Places*	97
Chapter XVII –	*Good Thoughts in the Midst of Business*	99
Chapter XVIII –	*Where There's a Will There's a Way*	101
Chapter XIX –	*Correcting Mistakes*	105
Chapter XX –	*Conquest of Evil Tempers*	106
Chapter XXI –	*Ill-gotten Goods*	111
Chapter XXII –	*Removals - Reasons Against it*	114
Chapter XXIII –	*Providence – Maxims*	117
Chapter XXIV –	*Peace and Forgiveness*	119
Chapter XXV –	*Kindness Among Neighbors*	125
Chapter XXVI –	*Self-Denial – to be Cultivated*	129
Chapter XXVII –	*Usefulness – How to be Useful*	130
Chapter XXVIII –	*Courtship and Marriage*	135
Chapter XXIX –	*Care of Children*	141
Chapter XXX –	*Family Prayer – Duty and Benefits*	154
Chapter XXXI –	*Observance of the Sabbath*	160

CONTENTS

Chapter XXXII –	Advice to Young Tradesmen	167
Chapter XXXIII –	Helping One Another	187
Chapter XXXIV –	Changing Places	189
Chapter XXXV –	Superstition	190
Chapter XXXVI –	Housekeeper's Chapter of Sundries	194
Chapter XXXVII –	Reverence to the Aged	202
Chapter XXXVIII –	Jesting, Foolish Sports etc.	210
Chapter XXXIX –	Christian Patriotism	214
Chapter XL –	Good and Ill Reports	216
Chapter XLI –	Companions and Secrets	217
Chapter XLII –	The Government of the Tongue	220
Chapter XLIII –	Reading – Advantages and Dangers	226
Chapter XLIV –	Common Sense – Its Value	229
Chapter XLV –	Politeness – A Christian Virtue	231
Chapter XLVI –	Help and Pity	237
Chapter XLVII –	Maxims Against Sin	239
Chapter XLVIII –	Conscience – A Blessing and Power	240
Chapter XLIX –	Maxims on Self-examination	243

CONTENTS

Chapter L –	Sayings on Repentance	245
Chapter LI –	The Awful State of a Wicked Man	246
Chapter LII –	Sickness, Recovery, Death	247
Chapter LIII –	True Riches – Sayings Worth Remembering	253
Chapter LIV –	Crosses and Afflictions	255
Chapter LV –	The Widow and the Fatherless	259
Chapter LVI –	Christian Contentment and Cheerfulness	264
Chapter LVII –	Hints for Young Persons	275
Chapter LVIII –	Rules for Daily Conduct	279
Chapter LIX –	Brothers and Sisters	281
Chapter LX –	Decision in Religion	288
Chapter LXI –	Consistency with Religious Profession	290
Chapter LXII –	Advice for Children	297
Chapter LXIII –	Remarks on Religious Education	309
Chapter LXIV –	Rich and Poor	318
Chapter LXV –	My Own Way	337
Chapter LXVI –	Only for Once	348
Chapter LXVII –	Instability of Religion	356

THE FAMILY AT HOME.

INTRODUCTION.

THERE is a well-known saying—"He that would end as his father ended, must begin as his father begun."—If the father through life acted wisely and well, the children cannot do better than follow his example. But it is possible that, in passing through life, the parents have been convinced of many errors; perhaps have smarted for their folly, and become wiser by bitter experience. In such a case, if the parents have candor and humility enough to point out to their children the mistakes into which they have fallen, with the inconveniences they have suffered in consequence, and the advantages they have found in correcting their sentiments and altering their habits, then the wisdom of the children will appear, not in blindly following their parents through all their errors, but in listening to their warnings, in avoiding their mistakes, and so arriving at as good a conclusion as their parents, without having so many painful steps to retrace. Such an act of parental kindness I have often wished to perform for my dear children; and with that view, I have long been in the habit of penning down such maxims and hints as I have gleaned in passing through life—some of them gathered from the lips of my parents or other friends; others resulting from observation, or experience of the inconveniences resulting from an improper course of conduct. "Experience keeps a dear school; but fools will learn in no other." I hope my children will not be guilty of such folly, but will be glad to take advantage of the experience of others.

The first step to obtaining true wisdom for ourselves, or imparting useful instruction to others, is to obtain a clear insight into human nature; to keep constantly in view our own depravity and the corruption of our hearts, as the great source of all our mistakes, both concerning the interests of time and eternity. We are too apt to look upon idleness, extravagance, neglect, incivility, and peevishness, as accidental faults, which stand alone, and which are to be corrected by arguing against this or that particular vice or folly; but the fact is, they are all so many streams issuing from a corrupt fountain, and the only effectual cure will be found in purifying the fountain. If the heart be renewed by the grace of God, though lesser faults may for a time be overlooked, yet, when they are fairly brought before the notice of the individual, they will be regarded in the light of *sins against God*, and on that ground steadfastly and successfully resisted. It is quite right that people should see the inconvenience and mischief resulting from improper conduct; and we have great reason to be thankful that sound policy is always on the side of duty, and that godliness is found "profitable unto all things, having the promise of the life that now is, and of that which is to come:" but then we must remember, that worldly interest is but a very inferior motive. The promise of advantage in this life, is to godliness and the minor virtues that godliness brings along with it—not to the minor virtues detached from godliness. Besides, in point of fact, they very seldom, if ever, are really separated. We sometimes see ungodly persons who are cleanly, industrious, frugal, and prosperous; but then there is so much ill temper and peevishness mingled with these good qualities, as deprives them, and those around, of the comfort their circumstances would lead us to suppose they enjoyed; or perhaps there is such a miserly spirit as embitters all; or such a worldly spirit as renders the thought of death dreadful, as the period which will terminate all these pleasures, and give them nothing better in their

INTRODUCTION. 11

stead; or there is such a self-righteous spirit, as induces persons really to suppose that heaven is their just due, as a reward for their industry, decency, and frugality in managing their little worldly affairs. One way or other it will surely be seen, that there is no complete character except the true Christian—and he, alas! is very far from perfect. There are two or three principles, however, constantly operating on his mind, which tend to secure that uniformity of character, which men of the world never attain, and for want of which, they are never thoroughly comfortable. In the first place, the Christian sees himself a *sinner*, unworthy of every good thing, and deserving every thing evil: this makes him humble, contented, and thankful. Then he habitually remembers that he is accountable to God for every moment of time, and every atom of worldly possession and influence with which he is intrusted. This teaches him carefully and diligently to employ all in the best possible way, so as to promote the happiness of his fellow-creatures, and the glory of God. Besides this, he habitually considers himself as only a passenger through this world to a better. This is the best guard against worldly-mindedness, and, at the same time, a great support under the sorrows and trials of life. Then, again, feeling that he is indebted for all his comforts here, and for all his hopes of heaven hereafter, to the free mercy of God in Jesus Christ, he finds the love of Christ constraining him in every thing so to live, as to glorify the Saviour, and to bring others to love and serve him too. The person who is habitually governed by these principles, will most successfully pursue the study of "whatsoever things are true, whatsoever things are honest, whatsoever things are pure, whatsoever things are lovely and of good report," and will most effectually secure his own happiness in this life, and the happiness of those around him. I therefore wish my children to remember, that, though I may often set down some particular instance of conduct, and the consequences resulting from it, it is my habitual conviction,—that whatever is bad in conduct flows from the inward depravity of the heart, and whatever is really good flows from the renewing influences of the Holy Spirit on the heart, making the tree good, that the fruit also may be good; moreover, that, though people without religion may act wisely in some particulars, there is nothing uniformly and permanently valuable in character, but what springs from Christian principles.

Being, as I have already observed, chiefly indebted to the instructions of my parents and friends for any useful knowledge I may be able to impart to my children and others, and not wishing to receive credit for what does not belong to me, I shall first introduce my reader to the acquaintance of those friends, and then proceed to give some of their maxims, and, when I can recollect them, the occasions of their being communicated.

CHAP. I.

MY FAMILY AND FRIENDS.

My parents were decent, respectable people, in a plain way, and spared no labor nor expense for the good of their children. My father had a laborious employment, and he was often exposed to night-watching and severe weather; but his health was good, and his pay according to his labor. My mother was one of the most cleanly, notable housewives in the town; and as both were frugal, industrious, and managing, our house and garden always looked creditable and comfortable, and our family was reckoned, among the neighbors, as "very well to do." I dare say, when we children were little, our parents had many sharp struggles to make both ends meet, which we little thought of at the time,— perhaps never thought of at all till we came to have families of our own. However, they brought us up in credit and comfort, and contrived to give us a better education than had fallen to their own lot. We each had two or three years' instruction at an evening school, where we learned to read, write, and cast accounts; besides which, the boys, as they grew up, were apprenticed to trades, and our good mother instructed us girls in household business, plain work, and knitting.

My elder sisters went into families. They were much respected by their employers, and scarcely ever changed their places, except to take a higher department in the same family. In course of time, both of them were respectably settled in life, and enabled to assist our dear parents in their declining years, which they justly considered but a small return for the benefits conferred on their childhood and youth, which, indeed, had laid the foundation of their prosperity through life.

My eldest brother was as steady as old Time. I scarcely ever remember his being blamed, or exciting an anxious feeling in the minds of our parents. My second brother was of a more fickle, roving turn; and they were often afraid, lest, by some rash, imprudent step, he should blast his own comfort, and disappoint their hopes—and indeed he was more than once on the point of doing so : but, with all his faults, he was a lad of principle. He would listen to the counsel of friends; and if a thing was pointed out to him as sinful and imprudent, he would conquer himself, and give it up. I need not say he had cause to rejoice in having done so. My youngest brother was, in some respects, the most highly favored of the family; for, in addition to the instructions we all enjoyed, in his childhood, a Sunday-school was set up in our village, of which he was one of the first scholars. The instructions imparted to him were a great blessing to the whole family; for, though our parents were conscientious, inquiring people, their advantages had been very limited, and their views of divine truth very imperfect. But the excellent friends who established the Sunday-school, and of whom I shall often have occasion to speak, in that and other plans of Christian usefulness, were the means of leading many, both parents and children, to a knowledge of the truth as it is in Jesus; and to their instrumentality, under God, I must ascribe it that my

THE FAMILY AT HOME.

dear parents, in their later years, were brought to know the way of God more perfectly, and to discern more clearly the glory and the authority of the gospel; and I trust not one of their children have been left strangers to its saving power. In religious things, my dear parents were pleasing illustrations of those sayings of holy writ—" Then shall we know, if we follow on to know the Lord "—" Though thy beginning be but small, thy latter end shall greatly increase "—" The path of the just is as the shining light, which shineth more and more unto the perfect day." Good books, lent by our excellent friends, became the delightful companions of my dear father's solitary labors. He read them with prayer, and he was enabled to " learn, mark, and inwardly digest " the sacred truths they contained. Our evenings were happily spent in listening to his profitable remarks—in hearing little Edward repeat the lessons appointed him, or the good instructions received in the Sunday-school—in searching the Scriptures whether these things were so—and in praying that the Holy Spirit would continually enlighten our minds, to discern the truth as it is in Jesus.

I have told you how the rest of the family were disposed of. I must just add, that, as we grew up, my mother often went out to ironing or household work, and occasionally to nursing. It was therefore necessary for me to remain at home, to make the house comfortable for my father, to keep the boys in order, and to have things in order against my mother's return. I took to my needle, and was pretty quick in imitating whatever I saw in that department. So I got pretty good employment both in taking in work at home, and going out, when mother could spare me, to work in various families.

My father died of a hurt in his back in the prime of life. He was many months confined to the house, during which time, he exemplified much of the power of true religion. After his death, my mother, brother Edward, and myself, lived happily together, till Edward was settled in his master's house as foreman; and about the same time I was settled in life, when my dear mother took up her abode with me, and, as my children well know, proved a great blessing to the family.

CHAP. II.

THE SUTTON FAMILY.

I WILL next give you such particulars as I have been able to collect of the excellent and judicious friends, to whom I have already alluded. On retiring from business, Mr. and Mrs. Sutton settled in the country, and they were in comfortable, moderate circumstances, but not what might be reckoned wealthy. Had they been intent on obtaining a large fortune, they would most likely have remained longer in a flourishing business; but they resolved rather to be content with moderation, and to retreat from the busy world, that they might have more leisure to devote to the cultivation of religion in their own souls, and to exert themselves for the good of their fellow-creatures. Accordingly, having seen their eldest daughter comfortably married, and given up business to two sons, they came, with two younger daughters and one little boy, to settle in our village; and many have had reason to be thankful that ever they came. Though the good old people have been dead many years, and the young ones settled far away, their names are still held in grateful remembrance; and perhaps some, who little think it, are to this day indebted to them for the comfort of a decent, respectable servant, or of a prudent, managing wife. It was my happiness, when a girl, to be often employed in this excellent family, by which means I had frequent opportunities of observing their good ways; and when, in course of years, I settled in life, and began house-keeping for myself, the good old lady often paid me a visit, and gave me such advice and admonitions as I have thought worth laying up for children's children. It seemed to be the constant study of this worthy family, how they might benefit others: there was no case of sorrow or suffering to which they did not attempt to afford relief. For this purpose they not only freely gave of their substance, but they spared no pains to put people in a way of bettering their own condition. It is surprising to observe how much every one's condition, under God, depends on himself; and how much things may be bettered by, as the saying is, taking hold of the tool at the right end. There was a wealthy man in the place, a kind-hearted, well-meaning man in his way, and who, as I have heard, had many more thousands a year than Mr. Sutton had hundreds; but which of them did most good among the poor? The latter, ten to one. The former, it is true, never refused to give relief to any case of distress, real or pretended; but then he did not trouble himself to go among the people, and find out the causes of their distress, and put them upon exerting themselves in the best way, and bringing up their families in an orderly, respectable and religious manner.

This good work, in our village, chiefly rested with Mr. and Mrs. Sutton: they were indefatigable in it, and, by this means, they were greater benefactors to the poor than if they had lavished among them thousands a year without discrimination and without personal exertion. Indeed, after they came into the village, what was otherwise given in charity was turned to much better account than it was before, for people often consulted them, and always attended to their recommendation.

When we see good fruit, we generally feel an interest in knowing something about the nature of the tree that produced it; and my children will, like myself, be inclined to inquire by what principles this amiable family were influenced and regulated, and what was the source of the excellency they discovered. I have already sufficiently intimated that it was a religious family; I may add, that, from what I constantly saw and heard among them, I was first led to form an idea what true religion is.

I have mentioned being frequently employed in the house

at needlework: besides this, I have several times travelled with the family; and once I was in the house several months together, on account of the dangerous illness of the youngest Miss Sutton. For several weeks, my mother, a domestic, named Mary, and myself, took turns in sitting up with the young lady; thus we had many opportunities of seeing and hearing what was good, and I do hope it was made a great blessing to us.

For the first three weeks, Miss Sutton was scarcely at all sensible: during that time her affectionate parents were filled with the deepest distress and anxiety, which, as we could find, both from their conversation and prayers, arose not so much from her state of suffering, or even the prospect of losing her, as from a deep concern to be assured of her everlasting safety and welfare. This was often a matter of surprise to my mother and myself; indeed there were many remarks made, and many practices adopted in this family, which we could not at all understand; and my mother used to think they were rather to blame in speaking so plainly about death and preparation for it, lest it should alarm the poor young lady. We were, however, soon convinced that, if the *soul* and *eternity* are of real importance, the attention paid to them was not greater than the subject justly demanded.

Old Mary, and Robert the gardener, had lived in the family a great many years. Robert had been gardener to Mr. Sutton's father, and, on his death, from attachment to the family, lived with Mr. Sutton, in the city, until his retiring from business to live in the country again placed him in a situation more agreeable to his early habits. Mary also had been in the family ever since Mr. Sutton's marriage. Both were completely identified with all the interests of the family, and seemed to look on the young people almost as if they were their own children. Old Robert was always on the watch, when any one came out of the sick room, to inquire what sort of a night his dear young lady had passed, or to offer choice flowers, or fresh ripe fruit, which he hoped she might fancy.

One evening, we were all sent down stairs to supper, while Mr. and Mrs. Sutton remained with their daughter. Old Robert began the conversation by asking my mother whether she thought there were any hopes of Miss Harriet's recovery. Mother replied, she had very little hope, but there was no certainty: she had seen persons still worse who yet had been restored.

Robert.—" I am sure many, many fervent prayers ascend on her behalf; and we know that God is a God hearing and answering prayer."

Old Mary.—" I am sure I, for one, should be most truly thankful for her recovery; and yet I pray more earnestly still, and so do her dear parents, that she may be enabled to leave some decided testimony of her safety for eternity. Dear child! she knows what is necessary to a sinner's salvation, and if she might but express that *her* mind is fixed on the Rock of Ages, I could resign her, and so could master and mistress. If the soul is safe, it little matters whether death come in youth or age. But it is not for us to dictate. She has been the child of many fervent prayers; she has been instructed in the way of salvation, and she has had holy examples set before her. We may hope that the Lord is working on her mind, though she is not capable of expressing it; yet it is very natural that her anxious parents should long to know from her own lips the state of her mind at this solemn period."

Mother.—" I wonder, for my part, that they should be so anxious on that particular: there is no doubt but what she is very safe. If she is not fit to go, what will become of thousands? Think how well she has been brought up; and so amiable and well behaved; and so good to the poor! 'Tis hard parting, to be sure, but I wish every child of mine were as fit to go. It is a pity her parents should distress themselves about it. If she had not been so good as she has been, yet God Almighty is very merciful; but she, dear innocent young creature, is sure to go to heaven."

Mary.—" Ah, my friend, these things cannot satisfy the

minds of her parents. Amiable and good as she has been,—and there could scarcely be a child more dutiful and amiable,—the Bible tells us we are all sinners in the sight of God; and except we believe on the Lord Jesus Christ for life and salvation, we must perish."

Mother.—"And do you suppose she does not believe on the Lord Jesus Christ?"

Mary.—" I have no doubt she believes that what the Bible says about him is true; but what we are anxious to know is, that she feels *herself* to be a lost, perishing sinner, and in deep concern commits her soul into the hands of the Lord Jesus, to be saved in his own appointed way. This is a very different thing from believing in a general, careless manner. If we believe to the saving of the soul, we apply to the Lord Jesus Christ, feeling that we need his salvation, as much as if we were the only beings who had sinned, and needed a Saviour; and we cannot rest satisfied without a well-grounded confidence and heartfelt experience of his salvation.

" You know, now Miss Harriet is sick, we are not satisfied with knowing that the doctor is a skilful man, and that he has plenty of excellent medicines in his shop, but we apply to him, and desire that he would come himself, and give his advice in this particular case, and we get the dear young lady to take the medicines he prescribes. So, every sinner must feel and bewail his own sin and misery, and seek Christ for himself, in fervent prayer, and have the remedy provided in the gospel applied to his own case."

Mother.—" Well, if all this belongs to believing in Christ, and obtaining salvation, I am afraid there are thousands who call themselves believers, and yet know nothing at all about it."

Robert.—" No doubt of it. I remember the time when I thought little about it myself: my parents taught me to be honest, industrious, and civil to my betters, and so I got the name of a good lad. As it was the custom of my parents, I went to meeting at least once every Sunday, and generally read a chapter in the Bible every evening: I used also to say the Lord's Prayer, and the Ten Commandments, night and morning, unless I was very much hurried or tired. This was more than many young men did; and I thought myself very good indeed. I was not over fond of thinking about death, but if ever the thought did come into my mind, I persuaded myself that I had done no harm, and was sure to go to heaven; but all the while I was as great a stranger to repentance, faith, and prayer, as if I had been born a heathen."

Mary.—" Yes, it was the same with all of us at that time; and oh, what a mercy that we were not left to perish in that state of ignorance! We may well say, 'God, who is rich in mercy, for his great love wherewith he loved us, even when we were dead in sins, hath quickened us together with Christ. By grace we are saved.'"

Mother.—" Well, it is a great mercy to be set right, if you were wrong before. And, pray, were Mr. and Mrs. Sutton of the same way of thinking? And how was it that you all took such a new turn?"

Mary.—" I will tell you all about it. When they were first married, they thought little about the religion of the heart. They were upright and kind to their fellow-creatures, and decent in their attendance on public worship; but at that time, it may be truly said of the whole family, we were living without God in the world.

" When Miss Ellen was born, (she that was married just before we came to live here,) a nurse was recommended to my mistress by an old lady whom she greatly respected. Mistress was not one of those mothers who leave their children entirely to the care of domestics, though at that time she loved pleasure more, and was more inclined to go out than she now is. However, let children be ever so well attended by their parents, it is a great matter to have a faithful, conscientious nurse, such as Fanny proved herself to be. When she came to be hired, she was very particular in engaging for liberty to attend public worship at least once every Lord's day, unless there was illness: this my mistress readily granted her, and it was the only liberty she required; indeed, there was no persuading her to leave sight of her charge for a single hour on any other business whatever; and even then, she was as particular in her directions to me and the housemaid, as if the child had been her own. She had very good ways with the children, (she lived with us till there were seven of them,) keeping them in strict subjection, and yet so cheerful and happy. Never were pleasanter children, nor children who gave less trouble to those about them, which I must, in a great measure, attribute to her good methods with them.

"Fanny generally spent her leisure, when she had any, (which was not very often, for she was industrious with her needle,) in the nursery, reading good books; yet she was by no means morose or gloomy. If we invited her, she had no objection to sit an hour with the rest of us in the kitchen; but she could not endure any light, vain conversation, or foolish song, or jest books, which, I am sorry to say, we at that time saw no harm in. However, she made herself very agreeable; having travelled much, and seen a great deal of the world, her conversation was always entertaining, though she never failed to give it also an instructive turn, and often proposed to read a chapter in the Bible, or an extract from some good book which she had by her, or had borrowed.

"By degrees she quietly wrought a great change in our kitchen: instead of vain, unprofitable talk, that one should have been ashamed to remember, we either spoke of something useful, or else Robert read to us as we sat at our needlework.

"As the children became old enough to understand any thing, Fanny spared no pains in teaching them sweet little hymns and catechisms, suited to their capacities; she used also to read the Bible, and pray with them, and took them with her to public worship. My mistress did not object to this, for, though she thought them too young to understand what they heard, she was always satisfied as to their being safe in Fanny's care. But children understand more than grown people are aware of. Their father and mother were fond of the children, and often had them into the parlor, but they did not at that time notice these things, and, perhaps, hardly knew the instructions that were bestowed on them.

" But what with Fanny's serious conversation and reading, and the children's pretty little sayings, we, in the kitchen, began to think there must be something in religion beyond a mere name. I believe Robert was the first who proposed to go with Fanny to her place of worship."

Robert.—" Yes, and never, I trust, shall I forget it. Every word the minister said came home to my conscience, and I could get no rest nor peace. I shall never forget how all my honesty, and civility, and prayers, (as I called them,) shrunk into nothing before the holy word of God; and I felt, at once, that I was a wretched, ruined sinner, deserving nothing but everlasting misery."

Mary.—" And how Sally, the housemaid, and I, laughed at you, when you were determined to go again in the evening! we little thought how soon we should feel in the same manner."

Robert.—" Yes, you all thought it was because I liked Fanny's company, and so I did; but that is nothing now; it was not to be. But we have all reason to be thankful that she was sent among us, to be the means of leading our feet into the way of peace."

Mother.—" But you said you could get no rest nor peace, your mind was so uneasy with what you had heard."

Robert.—" Indeed, I could not have peace, when I saw myself a perishing sinner, till I went again and again to hear the gospel, and read the Bible for myself, and so was enabled to see and believe, that 'Christ Jesus came into the world to save sinners, of whom I am chief!' And oh! what a different thing it is to read the Bible, and hear the preaching of the gospel, when one has the full impression that we are reading and hearing for the salvation of our own precious souls! Only think what a difference it would be, if we were reading a common newspaper, or if we had been told that that newspaper contained an advertisement of a great fortune which *we* might have on applying, and proving our relationship to such and such persons."

Mother.—" I believe it would, too! We should not be trifling about other people's affairs, but we should read that one advertisement over and over again, and try to understand every word of it, and consider how we might best apply, and how we could prove ourselves to be the parties described. And really, when one comes to think of it, it is a matter of far greater concern that we should know whether or not our souls are safe for another world; for we none of us know how soon we may be cut off by death.—And have you felt so ever since?"

Robert.—" I hope I have never lost the concern that was then awakened, nor ever been disposed to look upon sin as a trifle. It is still my grief that so much sin cleaves to me, and that I cannot do the things that I would. Sometimes the sinfulness of my heart so overwhelms me, that I seem to think it is scarcely possible for so sinful a creature to be pardoned and accepted: but then I go again to my Bible, and there I find that 'the blood of Jesus Christ cleanseth us from *all* sin;' that 'He is able to save to the *uttermost, all* that come to God by him;' and 'him that cometh he will in *no wise* cast out;' and thus I again find comfort and strength; and so, by the help of God's Holy Spirit, which he has promised to them that ask him, I hope to go on to the end, and so receive the end of my faith, even the salvation of my soul."

Mother.—" Well, that is a happy state of mind. I can only say I wish that mine was like it. And how was it that the rest were brought into the same way of thinking?"

Mary.—" Why, as opportunity offered, sometimes Sally went with Fanny and Robert, and sometimes I went; and the more we went, the more we liked to go; and we all took more pains to contrive our work on a Saturday, and as we all agreed together, and were willing to help one another, it was never necessary for more than one to stop at home. So we had many opportunities: and, as 'faith cometh by hearing, and hearing by the word of God,' the Lord was pleased to open our hearts, as he did the heart of Lydia, to attend to the things that were spoken by the minister; and we searched the scriptures daily whether those things were so, and prayed earnestly that we might be taught by the Holy Spirit, and 'made wise unto salvation, through faith which is in Christ Jesus.' And thus, having obtained help of God, we continue to the present day; still very ignorant, and very sinful, yet waiting on the Lord, and looking for the mercy of our Lord Jesus Christ, unto eternal life.—But you inquired how the change was brought about in the minds of our dear master and mistress with respect to religion."

Robert.—" Ah, that is a painful story! And yet we have all reason to say that joy arose in the midst of grief, and that, in the time of affliction, God remembered mercy, and bestowed that which more than made up for all he saw fit to take away. But you shall tell the story, Mary; I never can have the heart to go through with it."

Mary.—" Well, when we were all brought to know and love the truth, we used, as the Bible says, to take sweet counsel together, and walk to the house of God in company. Master and mistress were very kind, and as we always managed the work on a Saturday, and took turns in staying at home, so that they were never inconvenienced by our going out, they never interfered with it, but often expressed themselves pleased with our faithful services: it would be a shame indeed if Christian domestics were not faithful. But, as far as we could judge, our master and mistress had little or no serious concern about their souls. They generally went to church once on the Sunday, if the weather was fine, and spent the rest of the day in visiting and walking; they also, most days, read a chapter in the Bible: this was quite as much religion as most of their acquaintances possessed, and it seemed quite enough to satisfy them. You may suppose that, when we were brought, as we trust, to know something of a more vital and influential piety, we became anxiously concerned that our dear master and mistress should share our happiness. It would not do for us to set up for their teachers, but we took an opportunity, now and then, in a respectful way, to drop a hint, which never gave any offence, though it never seemed to make any deep impression. Good Fanny, being constantly with the children, saw more of mistress than the rest of us, and had more opportunities of speaking. She had been longer in the ways of God, and knew, better than the rest of us, what to say, and when and how to say it. However, we all prayed for them most earnestly and affectionately. I may say again, in the words of scripture, 'Then they that feared the Lord spake often one to another, and the Lord hearkened and heard, and a book of remembrance was written before him, for them that feared the Lord, and that thought upon his name.'

"But when we pray for spiritual blessings, how little do we think in what way our prayers are to be answered! We were living very happily together, delighted to see the docility and improvement of the sweet children, and only desiring the conversion of our master and mistress, when Miss Ellen came home, very poorly: the complaint proved to be the measles. She had it very favorably; but the rest of the children took it, and two of them died; the youngest a sweet little babe of ten months old, and the other a fine boy of six years. Oh what a house of mourning was ours when death first entered it! Master and mistress were dotingly fond of their children, and, when that fine lovely babe was taken, it seemed as if they would break their hearts; but that was only the beginning of sorrows. Don't you remember, Robert, how affectingly master spoke to you about it, some time afterwards?"

Robert.—"Yes, quite well. He said, 'The first stroke seemed too heavy to be borne. We were rebellious under it; we struggled like a wild bull in a net; and felt as if God had no right to touch *our* treasures. It took more and severer strokes to bend our stubborn souls; but God, who is rich in mercy, opened a way to our hearts by means of affliction, and then came in himself and filled the painful void.'"

Mary.—"Well, when this dear little William died, it was hoped that all the rest were going on favorably; but a cold easterly wind set in just at the time, and, though every care was taken of the dear little sufferers, Master Herbert, the flower of the flock, was seized with inflammation of the lungs, and died."

Robert.—" But oh, what a happy death was his! His kind nurse had been the means of bringing this dear little lamb to the Good Shepherd, and while he lay suffering, and his dear parents were weeping over him, he was continually saying some sweet verse of scripture, or of his little hymns, about the love of Jesus to children, and assuring them that he was quite happy and willing to go to Jesus; or fervently praying, in his own simple language, for his dear papa and mamma, and brothers and sisters, and even every one of us servants by name. It was a melting scene; and his dying sayings surely sunk into the hearts of his dear parents."

Mary.—" Yes, that they did. I remember, when we had laid the dear little corpse in the coffin, my poor dear mistress bent over it, and said, ' Would to God I were where my child is! I can bear this stroke better than the former; and, dearly as I love my remaining children, I could gladly part with them all, and go myself, if we were all sure of dying as happy and as well prepared as this precious babe!' Poor Fanny, though herself almost broken-hearted, as indeed we all were, talked sweetly to mistress, and begged her to carry her sorrows to God in prayer, and beseech him to make the affliction a blessing, by leading her to that gracious Saviour, who had been so gracious to the dying child. Then she gave her the little books with which he used to be so delighted, and marked the passages of scripture he loved to repeat. The bereaved mother withdrew with them to her chamber, where she remained some hours; and I do believe she then began to seek a throne of mercy for herself the few remaining days that Fanny was with us."

Mother.—" What! did she leave you soon afterwards ?"

Mary.—" Yes, indeed, she did, never to return ! When little Herbert's funeral was over, mistress was continually going into the nursery, and asking questions about him; she seemed like a little child among the children. Her attention was awakened to those things which she never had before regarded. She found the need of consolations which the world could not bestow; and she felt assured, that her dear dying child had enjoyed those consolations through the truths impressed upon him by his faithful nurse. A fortnight had elapsed from the time of his death, when Fanny herself was seized with the complaint, which she did not know but she had passed in childhood: she had it very severely, and, though she did not actually die under the disease, she never recovered from it. A cough settled on her lungs, and she went off in a rapid consumption. You may suppose that master and mistress were greatly distressed at the prospect of losing so valuable a servant, and one who had been so great a blessing to their dear children. They kept her in the house, and paid her every possible attention; but it was all in vain, as to this world. However, even this additional trial proved a great blessing to all the family. The good old lady who first recommended Fanny to the place, often visited her in her illness, and her conversation was very consoling and profitable to my mistress, who, though she had long respected her, never till now knew her real worth. With some hesitation, Fanny expressed a wish to see the faithful minister on whom she had long attended. To this our master and mistress readily consented: whatever prejudices they might formerly have felt on such a subject, had now given way; their hearts were softened and inquiring; and they were ready to receive, as an angel of God, any one who could instruct them in those sacred truths which they now perceived to be of infinite value. The good man became a frequent visitor, and, by the bedside of the dying servant, he uttered many a sentiment, and breathed many a prayer, which, through the Holy Spirit's influence, sunk deep into the hearts of our master and mistress.

"The last days and hours of this excellent young woman were rich in heavenly hopes and consolations: many precious instructions flowed to us all from her dying lips; and her memory is to this day fondly cherished in all our hearts. The whole family followed to the grave the remains of faithful Fanny, and were present at her funeral sermon. The preaching was of a totally different kind from the cold, trifling, and formal sound which our master and mistress had been used to attend. They at once perceived that the minister was in earnest, and that he really believed the things he uttered were true and important. This naturally excited serious attention. Then he so carefully proved from scripture whatever he advanced, that there was no gainsaying it; and his tender and affectionate spirit tended to win the heart. From that time the family regularly attended his ministry, as long as we resided in the city; and he has been to visit the family since we came into the country.

"Under these various means, our master and mistress were gradually enlightened to perceive their own state, however amiable and estimable their characters before men, as guilty and polluted in the sight of God, and altogether without hope, except from the free mercy of God, in Jesus Christ. Like the apostle, they have been brought to say, 'What things were gain we count loss; yea, doubtless, and we count all things but loss for the excellency of the knowledge of Christ Jesus our Lord; and do count them but dung, that we may win Christ and be found in him, not having our own righteousness which is of the law, but that which is through the faith of Christ, the righteousness which is of God by faith; that we may know him, and the power of his resurrection, and the fellowship of his sufferings, being made conformable unto his death.'

"I need hardly tell you, that, when these sentiments and feelings had taken possession of their hearts, a suitable change was soon seen in the conduct of their family. The Sabbath was entirely devoted to its sacred purposes; family worship was established; worldly pleasures abandoned; and the great concern about the children, was, that they might be brought up 'in the nurture and admonition of the Lord;' and, as they advanced in years and understanding, the utmost anxiety was evinced by the affectionate parents, that each might become a personal subject and possessor of divine grace. They have often spoken of it, as a great mercy, that they were brought to a knowledge of the truth while their children were yet young and tender: the eldest was not more than nine or ten years old, and the instructions of their nurse had prepared them to fall in with those of their parents; and I suppose they can scarcely remember the time when things were different from what they now are. The fervent prayers of the parents have been answered, and their pious endeavors succeeded and blessed in a good degree. The eldest four of the family have long been decidedly pious, and the two younger are amiable and hopeful. This dear Miss Harriet is, as you say, a kind, gentle, lovely young lady; but, from what we have told you of the views and experience of the parents, you cannot wonder that they should be deeply anxious to obtain decisive evidence that she knows the grace of God in truth, and is enabled, in this trying hour, to rest a firm hope for eternity on Jesus Christ, the Saviour of sinners."

Mother.—" Indeed, I do not wonder at it; and I hope it may please God to grant their desire. But I want to know who took care of the children after the death of your fellow-servant Fanny?"

Mary.—" Why, master and mistress were sadly afraid of engaging any one on whom they could not rely for acting in the fear of God, and instilling holy principles into the minds of the children. As there was not a young infant to mind, and Sally the housemaid, and myself, were very fond of the children, we begged mistress not to hurry about getting any one, assuring her we would do our best to make things comfortable, and should prefer engaging in a little extra work, rather than running the hazard of having a fellow-servant who might not be a comfortable companion in the best things. I must say, Robert was as willing as either of us to make this bargain, and never objected to put his hand to any thing by which the general comfort might be promoted; and so we have gone on very happily ever since.

" Mistress, having given up her gay engagements, resolved to devote herself to the education of her children. In this great work she found the advice of the good old lady highly valuable; indeed, the intimacy was like that of a mother and daughter.

" At first, mistress was sadly afraid she should experience great interruption in her new plans, from the visits of her irreligious acquaintance; but the difficulty did not prove nearly so great as had been expected. Most of them were sickened at the change they perceived, and dropped off one after another, saying that Mr. and Mrs. Sutton had gone melancholy since the loss of their children. Never was a greater mistake; for it was then they began to know what true happiness means. However, it is a pleasure to say, that *all* did not thus forsake them in disgust, but that several families of their acquaintance were induced by their example to think seriously about religion, and, in time, became their companions in the ways of God.

" About two years after the death of the two children and their nurse, it pleased God to bestow on our dear master and mistress another son, whom they called, after his departed brothers, William Herbert. Being so much younger than the rest, he has always been the darling of the family; I hope and trust he will not be spoiled. He is the child of many prayers, and of wise parental government; and, from many little circumstances that have come under our observation, we have great hope that his dear young mind is inclined to seek the God of his parents. About the time of his birth, a governess was engaged to assist mistress in teaching the young ladies: she was a pious person; and, as all went hand in hand with the parents, great success has attended their endeavors. Never was a more lovely and well-behaved family than ours; at least, I think so, and so do many who are better judges. But the great care and anxiety is, still, to ascertain that the root of the matter is in them; for, humbling as it may be, it is a truth, that the loveliest babe that ever was born, and the most amiable youth that ever eyes beheld, is a guilty, depraved creature, and *must* be born again before it can see the kingdom of God."

Mother.—" I thank you for telling me all this, and I shall often think of it; for, if such a change was necessary to those good people, it is surely as necessary to me and mine.

"I must ask you one more question: What became of Sally, the housemaid? She did not come into the country with you."

Mary.—" No: she was married to one of master's young men, just before we came down; and she keeps house, and attends upon the two young gentlemen, who are now in business. They highly value her, as trusty and faithful, and master and mistress are satisfied in knowing that there is a prudent, careful person to look after their comfort and expenses; for young men, especially in London, are exposed to great snares and dangers. But, as Sally said in her last letter, it is such a comfort to see them steadily following the ways of their dear parents,—useful and honorable in the church of God, and promoters of every good word and work."

At the close of this long conversation, the bell rang for one of us to sit by Miss Harriet's bedside, and the rest to come in to family prayer. Mr. and Mrs. Sutton had evidently been weeping much; they, however, appeared placid and resigned. Mr. Sutton read the 126th Psalm, and, in prayer, committed their dear dying child, as she then appeared, to the care and protection of Infinite Mercy, at the same time expressing a grateful hope that she herself had not been a stranger to the throne of grace.

We afterwards learned that the conversation had been very satisfactory and consolatory. She had opened her mind to her parents, and had relieved theirs. Timidity and reserve had hitherto restrained her lips; but now, in the near prospect of eternity, she ventured to state, that she had long sought the Lord in humble prayer, and was now permitted to enjoy his supporting presence. She had still a faint recollection of the scene when the children were taken into the chamber of their dying nurse, to receive her last farewell, and when she entreated each of them to apply to that gracious Saviour who said, "Suffer little children to come unto me, and forbid them not, for of such is the kingdom of heaven." At that time, the children wept, they scarcely knew why. The next day, they were told that Fanny was gone to heaven, to their dear little brothers, and to that Saviour whom she had taught them to love; and the passages she had urged on their attention became permanently associated in their minds with the affectionate tenderness of one they had so dearly loved, and the happiness on which she had so soon entered.

The happy change that took place in the minds and habits of the parents tended to confirm these early impressions on their children; and they had now the unspeakable happiness of seeing the elder four walking in the truth; and now, concerning the youngest, who had shared the instructions and solicitude of their long-lost pious nurse, of cherishing the pleasing hope, that, "whether she lived, she would live to the Lord, or whether she died, she would die unto the Lord; and so, living or dying, she would be the Lord's."

It pleased God to raise Miss Harriet from her bed of sickness, and to spare her to become an ornament to religion, and a great blessing to all connected with her.

I may add, that, during many weeks, in which she was slowly recovering, it was my happiness, and that of my dear mother, to gather those instructions from the reading, the conversation, and the prayers of this pious family, which, I trust, have proved a great and lasting benefit to us.

CHAP. III.

DEFERENCE TO PARENTS.

I ONCE received a useful lesson from some kind friends, which leads me to look back with keen self-reproach; and that, perhaps, is generally the case with the most profitable lessons we receive; for the more clearly we are taught what we ought to do and be, the more we shall be humbled at observing how far we have fallen short of it.

The point to which I allude is deference to parents—one on which I believe many young persons transgress, more from want of due consideration, than from really bad intentions.

I have observed, that, when my mother was out at work, or nursing, it fell to my lot to keep house for my father and brothers: I grieve to think how often, in this respect, I failed in my duty. Having an employment of my own, I was too apt to regard my time and earnings as entirely mine, and to grudge any interruption. Often my dear father has come in, cold and weary, and found the fire out, the house untidy, and no supper prepared. Instead of attending to these things, I have been eagerly busy at my needlework, pleasing myself with the thought of what I should gain, if at work for others, or, perhaps, amusing myself with altering my own clothes to the newest fashion that had come to my knowledge. Father was a mild, quiet man, and seldom found fault; but I am sure my unkindness and neglect must have given him pain at the time, as they have given me many an uneasy feeling since.

One day, when I was about seventeen years of age, a gentleman from a distance came to reside in our neighborhood, and both my mother and myself got many days' employment in settling the family. Mother got the house in order, and cleaned the furniture as it arrived by the wagon; and I set at work with the young ladies, making up window-curtains and other things of that description.

Just as the house was got to rights, mother was called away to a neighbor whom she had engaged to nurse. As I had only two or three hours' work to do, she left the key of our house with me, and charged me to be sure and go home in good time to get my father some supper.

In the course of the day, the ladies bethought themselves of some more work they wanted done, and asked me when I could be spared from home. I replied, that, if they pleased, I would stay then, and not go home at all; for I was delighted at working with the young ladies, and getting such profitable employ. But the lady of the house, who had heard my mother's charge to me, asked me who was at home to provide for my father's comfort. I answered her with some degree of confusion; for, though I had never thought much about the matter before, my conscience felt as if I had neglected a duty. She then very kindly said to me, "My good girl, it is quite right that you should be diligent in your business, and desirous of honest gain; but let your duty to your parents have its proper place: they have the strongest claims on your gratitude and obedience. Think how much of their own comfort they have relinquished to provide for and make you comfortable when you could do nothing for yourself! Think what they have sacrificed to procure you the knowledge by which you are enabled to maintain yourself now, and to assist in the support of the family!"

My confusion increased; for I felt conscious that, as I approached to womanhood, I had fancied myself my own mistress, and especially since I had been out to work, that I had spent most of my earnings on myself, and had in many respects been very deficient in consulting the comforts and wishes of my parents. Perhaps they, too, had erred in indulgence towards me, and leaving me too much to my own disposal. They would not have done this had they observed in me any particular vicious propensity; but, seeing me, in the main, tolerably steady and industrious, they were thrown off their guard. This is a danger to which well-disposed parents are often exposed, especially when the children have had any thing like an education of which the parents have been destitute: they are apt to think too highly of the little attainments of their children, and to treat them with deference as a superior kind of beings. Such conduct too frequently leads children to forget their dependence and obligations, and the respect and deference due to parents. During the remainder of the day, nothing more was said to me on the subject, and it is very likely that the lady thought no more about it; but a train of reflections was awakened in my mind, which proved of lasting benefit. I resolved from that hour to be more observant of the wishes of my parents; and it was my happiness, years afterwards, to receive from each the dying parent's blessing on a dutiful child.

Let me set down, by way of admonition to all other young people, a few instances in which I recollect my own early failures, and in correcting which, the happiness of my dear parents was promoted, as well as my own peace of mind.

One thing to which I have already alluded is, prompt and punctual attention to their requests and comforts. Though my parents had borne much, and complained little, I shall never forget the fond pat which my dear father gave me that first night, when, on coming home, weary and hungry, he found a cheerful fire, a clean-swept hearth, and a bit of hot bacon and potatoes ready to set on table; nor the tender tear that started in my mother's eye, when I carried her gray cloak to the house where she was nursing, to keep her warm if she should have to sit up all night: these were the first fruits of my friend's admonition.

Another point on which I had not sufficiently consulted my parents' comfort was that of regularity at meals. Regularity is at all times desirable, and as people advance in life, it becomes of more consequence that they should take their meals and retire to rest with punctuality. When awakened to think more particularly of my duty to my parents, I recollected with pain, that I had sometimes suffered my mother to rise and prepare breakfast, and to call me again and again before I could shake off sloth and obey the summons; that I had often been sitting eagerly at my work, or gossipping at the door with a neighbor's daughter, when my parents were waiting for dinner or supper; that I had sometimes been out when I ought to have been at home; or had brought my young companions uninvited, and when, perhaps, their company was an intrusion on the rest or quietness my parents wished to enjoy. It only required an habitual and conscientious sense of what my parents had a right to expect, and what it ought to be my pleasure to yield, to do away with all these improprieties. And here I cannot help noticing, that proper behavior towards parents is the safeguard of many other virtues, and the security against many temptations. It checks *indolence;* for a dutiful child cannot be idle, and suffer a parent to toil. It checks *extravagance;* for, so far from appropriating all earnings to his own use, much less sponging on the resources of his parents, the dutiful child will be intent on sparing from his own gratification for the comfort of those so dear to him, and to whom he is so deeply indebted. It checks *self-conceit;* for a child accustomed to consult the wishes and opinions of parents, so often sees his own mistakes corrected, and perceives the advantage of looking to those wiser and more experienced than himself, that it very much tends to sober his opinion of his own judgment. It tends to break the snare of *unprofitable or injurious company;* for the youth who drops an intimacy, in compliance with the wishes of wise and good parents, generally lives to see that the connection would have done him no good. I can look back on several characters who have turned out very worthless, and have involved in ruin those connected with them, concerning whom, years before, my parents had said to one or other of us, "I'd have you beware of such a person; don't be hasty in forming a friendship; I think he (or she) will not prove a profitable acquaintance." *Once* I thought my parents narrow-minded in these remarks; but subsequent events have so frequently showed that their judgment was right, as to lead me almost to attach an oracular authority to their sayings.

Another advantage resulting from dutiful conduct to parents is this—It is the best preparative for filling up every other relation in life with propriety. The best child bids fair to make the best husband or wife, and best knows what to expect and claim from children, and how to enforce those just claims and expectations.

To return to the time when that lady's remark made such an impression on my own mind.—As soon as I could be spared from home, I went there to work again. At family prayer, that evening, a chapter was read out of one of the epistles, (I believe it was Ephesians,) in which a great deal is said about the duty of children to their parents. At that time, I thought it was all meant for me; however, I resolved not to take offence, but attend to good instructions, and endeavor to improve them. I afterwards found that the chapter occurred in the regular course of family reading; but the instruction was just as applicable as if it had been read, or even written, on purpose for me.

It was a custom in that family, as they sat at work, to converse about the passage of scripture which had been read; or sometimes a page or two would be read from some other book that served to explain it. That day, a beautiful address to young people on Filial Duty, was read, in which it was explained, that the word used in the fifth commandment, "*honor*," comprehends more than any other single word that could have been put in its place: it includes *reverence, love,* and *obedience*. Parents should be treated with great reverence and gratitude, as the best friends and benefactors; their opinions should be received with deference; their feelings and their characters regarded with the greatest delicacy and respect; they should never be spoken to but with modesty and submission; nor spoken of but with tenderness and veneration; their instructions should be gratefully received and regarded; their commands cheerfully obeyed; their counsel sought in every matter of importance; and every effort should be made, by a dutiful and affectionate child, to render their last days comfortable. Perhaps the expenses of bringing up a family have straitened the parents through life, and disabled them from laying by any store for the support of their old age. Perhaps the incessant care and attentions bestowed on their children may have impaired their strength, and brought on weakness and disease. Perhaps their privations have laid the foundation of their children's success in life: they denied themselves to give education to their children, and to set them up in life; and the children have prospered, but the parents are fallen to decay. Then what can be more reasonable or more equitable than that the children should "requite" the parents, and consider it a most sacred duty to provide for their comfort to the very utmost of their ability, even at the sacrifice of many personal and family indulgences?

This is the substance of what was read to us, and which, I hope, made a deep impression on my mind. The gentleman also mentioned, that he once heard an aged minister say, that, having, through the course of a long life, made observations on the dealings of Providence with the children of men, he had rarely, if ever, met with an instance in which the three following crimes escaped evident punishment, even in this life: murder, infidelity to the marriage covenant, and disobedience to parents. Of this he gave some striking instances, as also of the blessing of God eminently resting on dutiful and affectionate children in fulfilment of "the first commandment with promise: Honor thy father and thy mother, that it may be well with thee, and that thy days may be long in the land."

He told us of one wicked son, who not only refused to give his aged father any thing to support him, but even thrust him out of his house, and dragged him by the hairs of his head. When they came to a certain part of the grounds, the old man cried out, "Stop, son! stop! You have no

DEFERENCE TO PARENTS. 39

right to drag me any farther. To this point I dragged my father; and now I see and feel that God is just!"

Another affecting story that he related was this—" In a town in the centre of England, lived a family of humble circumstances. Some of the younger children and their father died, leaving the aged mother with two sons grown up, and able to assist her. This, however, they refused to do, and she was obliged to apply to the parish for relief; and, for some years, two shillings a week were allowed her by the overseers, which, with a trifle added by some Christian friends, was all which she had for subsistence.

" During this time her youngest son died. He had lived without the fear of God, and died under a sense of his wrath, in deep agonies, both of body and mind, and uttering dreadful expressions. The eldest was clever in his business; he got forward in the world, and became possessed of considerable property. But he still refused to assist his mother, and, even while holding offices of consideration and importance, left his mother to her allowance from the parish. This conduct, of course, was noticed; he was repeatedly spoken to upon the subject; at length, he ordered her name to be taken off the parish books, and *allowed her the two shillings a week out of his own pocket*, at a time when he possessed thousands of pounds, and was without a family.

" One day some friends were assembled, and her case being mentioned, they proposed to remonstrate with the ungrateful son. 'No,' said an aged minister, 'let him alone; if he dies possessed of the property he is now worth, I shall be deceived. God will never suffer such base ingratitude to prosper.

" In a short time afterwards the mother died; and such was her humility and Christian spirit, that she died imploring a blessing upon her son. He buried her with more attention to his own situation than he had bestowed upon her while alive.

" Years passed on; she was forgotten, and his behavior towards her was only remembered by a few, who had been impressed with the vileness of his conduct. His circumstances at length began to change; repeated losses ensued, and after some time he became *a bankrupt*, and lived in *abject poverty.*"

The following interesting anecdote I have somewhere read in ancient history. A certain city was besieged, and at length obliged to surrender. In the city there were two brothers, who had in some way obliged the conquering general, and in consequence received his permission to leave the city before it was set fire to, taking with them as much of their property as each could carry about his person. Accordingly, the two generous youths appeared at the gates of the city, one of them bearing their father, and the other their mother.

I shall here set down another pleasing fact. A recruiting officer was applied to by a very fine young man, who desired to be enlisted into his company. He appeared greatly agitated, and expressed a fear lest the bounty he required should be considered too high, and his offer rejected. He asked ten guineas, assuring the officer that it was no unworthy motive that compelled him to demand so large a sum, and that he should be the most miserable of men if he refused. The officer complied with his request, handed him the money, and told him the company would depart on the next day. He then requested leave of absence for one hour to perform a sacred duty at home. This the officer granted, relying on his honor; but, observing something mysterious in his manner, he had the curiosity to follow him at some distance. He hastened to the town prison, knocked, and was admitted. At the door of the prison, he presented the ten guineas to the jailer, saying, "Here is the sum for which my father is confined; I put it into your hands, and request you to conduct me to him immediately, that I may release him from his misery." In a few moments the officer saw the venerable old man locked in the arms of his son, and bedewing him with his tears. The officer was not immediately perceived, until, deeply affected by the melting scene, he approached the old man, and said, "Be composed; I will not deprive you of so worthy a son. Permit me to restore him to you, that I may not regret the money which he has bestowed in so virtuous a manner." The father and son fell on their knees at his feet; the youth hesitated to accept the proffered freedom, until constrained by the generous officer, who accompanied them both from the prison, and took his leave with the pleasing reflection of having contributed to the happiness of a very worthy son and an unfortunate father.

CHAP. IV.

SPECULATION AND SURETISHIP.

My father had a brother, who was a painter by trade. He was reckoned an ingenious and hard-working man; but, I suppose, there must have been some extravagance or bad management in his family, for they were always poor. My father used to ascribe it to two particulars; and, I believe, he was pretty near the truth. One of my uncle's habits, which my father disapproved, was that of paying and receiving money at a public-house. This drew him into much needless expense, and also led him into very unprofitable society. Another failing was this: he was much fonder of idle speculation than of steady perseverance; and, though he was both a clever and quick workman, and would sometimes get through a job of work to the amazement of all who witnessed it, he would often lose as much time in vain projects as would have wrought two or three such wonders. My father used to say to him, " Brother Tom, you build too many castles in the air, and some day or other you will tumble down and break your neck; small gains and steady would do far better in the long run." But uncle was none of the sort to take advice; and true enough is the saying, " Those that will not be counselled, cannot be helped." He was continually starting some new scheme in business, or losing time in trying to get the notice of some great man, and always certain that the last new project would be the making of himself and his family. Meanwhile, he was always in distress; sometimes quite destitute; sometimes borrowing a few shillings to carry him on, and then grudgingly working it out; and sometimes reduced so low as even to sell or pawn his ladders and brushes.

One time he came to my father in great haste, and begged him *just to put his hand to a note* for a payment of twenty-five dollars. My father declined to do it, saying he had not twenty-five dollars to spare. "Spare!" replied my uncle, " nobody wants you to spare it, or a farthing of it. I shall have the money over and over again before the day comes. It is only just to set your hand to this bit of paper; and depend on it you will never hear another word about the matter." After much pleading, he prevailed on my father to do it. I recollect mother was out at the time; and when she came in, and father told her what he had done, she replied, "Well, then, we must wait a few years longer for our clock, and, perhaps, never get it; for, depend upon it, you will have to pay every farthing of the money." At that time there was about twenty-five dollars in the house, which had been long collecting, in order to purchase a handsome clock, which was to be sold, and which my parents, and, indeed, the whole family, greatly desired to possess. However, sure enough, according to mother's words, my father was called on to pay the money. It was in vain for him to assure the creditor that he never received one farthing value for it, and that his brother desired him only just to put his name to a bit of paper. "And, for doing so," replied the creditor, "you have only just to pay the money. This is what comes of giving people credit that they do not deserve. I should never have thought of trusting your brother for that sum; but I knew you to be an honest, careful man, and, as the story goes among the neighbors, a man of some little substance; and when I saw your name, I was satisfied. One or other of us must be the loser; and since you have been fool enough to put your name to another man's engagement, it is fitter you should lose it than I."

SPECULATION AND SURETISHIP. 43

This was a rough lesson; but, I believe, on the whole, it was profitable. I do not think my uncle's intentions were dishonest; he thought he should be able to meet the bill; and although "he received the money over and over again," he had been tempted to part with it, and so at last, when the time came, he had not a shilling left to help himself.

Having paid the money, my father and mother wisely resolved never to speak about it, lest it should lead to useless vexations and reproaches; but they set about to earn and save again as fast as they could. If my uncle had done the same, he might, perhaps, in time, have got over his difficulties, and gained a *solid house*, which, as my father often told him, would be worth twenty *air castles*. But, as I said before, he was not a man to learn wisdom, even by experience. Sometimes, when my father knew of his taking money, he would try him hard, and perhaps get a dollar or two of him at a time; but he never in the whole got one quarter of the money. In course of time, we had a clock, but it was not the handsome one, on which we had at first set our minds.

Some years afterwards, my uncle came again to ask my father a like favor, but to a much larger amount.

"No," replied my father firmly, "a burnt child dreads the fire. You don't catch me again putting my hand to a bit of paper that don't belong to me. The wise man says, 'He that hateth suretiship is sure.'"

"But," replied my uncle, "this is quite a different sort of a story. I want to get the sum of two hundred dollars, which was left in the hands of trustees, to be lent for seven years without interest to a poor tradesman, only he must get two friends just to put their names to it. My cousin Jones is willing to be one, and you surely can't be so unnatural as to refuse to be the other. It won't cost you a farthing, and will be the making of me and my family through life. Think what a stock of goods I shall be able to lay in, and buy every thing at the best hand. Why, I shall save the money ten times over in the course of seven years, and live like a gentleman besides."

"Ah, brother!" said my father, "that's the very mischief of it. Such a loan might help one who is content to live and labor like a poor man; but the living like a gentleman will turn it into more harm than good."

"Well, then, I will promise you not to live like a gentleman. I will do any thing you desire, if you will only just put your name."

"Brother, I would gladly help you, if it were in my power; but, as an honest man, I cannot and will not do what you desire. I fear you would be just as unable seven years hence to pay the money, as you are at present; and I am sure I shall not have it then to spare. Perhaps I may not live to see the time; and should I not have acted a very bad part, to leave my poor wife and children chargeable with such a debt, or to wrong the trustees of the charity, if they were not able to pay it? As the wise man says, 'Be not thou one of those who shake hands, or of them that are sureties for debt. If thou hast nothing to pay, wherefore should he take thy bed from under thee?'"

When my uncle had said all he could by way of persuasion, and found my father resolute, he fell into a violent passion, calling him cruel, unnatural, and many other hard words that I need not repeat, and declaring that he would never again enter the house, or own him as a brother. Away he went, and represented to a neighbor the cruelty and unkindness of his own brother, and so wrought on his feelings, that, with more good nature than prudence, he engaged to do for him what his own flesh and blood had refused.

Thus he obtained the money, and carried himself with a high head towards my father whenever he met him, as well as said many unkind things to his prejudice behind his back. My father felt it keenly, but was supported by the consciousness of having done his duty.

The money just served to stop the mouths of a few creditors, and to give a dash for a little while both to business and housekeeping; but it was soon gone, and nothing to show for it. The bondsmen often reminded my uncle that pay-day was drawing on. Almost to the last, he assured them that he should be able to meet it; but when the time came, not a shilling was forthcoming from the right quarter, and the two bondsmen had to make up the money between them. So far from the loan proving any real advantage to my uncle and his family, my father often said he thought it proved a great calamity, as it only fostered them in habits of extravagance and self-delusion.

But though my father refused, in this instance, to grant my uncle's request, he was always ready to act a brother's part by him and his family. Many a portion has been sent them from our own table; and in times of sickness and affliction, money that had been laid up has often been brought out for them; and through life my father was enabled to do kindnesses for them, which would never have been in his power, if (to use his own expression) he had consented to be pulled under water to please a drowning brother.

At last my uncle and his family went to America, which, they say, is a fine land for repairing shattered fortunes, though some have found it otherwise; but what became of them afterwards, I never knew

CHAP. V.

SELF-CONCEIT.

A LADY once took a poor motherless girl into her family as housemaid, and was determined to take pains in instructing her, in order to make her a good servant. Molly was a good-tempered, active, lively girl; but she had one great fault, which defeated all the good intentions of her friends— she was terribly self-conceited. By her own account, you would have supposed her a very clever person, and experienced in work of all kinds; but when it came to the trial, there was not a thing she knew how to do properly; and the worst of it was, she would spoil twenty things in trying her own way upon them, rather than humble herself to ask how it ought to be done. The lady who engaged her was a truly good mistress; she knew how things ought to be done, and she never grudged the trouble of teaching a servant; but she insisted on having things done properly. Many a time I have heard her say, "Molly, I wish such a thing done; do you know how to do it?" Molly was sure to answer, "O yes, ma'am, I know very well how to do it; I have seen it done many a time." In an hour or two's time the thing would be found done in any way but the right; perhaps some valuable piece of furniture injured or spoiled through her conceit and ignorance. When told of her fault, instead of owning her mistake, and desiring to be better taught for the future, she would pertly reply, that was the way she had always been used to see it done; though the truth was, she had never seen it done at all.

I remember once the old cook played a joke upon her, which she did not soon hear the last of. It is a common saying among cooks, that, "If you beat a batter-pudding too much, it is rank poison;" the plain meaning of which is, that the more it is beaten, the better; it is impossible to beat it too much. One day, cook was busy making wine, and asked Molly to make her a batter-pudding. Molly readily agreed, for she was always willing to help any one, and pleased to be employed; and, had it not been for her foolish conceit of her own abilities, she would have been a general favorite. "But,' said cook, "are you sure you know how to do it? for mistress is very particular: don't go and beat it too much, lest it should 'turn to poison.'" "O no; I know very well how to do it," replied Molly. "Mrs. Bell, with whom I lived before I came here, was quite as particular as our mistress. I know how it must be beaten." To work she went, pleased at having, as she thought, got a bit of knowledge slyly; and, determined not to spoil the pudding by over-beating it, she scarcely ventured to turn the spoon at all. When the pudding came to be served up, it was lumps of flour in some parts, and hard-boiled egg in others. On this occasion, the lady spoke to her very kindly, pointing out the folly and mischief of self-conceit. "Conceit of knowledge," said she, "is the greatest enemy to knowledge, and the greatest proof of ignorance. 'Seest thou a man wise in his own conceit? there is more hope of a fool than of him.' The most ignorant person may be taught, if he has humility enough to learn; but the self-conceited is likely to spend his life in ignorance. He shuts up the very door by which knowledge enters to the soul. If we could once see you, Molly, convinced of your own need of instruction, we might hope that instruction would be bestowed upon you to good purpose; and the spoiling of this pudding will be the best bit of cookery you ever performed, if it should lead you to be less confident of your own knowledge and abilities."

The spoiled pudding was a standing joke in the kitchen against Molly; but I could never see that either the kind and serious instructions of her master and mistress, or the sharp rubs of her fellow-servants, succeeded in curing her of her unhappy propensity.

A very favorite saying of Molly, when remonstrated with on any course she was pursuing, was, "It won't hurt—I am certain there is no danger." In this way she often met with accidents; some of a serious nature. There was an old ladder about the premises, unfit for use, which was to be cut up for fire-wood. The gardener had laid it aside for that purpose; but seeing Molly set it up against the loft door, he begged her to wait a moment, while he ran round and fetched the new ladder, assuring her that the old one was not fit to venture on. But Molly persisted, saying, "I'm certain it will bear *me*." Just as she got on the top round, the rotten spar gave way, and she fell to the ground, dreadfully bruised, and with two broken ribs.

It is a saying of the wisest of men,—and, of all kinds of folly, self-conceit is, perhaps, that to which it most universally applies,—"Though thou shouldst bray a fool in a mortar among wheat with a pestle, yet will not his foolishness depart from him." So it was with poor Molly: all her experience of the mischiefs resulting from self-conceit, could not prevail to cure her of it.

This disposition was no less injurious to her in matters of the greatest moment than in trifles. On leaving this lady's, in spite of all remonstrance, she engaged in a situation, to the duties of which she was quite incompetent, and which exposed her to temptations that she was not likely to resist. She was *certain* that she could do it very well, and *certain* that *she* should be in no danger of having her morals corrupted. In vain was she admonished of the weighty sayings of holy writ: "He that trusteth his own heart is a fool," and "Let him that thinketh he standeth, take heed lest he fall." Molly went to her ill-chosen place, and, as her friends forewarned her, soon fell into sin and disgrace, misery and want. Those whose kindness she had rejected did not cast her off in the time of her distress. They kindly visited her, and endeavored to impress on her mind the humbling, yet salutary truths of the gospel; but, alas! self-conceit was still the bar to their admission. She fancied herself too well informed to need instruction, and disdained to be catechised, as she called it.

Notwithstanding her gross misconduct, she could not believe herself to be a great sinner, and in absolute need of mercy, but still flattered herself, that she possessed something by which to recommend herself to the favor of God. She said she had not been so bad as many others, and she repented of what was past, and resolved to do better in future; and on this miserable foundation, to this refuge of lies, she ventured to trust her immortal hopes. Poor girl! she died in early life, and, as far as appeared to those who visited her, satisfied with herself to the last, depending on her own righteousness, and in a spirit as far as possible from his who exclaimed, "God be merciful to me, a sinner!"

O, my children, if you wish to excel in what you attempt of worldly business, and especially if you wish to tread a safe and happy path as it respects futurity, shun pride and self-conceit, and cultivate a spirit of humility and self-distrust. "Before honor is humility." "He that exalteth himself shall be abased; but he that humbleth himself shall be exalted." "With the lowly is wisdom." "God resisteth the proud, but giveth grace to the humble."

CHAP. VI.

PUNCTUALITY.

I was once employed in a family which was remarkable for punctuality. Every thing went on as regular as clock-work. Every person in the house had his or her regularly-appointed duties, and allotted times for performing them. Things were not left to be done by somebody or other, just as it might happen, and just when it might happen, if indeed it happened at all; but time and business were regularly portioned out. It often put me in mind of a dissected puzzle: instead of lying in a heap, a parcel of odd-shaped bits of wood, every little bit was just fitted into its own place, and so the whole was complete and beautiful; and, in a higher degree than almost any other family I ever visited, in that family the work of every day was done in its day, according as the duty of the day required. They were not much in the habit of changing; but whenever a new person was in any way employed in the house, one of the first things was, to teach them habits of punctuality. From among the instructions given in this particular, addressed to myself or to others in my hearing, I have preserved the following observations and anecdotes, some of them copied from books lent me.

"Method is the very hinge of business; and there is no method without punctuality. Punctuality is very important, because it subserves the peace and good temper of a family. The want of it not only infringes on necessary duty, but sometimes excludes this duty. Punctuality is important, as it gains time. It is like packing things in a box: a good packer will get in twice as much as a bad one. The calmness of mind which it produces is another advantage of punctuality. A disorderly man is always in a hurry: he has no time to speak with you, because he is going elsewhere; and when he gets there, he is too late for his business, or he must hurry away to another before he can finish it. It was a wise maxim of the duke of Newcastle,—' I do one thing at a time.'"

Punctuality gives weight to character. " Such a man has made an appointment—then I know he will keep it;" and this generates punctuality in you; for, like other virtues, it propagates itself. Servants and children must be punctual, when they know that the head of the family is so. Appointments, indeed, become debts. "I owe you punctuality, if I have made an appointment with you. I have no right to throw away your time, if I do my own."

The Rev. S. Brewer was distinguished for punctuality. When a youth in college, he was never known to be a minute behind time in attending the lectures of the tutors, or the family prayers, at which the young men who boarded in private families were expected to assemble. One morning, the students were collected; the clock struck seven, and all rose up for prayer; but the tutor, observing that Mr. Brewer was not present, paused awhile. Seeing him enter the room, he thus addressed him: "Sir, the clock has struck, and we were ready to begin; but as you were absent, we supposed the clock was too fast, and therefore waited." The clock was actually too fast by some minutes.

The celebrated reformer, Melancthon, when he made an appointment, expected that the *minute* as well as the *hour* should be fixed, that the day might not be run out in idle suspense. An idling, dawdling sort of habit, which some people have, and which makes them a little too late for every appointment, however trifling it may appear, is often the cause of their ruin; for the habit goes along with them into every thing they do: and, moreover, the loss of time, and the plague which it causes to others, make the habit injurious to our friends, neighbors, and dependants, as well as to ourselves.

When a man is in a hurry at the last moment, every thing is confused and wrong. He tears his stockings, breaks his bootstrap or his shoe-strings, or he gets some string or other in a knot, and all from being in a hurry; and these trifles take up time just as much as weighty matters; and then, his letter is too late for the post, and his absent friend is kept in anxiety and suspense; or the coach has gone without him; or a dinner to which he was invited is spoiled with waiting, or the company is disturbed by his entrance after the rest are seated.

A punctual man generally has a quiet, leisurely way of going about things. There is no hurry and bustle, but the work is done in time; so making good the old saying, "Make haste slowly," or "Take time to be quick."

It is a good maxim, "That you may be always in time, take care always to be ready a little before the time."

King George the Third is said never to have been a minute behind any of his appointments. Another of our kings, by his dilatory habits, fixed on his name the disgraceful stigma, "Ethelred *the Unready*."

The celebrated Lord Nelson said, he owed all his success in life to being ready for every appointment a quarter of an hour beforehand.

A committee, consisting of eight ladies, was appointed to meet at twelve o'clock. Seven of them were punctual, but the eighth came bustling in with many apologies for being a quarter of an hour behind time. "The time had passed away without her being aware of it; she had no idea of its being so late," &c. A Quaker lady present said, "Friend, I am not so clear that we should admit thine apology. It were matter of regret that thou shouldst have wasted thine own quarter of an hour; but here are seven besides thyself, whose time thou hast also consumed, amounting in the whole to two hours, and seven eighths of it was not thine own property."

The following judicious remarks I have copied from a living author.*

* Rev. W. Jay.

THE FAMILY AT HOME.

" Hear the apostle : ' Let every thing be done decently and in order.' The welfare of your household requires that you should observe seasons. Every thing should have its season ; your businesses, your meals, your devotional exercises, your rising, and your rest. The periods for these will vary with the condition of families; but labor to be as punctual as circumstances will allow. It is of importance to peace, and temper, and diligence, and economy. Confusion is friendly to every evil work. Disorder also multiplies disorder; for no one thinks of being exact with those who set at nought all punctuality."

Want of punctuality has a great and grievous influence on religious matters. By indulging a few minutes too late in bed, secret devotion is hurried, and family prayer is interrupted, or perhaps some member of the family is obliged to leave before it can be attended to; the first supplications of the sanctuary are lost; the congregation and minister are disturbed; often the mind is agitated and kept in an uncomfortable and unprofitable frame during the whole service, and all for want of *being in time*. Who, then, will venture to say that it is but a trifle—there is no sin in being a little too late?

CHAP. VII.

PROCRASTINATION.

THERE are more people in the world who fail to perform their duty through procrastination than through wilful, direct neglect. Many persons, who dare not say " I will not do it," satisfy themselves with admitting that the thing ought to be done, and resolving to do it to-morrow. The mischievous consequences of such conduct are perpetually seen in matters the most trifling and the most important. A hook or fastening to a window is observed to be loose ; a youth is desired to go directly and get a hammer to fasten it; he thinks an hour or two hence will do just as well; perhaps it has been in that state for months, and no harm has come of it; it cannot signify leaving it an hour or two longer. A high wind rises, and the whole window, for want of that little fastening, is carried away, dashed in pieces, and injures some person in its fall.

A poor man had received some money, with which he intended to pay his rent. He had been exceedingly anxious to receive it for that purpose; but having got it, he was satisfied; and, though his wife urged him to take it that evening, observing, that it would look well to the landlord to be able to say that they brought it the same day it was received, he thought the next day would do just as well. In the night the cottage was broken into, and all the money stolen, by some villains who happened to know of his receiving it.

"That kitchen chimney ought to be swept."—The remark had been made day after day, and still the execution of it put off till to-morrow; when at length the soot caught fire, and communicating to a beam in the chimney, the house was presently on fire. Happily no lives were lost; but one of the family broke his leg in jumping from a window; and the loss of property was considerable.

A very worthy and estimable person, having been unkindly treated by her nearest relatives, (an uncle and cousins,) in her distress, sought the assistance of a family of relatives much farther removed. They exerted themselves in her behalf, assisted in setting her up in a little way of business, and showed her every kindness in their power. Providence smiled on her endeavors; her shop succeeded; she not only supported herself in comfort, but laid by a little property and purchased her house. She was not deficient in gratitude to her benefactors. Her distant cousins and their children received many kindnesses from her, in return for the kindness they had shown her in time of need; and she pleased herself with the idea of leaving the business to their son, and dividing her little savings between the daughters; but she neglected from day to day to make her will. She was seized with a sudden and alarming illness; no interval of consciousness occurred in which she could execute her often-expressed purposes. She died without a will; and the nearer cousin, from whom she had received nothing but unkindness, came forward as heir-at-law, and laid claim to the whole of her property.

A child was observed to be very languid and feverish. The parents agreed that he ought to have a dose of medicine; but the child was averse to take it: a neighbor called in, and the mother was diverted at the moment that she ought to have given it him. She consoled herself with thinking that she would give it him the first thing in the morning, and that would make very little difference. It was given to him, but it produced no effect; another morning came, and the child was much worse. Then it was agreed to send for the doctor, and the servant was told to go directly, as the doctor was in the habit of leaving home at ten o'clock, and not returning for several hours. She received the order; but, thinking a few minutes could not make much difference, she delayed till the time was past: it was *only* a few minutes: but the doctor was as remarkable for punctuality as the family to which he was summoned was for procrastination; he had left home, and was gone several miles to visit his patients. Some hours elapsed before his return; he then hastened to the bedside of the sick child; but his efforts were too late: a fatal disease had laid hold on the frame, which, in all probability, might have been checked by timely application.

Julius Cæsar, one of the Roman emperors, was assassinated in the senate-house. On the morning of his death, he received a letter, intended to admonish him of the conspiracy formed against him, and to suggest the means of escaping it. Being much engaged, he gave the letter unread to his secretary, saying, "To-morrow, to-morrow." Alas! his to-morrow, like that of thousands, was in eternity!

And oh, how often is this fatal habit allowed to act upon the concerns of the soul and of eternity, and how awful are its consequences! The youth, when urged to attend to the salvation of his soul, says, "It is too soon to become reli-

PROCRASTINATION.   55

gious; there is time enough yet." Perhaps he lives to old age, and, when the matter is again urged upon him, he says, "Now it is too late."

The following affecting facts, as related by a minister of the gospel, will serve to illustrate this melancholy subject. Calling at the house of one of his friends, the minister found them in the deepest distress, having suddenly lost their only child. He attempted to console the distracted parents; but the mother replied, "Ah, sir, these consolations might assuage my grief for the loss of my child, but they cannot blunt the stings of my conscience, which are as daggers in my heart. It was but last week I was thinking, 'My child is now twelve years of age; his mind is rapidly expanding; I know he thinks and feels beyond the measure of his years, and a foolish backwardness has hitherto kept me from entering so closely into conversation with him as to discover the real state of his mind, and to make a vigorous effort to lead his heart to God.' I then resolved to seize the first opportunity to discharge a duty so weighty on the conscience of a Christian parent; but day after day my foolish, deceitful heart said, 'I will do it to-morrow.' On the very day that he was taken ill, I had resolved to talk to him that evening; and when he at first complained of his head, I was half-pleased with the thought that this might incline him to listen more seriously to what I should say. But oh, sir, his pain and fever increased so rapidly that I was obliged to put him immediately to bed; and, as he seemed inclined to doze, I was glad to leave him to rest. From that time, he was never sufficiently sensible for conversation; and now he is gone into eternity, and has left me distracted with anxiety concerning the salvation of his precious soul! Dilatory wretch! had it not been for my own sin, I might now have been consoling myself with the satisfactory conviction of having discharged the duty of a Christian parent, and enjoying the delightful assurance of meeting my child before the throne of God and the Lamb. Oh, the cursed sin of procrastination! Oh, the ruinous delusion that lurks in the word *to-morrow!*"

Every word of the distracted mother was like a dagger in the minister's heart; for he, too, was agitated by feelings similar to her own. "I have just returned," said he, "from a house which to me, as well as to the family, was the house of mourning. I was sent for *yesterday* to visit a sick man, and, as I fancied that I was then engaged, I promised to call and see him *to-morrow;* but when I went there *to-day*, I was shocked to find that he was dead, especially as I had reason to fear for his eternal state, and his wife said he was very anxious to see me." The minister returned home, bitterly reproaching himself for suffering any inferior engagement to stand in competition with a sinner's eternal interests, and praying, "Lord, lay not this sin to my charge, nor let the blood of my brother's soul rest upon my mind, and blast the future success of those employments for which I left him to perish in his sins! Grant me to learn hence, to abhor, through all my future life, the thought of deferring the concerns of souls till *to-morrow!* Christians, parents, ministers, learn wisdom from my folly; obey the voice that says, 'Son, go work *to-day* in my vineyard; to-morrow is none of yours. Sinners, *to-day*, if ye will hear the voice of Christ, harden not your hearts, lest he swear in his wrath that ye shall not enter into his rest.'"

It is an awful saying, yet true, "The way to hell is paved with good resolutions." The very *intention* of doing good lulls the conscience to sleep, in the neglect of *doing* it, and thus leads on to condemnation for leaving it *undone*. In the matter of individual salvation, this should be the motto, "Now is the accepted time, now is the day of salvation:" but in no part of the Bible is this written of to-morrow.

In our endeavors to do good to others, especially spiritual good, in which we are most apt to be neglectful, this should be ever before our eyes—"Whatsoever thy hand findeth to do, do it with thy might; for there is no work, nor counsel, nor wisdom, nor device, in the grave, whither thou goest."

If we defer till to-morrow what ought to be done to-day, without one shadow of reason to expect a more advantageous opportunity, or greater ability than at present, we add seriously to the difficulty, and awfully to the uncertainty of its being ever done at all.

"When once life is past, it will be vain to think of repenting; you will then have no more sermons, no more offers of Christ and grace. Heb. ix. 27. God will be patient no more. And if God should take away your life to-morrow, you would perish inexcusably for refusing his grace to-day. *One* offer of grace refused, renders a sinner inexcusable, though God should never offer his mercy more. Then trifle not away this moment, upon which depends eternity."

> "He who defers his work from day to day,
> Does on a river's brink expecting stay
> Till the whole stream that stops him shall be gone,
> Which, as it runs, forever will run on."

"Between the more stated employments, and more important occurrences of human life, there usually happens to be interposed certain intervals of time, which though they are wont to be neglected as being singly, or within the compass of one day, inconsiderable, yet, in a man's whole life, they amount to no contemptible portion of it. Now, these uncertain parentheses, if I may so call them, or interludes, that happen to come between the more solemn passages (whether business or recreations) of human life, are lost by most men, for want of valuing them aright; and even by good men, for want of skill to preserve them. But as, though grains of sand and ashes be but of a despicable smallness, and very easy and liable to be scattered and blown away, yet the skilful artificer, by a vehement fire, brings numbers of these to afford him that noble substance, glass; by whose help we may both see ourselves and our blemishes lively represented, as in looking-glasses; and discern celestial objects, as with telescopes; and with the sunbeams kindle disposed materials, as with burning-glasses;—so, when these little fragments or parcels of time, which, if not carefully looked to, would be dissipated and lost, come to be managed by a skilful Christian, and to be improved by the celestial fire of devotion, they may be so ordered as to afford us both looking-glasses to dress our souls by, and perspectives to discover heavenly wonders, and incentives to inflame our hearts with charity and zeal: and since goldsmiths and refiners are wont, all the year long, carefully to save the very sweepings of their shops, because they contain in them some filings or dust of those richer metals, gold and silver, I see not why a Christian may not be as careful not to lose the fragments and lesser intervals of a thing incomparably more precious than any metal, *time;* especially when the improvement of them may not only redeem so many portions of our life, but turn them to pious uses, and particularly to the great advantage of devotion."

CHAP. VIII.

DECISION OF CHARACTER.

"I HARDLY know what to do." "I have a great mind to go." "I have a great mind not to go." "I should never have done it, if I had not been over-persuaded." All these, and many such like sayings, are the expressions of weak minds; people who, without intending ill, are almost sure to act ill, for want of decision of character. To avoid such folly and weakness, make up your mind as to what is right, and let no persuasion induce you to swerve from it, against your better judgment.

To be *infirm of purpose*, is to be at the mercy of the artful, or at the disposal of accident. Look around, and count the numbers who have, within your own knowledge, failed from want of firmness. An excellent and wise mother gave the following excellent advice to her son, with her dying breath— "My son, early learn how to say *No*."

A failure in this particular is one of the most common faults of mankind, from the highest to the lowest classes of society, and is alike productive of mischief and misery in all. The following sketch is from humble life; recorded by a worthy clergyman.

"How many of our misfortunes might be prevented if we could each of us learn to say the little word *No!* I remember, when I was a boy, an incident took place, which serves to show the importance of the above little word. In our village there lived a very fine young fellow, named Jones: he was one of those who could never say No. It happened that a recruiting serjeant came there, to enlist soldiers, and, being pleased with the appearance of Jones, he invited him into the public-house, where he was drinking. Jones did not like to say No, but went in. Though a sober lad, not being able to say No, he soon got tipsy. He then enlisted, and went abroad. Not being able to say No, he fell into bad company, and got connected with them in their crimes. The last I heard of him was, that he was in jail, under sentence of death, for sheep-stealing; but, through the influence of his friends, his sentence was mitigated to transportation for life. Before his reprieve arrived, he spoke to some friends who visited him, to the following effect:—'My ruin has been that I never had resolution enough to say *No*. All my crimes might have been avoided, could I have answered *No* to the first invitation to do wrong; but, not being able to say *No* to a merry companion, even when he invited me to commit a crime, I thus became his accomplice."

Reader, doubt not the truth of this story, but learn from it to take courage to say *No*.

> "In vain the world accosts my ear,
> And tempts my heart anew;
> I cannot buy your bliss so dear,
> Nor part with heaven for you."

CHAP. IX.

MUTUAL FORBEARANCE.

Among the duties which a good man ought to discharge, few are more important than those of the peace-maker. The peace-maker will be applied to in many of the quarrels and misunderstandings, which occur among families and neighbors. On these occasions, he will be not so much concerned to hear the particulars of the quarrel, as to impress on both parties the duty of mutual forbearance. There is little done towards settling a difference, to prove who was most in the wrong in beginning it, or to hear all the angry things that may be said by both parties. The great means of harmony is the promotion of a spirit to bear and forbear; forget and forgive; and that upon the principles of the gospel, which enjoin us to be gentle towards all men, pitiful and courteous, kind and tender-hearted, forgiving one another, even as God, for Christ's sake, hath forgiven us.

There is a difference in the natural tastes and dispositions of mankind: besides this, early habits, education and connections, make a great difference in individuals, in things which are in themselves innocent or indifferent. Circumstances sometimes throw together, in after life, persons whose previous modes of thinking and acting have been widely different. This is a call for the exercise of mutual forbearance. If both parties are determined to censure, despise, or be disgusted with every thing to which they have not been accustomed, their differences will be a source of perpetual altercation and discord. But if both parties resolve to be pleased with each other; to bear with the imperfections of others, and to correct their own; occasionally, also, giving a gentle and friendly hint which may benefit those with whom they associate; then, notwithstanding little differences, persons may happily unite and harmoniously coöperate in the family, the neighborhood, and in religious society; and, indeed, their very differences may prove useful, as peculiarly fitting them for different departments in the general cause.

CHAP. X.

MAXIMS ON WASTE.

I ONCE heard a gentleman relate, that the collectors for some benevolent society in London, calling on a wealthy gentleman to solicit contribution, overheard him reproving his maid-servant for throwing away a match of which only one end was burnt. One of the collectors proposed immediately to leave the house, observing that it was quite in vain to hope for assistance from such an old niggard; but the other was disposed to wait. The gentleman soon made his appearance, and, having examined the case, went to his bureau, and, taking out a fifty pound note, presented it to the astonished collectors. "Gentlemen," said he, "you appear surprised at this donation; and probably consider it inconsistent with what you have just now heard; but, I assure you, it has been by scrupulous attention to economy in little things, that I have been enabled to exercise liberality in great ones."

This story brings to my mind that famous saying of poor Richard, "Take care of the pence, and the pounds will take care of themselves." Like most of his sayings, it contains a great deal of good sense, shrewdness, and knowledge of human affairs. I wish a regard to the disposals of Providence was more constantly kept up; but while every pious person will humbly and gratefully acknowledge that "the blessing of the Lord, it maketh rich, and addeth no sorrow," we cannot but observe that the blessing of God is generally seen to rest on those who are diligent, thrifty, and frugal; we are quite sure it never rests on indolence and extravagance. Every day shows the general truth of the following maxims :—

"Waste not, want not."

THE FAMILY AT HOME.

"Wilful waste makes woful want."

"Waste a crumb and you are likely to want a loaf. Squander a penny, and you are likely to want a pound."

"Beware of small expenses and small imprudences: a small leak may sink a great ship."

"The rich should not suffer the waste of their property, while there are poor in want of it, and while they know not but they or their families may one day want it themselves."

The following beautiful remarks I copied from a sermon on frugality:—

"The Creator of the world is infinitely rich and infinitely bountiful; and yet in all his provisions he allows no waste: 'He *weighed* the dust, and *measured* the waters' when he made the world; and calculated to a nicety,—so much earth, so much air, so much fire, so much water, went to make up such a world as this. The first quantity is still here; and though man can gather and scatter, move, mix, and unmix, yet he can destroy nothing. The putrefaction of one thing is a preparation for the being and bloom of another. Thus a tree gathers nourishment from its own fallen leaves when they are decayed, and something gathers up the fragments, that nothing is lost.

"And when the Son of God was on earth, and went about scattering blessings; when with a word he multiplied five barley loaves and two small fishes to feed many thousand persons, he could in the same manner have provided another meal whenever the need of his followers required it; but, instead of that, he commanded them to gather up the fragments, that nothing might be lost; thus teaching us to regard frugality as a Christian virtue."

The following are useful rules for those who wish to leave something good to children's children.

1. Buy nothing but what you really need. Those who accustom themselves to buy things merely because they are pretty,

or curious, or are offered a great bargain, are likely to fill their house with NEED-NOTS, and to deprive themselves of the means of obtaining what they need.

2. In purchasing, choose such things as are durable, rather than such as are showy; and what is in itself neat and becoming, rather than what is just the top of the fashion. Fashions soon change, and that which is glaringly fashionable now, will be notoriously unfashionable a little time hence.

3. Though it may sometimes call for the exercise of self-denial, whatever you purchase, or whatever you think you want, be resolute in retaining something in your power to meet an unforeseen, an indispensable need. For want of this precaution, many have been compelled to part with what they wished to preserve, to obtain something that they could not do without.

4. Endeavor to have different things for different purposes, and to keep each to its proper use. Nothing is more destructive than to make one thing do the work of two or three.

5. Never use a better thing of its kind without being satisfied that a worse would not answer the purpose. Many people, whenever they obtain a new thing, directly lay aside the old one, and forget to use it, or perhaps suffer it to be thrown about and destroyed. Such are not likely to leave behind them much that is worth having.

6. If intrusted with the property of others, be as careful of it as if it were your own. This is the likeliest way to be honestly possessed of property yourself, and to acquire a habit of taking care of it.

7. If children are committed to your care, bring them up in habits of knowing the value of property, and the importance of taking care of it. Those who are careful themselves, but suffer their children to be extravagant, have little encouragement to lay up property for them to squander.

8. See that, in all your gains, and savings, and prospects, you keep the fear of God before your eyes. His blessing alone maketh rich, and addeth no sorrow. Wealth gotten by vanity (that is, unjust, selfish gain) will be soon minished. It is like

putting money into a bag with holes; but a good man shall leave an inheritance to children's children.

9. Whatever you leave your children, do not neglect their best interests. Teach them to read; provide them with a Bible; store their minds with good principles, that so they may be prepared to be content with a little, or faithfully to improve and safely to enjoy more; and be sure to lay up for them a good store of prayers. The effectual fervent prayer of a righteous man availeth much; and a parent's prayers have often been answered in rich blessings on his offspring, long after his head has been laid in the grave. Let the chief concern be for yourselves and them, that you may all be possessors of durable riches and righteousness, a treasure in the heavens that faileth not, where neither moth nor rust can corrupt, nor thieves break through and steal.

CHAP. XI.

FEMALE DRESS.

Among the many evils which judicious ladies will labor to oppose as far as their influence extends, I ought to mention extravagance and vulgar finery in dress. They will set an example of neatness and modesty in apparel, without approaching to singularity. They never adopt a ridiculous fashion, nor are they backward in adopting what is convenient and becoming. I have often observed that the example of ladies in this respect has a great influence on those around them. I have seen domestics imitating the dress of their ladies in every thing but the quality and texture of the materials, and even Sunday-school children aping the bows and feathers and necklaces of their teachers.

It very often, however, requires some care and pains to bring young girls into the right habits in this respect. In fact, I believe that I have sometimes myself received a hint or two on the subject; at all events, I have gathered a few hints, which, for whomsoever they might be originally intended, are much at the service of all to whom they may be applicable.

To many young women the love of dress is a great snare; it leads them into a series of mistakes from beginning to end. In the first place, they mistake by thinking that fine clothes set off their persons to advantage; whereas all persons of taste acknowledge that real beauty does not need the aid of finery, and that ugliness is only displayed and rendered conspicuous by it.

Next, they imagine that fine clothes give them the appearance of belonging to a higher class of society, and prove their introduction to it. No such thing. The real lady is discovered in her education, speech, and manners, which are not so easily imitated; and is more frequently distinguished by plainness of dress than by finery, which generally bears the stamp of vulgarity.

Another mistake is, that fine clothes will recommend them to the notice of young men, and lead to an advantageous marriage—a very unlikely thing! There are many young men who will admire such a girl as they would a peacock, and play with her as with a doll; but no sensible, discreet young man would ever think of making her his wife. "No, no," says he; "give me a wife who does not carry her chief beauty outside, and all her wealth on her back. I must see the ornament of a meek and quiet spirit, which is of great price; and the treasures of understanding and discretion, and the fear of God, which are more precious than rubies, and more rare than diamonds."

Another mistake of dressy girls is, that they believe that foolish fellows, who flatter them about their beauty and fine appearance are really sincere, and mean what they say; while the truth is, that they in heart despise and ridicule them; or, if they feel any of the fondness they profess, it is but a low, selfish passion, to which they will not hesitate to sacrifice their pretty, garnished victim. But oh, when the silly girl is induced by the love of finery to receive presents with which to indulge it, or perhaps to make free with the property of others!—but these are mistakes too dreadful to be entered on here. Alas! by these mistakes thousands are every year brought to ruin and disgrace; and she who thoughtlessly begins with the first and simplest of these mistakes, is in danger of proceeding to the last and grossest.

I recollect a remark which I heard many years ago, which my own observation has never contradicted, namely, that a dressy girl generally makes an untidy, slatternly wife and a negligent mother. I can look round me and see it confirmed in the dirty, blowzy finery of mothers and children, and the untidiness of the dwellings they inhabit; and in the remarks of occasional visitors: "Is it possible that that dirty, untidy slattern is the once smart, dressy Betsy ——? I could not have believed that a few years would have made such an alteration. And who is that neat, respectable matron at the next house, surrounded by her little, cleanly, orderly group of children? I certainly recognize the cheerful, modest countenance and respectable appearance that I used so to admire in Mary ——. Well, the only change in her is as natural and pleasing as from the chaste blossoms of spring to the ripening fruits of autumn; but in the other, it is as contrary and as disgusting as if the flaunting poppy should ripen to the loathsome toadstool."

Many a husband, who has been won by finery, has been weaned by slatternly negligence.

It was a saying of Augustus Cæsar, the Roman emperor, that rich and gay clothing is either the ensign of pride or the nurse of luxury.

A profusion of fine bows, feathers, necklaces, and ear-rings, may be regarded as the outward and visible sign of inward emptiness and vanity.

A minister, calling to visit a lady, was detained a long time while she was dressing. At length she made her appearance, bedizened in all the frippery of fashion and folly. The minister was in tears. She demanded the cause of his grief;

when he replied, "I weep, madam, to think that an immortal being should spend so much of that precious time which was given her to prepare for eternity, in thus vainly adorning that body which must so soon become a prey to worms."

A lady once asked a minister whether a person might not be fond of dress and ornaments without being proud. "Madam," replied the minister, "when you see the fox's tail peeping out of the hole, you may be sure the fox is within." Another lady asked the Rev. John Newton what was the best rule for female dress and behavior? "Madam," said he, "so dress and so conduct yourself, that persons who have been in your company shall not recollect what you had on." This will generally be the case where singularity of dress is avoided, and where intelligence of mind and gentleness of manners are cultivated.

Two holy apostles have not considered it beneath them to describe a well-dressed woman. St. Paul directs, "That women adorn themselves in modest apparel, with shamefacedness and sobriety; not with broidered hair, or gold, or pearls, or costly array; but, which becometh women professing godliness, with good works." St. Peter also exhorts, "Whose adorning, let it not be that outward adorning of plaiting the hair, and of wearing of gold, and of putting on of apparel; but let it be the hidden man of the heart, in that which is not corruptible, even the ornament of a meek and quiet spirit, which in the sight of God is of great price."

Solomon winds up his description of a virtuous woman, and one that is worth seeking in marriage, in these words: "Favor is deceitful, and beauty is vain; but a woman that feareth the Lord, she shall be praised. Give her of the fruit of her hands, and let her own works praise her in the gates."

This is a good place to set down the following remarks on the importance of teaching young women to pay attention to something better than mere outside show and finery. "The importance of female education will rise in our opinion, if we consider women as persons who may become wives and mistresses of families   In this situation, they have duties to perform which lie at the very foundation of human life. The support or the ruin of families depends on their conduct. A judicious woman, that is diligent and religious, is the very soul of a house. She gives orders for the good things of this life, and for those also of eternity."*

It was a judicious resolution of a father, as well as a most pleasing compliment to his wife, when, on being asked by a friend what he intended to do with his girls, he replied, "I intend to apprentice them to their mother, that they may learn the art of improving time, and be fitted to become like her—wives, mothers, heads of families, and useful members of society." Equally just, but bitterly painful, was the remark of the unhappy husband of a vain, thoughtless, dressy slattern :—"It is hard to say it, but if my girls are to have a chance of growing up good for any thing, they must be sent out of the way of their mother's example."

CHAP. XII.

SOBRIETY AND MODERATION.

I ONCE knew a girl of excellent, steady habits, who came to live in a gentleman's family. She had fared hard at home, for there was a large family to keep upon small earnings; but she was healthy and industrious, well behaved, and willing to learn.

In the course of two or three months, she began to grow so fat, that you would hardly have known her; and when any of her old friends met her, they generally accosted her with, "Well, Nancy, how hearty you look! You credit your keeper." Nancy always replied, that she had a very comfortable place, and plenty of every thing; and her father and mother

* Gisborne.

often remarked, what a great thing it was for a healthy, growing girl to live where she could have plenty. True enough, it is a great blessing to have plenty, and one for which we ought to be very thankful; but there is a danger, of which many people are not aware, of taking a little more than enough; and, as the saying is, "Enough is as good as a feast; more is as bad as a surfeit."

There are two sorts of people principally in danger from this, namely, those who have not much to do, and can have what they please to eat—one delicacy after another is contrived to make them eat a little more than is necessary; and those who are suddenly removed from the hard fare of a parent's cottage to the plenty of a gentleman's house—all is new and tempting to them; they wish to taste every variety that is set before them, and at almost every meal, they eat a little more than nature requires, in order to gratify the palate with the taste of something new; and health is soon injured by it. Nancy Cox had not been many months in this family before she became less nimble in her movements; her eyes looked heavy, her clear, ruddy complexion assumed a yellowish hue; she often complained of head-aches; and as soon as she sat down, was sure to drop asleep. Her mistress now and then gave her a dose of physic, and then she was better for a little while; but at last she was quite laid up, and they had the doctor to her. He said it was a bilious fever, and something about the blood flowing to the head. I did not rightly understand his learned words, but by what I could make out, it meant that the blood was clogged up, and could not flow freely, and that this made her so heavy and stupid; but I have never forgotten what he said when he cautioned her, as she recovered, against eating much meat or drinking much beer. He said, "I dare say your health was much better when you had only water to drink, and but little meat to eat. Now, if you wish to keep well, you must have resolution to bring your diet much nearer to what it was then. Though you can get so much more victuals and drink, it is no proof that more would do you good; indeed, this illness is a proof to the contrary. It is a sad mistake to suppose that a great quantity of food is nourishing and strengthening. It is not what persons *eat*, but what they *digest*, that strengthens them; and if they eat a little more than they can digest, this is all so much hoarded up towards making them ill. It is against my interest to say so, for I can assure you that more than half the doctor's work consists in attempting to undo the mischief that people have done themselves by habitually taking a little too much."

I am afraid that Nancy had not resolution enough strictly to follow the doctor's directions. As her appetite returned, she was eager after a little more meat, and beer, and pastry, than was quite proper for her. She could not be persuaded but that it would help her to get up her strength, which, however, was very long in getting up; and as long as she was in that family, which might be five or six years, she was more or less unwell, and obliged to take physic.

At length she was married to a poor, laboring man, and once more restored to cottage fare. She found it very hard at first, and indeed I have heard her say, she was years before she could get a relish for the plain food to which in her childhood she had been accustomed. A few months after she was married, she was very ill, and had gatherings on the tops of all her fingers. Dr. Collins attended her again, and told her that it was owing to the sudden change of living; but that he thought, if she once got over the change, she would have better health than she had known while living in the midst of plenty, and feeding to the full; and so indeed it turned out. She became a very healthy woman, and the mother of a fine healthy family. She often looked back with regret on the years of her self-indulgence, and she brought up her children to be content with the homeliest fare, and to drink nothing stronger than water; and when they grew up and went to service, it was one of her great concerns that they should not learn to eat or drink more than was good for them. In particular, she used to caution them against getting fond of strong beer, porter or wine, and especially spirits, even in the smallest quantity. Some masters and mistresses, out of false kindness, allow these things, when there is washing or any extra work about; but these things neither give strength, nor prevent taking cold, nor indeed do any real good whatever; and too often they form a habit that lasts through life, and proves very injurious in every respect.

I remember a poor, dirty, half-starved old woman, who, it was often said, had seen better days, and who, if she had but a few pence to provide for all her wants through the day, might be seen every morning coming out of the public-house with her little cream-jug of gin. She said she learned to take it, from having a glass allowed her before she began washing, by a very excellent and pious lady, who would have shuddered at the thought of being the occasion of sin to any one; but so the poor creature got the wretched habit, and though she owned it was the cause of her poverty and misery, she said it was *impossible* now to do without it. I fear she never tried in good earnest; but oh, how important is it that young people should guard against forming habits which may bring them into such disgraceful bondage! The only way to keep quite free from it, is by resolutely resisting the *first* temptation, from whatever quarter it may proceed.

I shall now set down a few maxims, both from the holy scriptures, and from the writings of wise and good men, which, I hope, will impress on the minds of the young the importance of strict sobriety and moderation; also some verses I lately met with in a magazine, and a piece called *The Drunkard's Will*, which I am sure ought to warn young men against once entering the public-house, or indulging the love of liquor.

"He that loveth pleasure shall be a poor man. He that loveth wine and oil (that is, luxurious living) shall not be rich."

"Dainties are deceitful meat."

"Hast thou found honey? Eat so much as is sufficient for thee, lest thou be filled therewith, and vomit it."

"Wine is a mocker, strong drink is raging, and whosoever is deceived thereby is not wise."

"Who hath wo? who hath sorrow? who hath contention? who hath babbling? who hath wounds without cause? They that tarry long at the wine; they that go to seek mixed wine. Look not thou upon the wine when it is red, when it giveth its color aright in the cup, when it moveth itself aright. At the last it biteth like a serpent, and stingeth like an adder."

"Take heed to yourselves, lest your hearts be overcharged with surfeiting and drunkenness, and cares of this life, and so that day (the day of death and judgment) come upon you unawares."

"Let us who are of the day be sober."—"Let your moderation be known unto all men: the Lord is at hand."

"He is the greatest slave who serves none but himself. He is the most beastly idolater who makes a god of his own belly." "The luxurious live to eat and drink, the wise and temperate eat and drink only to live."

"Always rise from table with an appetite, and you will not be likely to sit down without one."

"He that hankers after dainties, must often feel dissatisfied, and sometimes lie at the mercy of a dear market."

"Who dainties love, will beggars prove."

A celebrated Roman epicure consumed the principal part of his property on sumptuous delicacies. He had still enough left to support himself in moderation and comfort, but he put an end to his life, lest he should not have enough to furnish the costly luxuries to which he had been accustomed.

"Nature is satisfied with little, grace with less, but lust with nothing."

"An intemperate patient makes a cruel doctor."

"The glutton digs his grave with his own teeth."

"Wine and strong drink have drowned more than the sea, and the teeth of intemperance have slain more than the sword."

When disease is abroad in the land, it generally selects its victims from among the intemperate and self-indulgent.

Disease will be often knocking at the door, while his old friend, intemperance, dwells within.

It was the saying of a celebrated physician, "When I see a group of persons surrounding a splendid banquet, and feasting themselves without fear, I think if the prophet's prayer could be granted, 'O Lord! open their eyes that they may see,' the thoughtless creatures would then discover, under the disguise of luxurious viands and inviting bowls, fevers, dropsies, palsies, gouts, consumptions, death; and would flee in terror and amazement from the untasted repast."

"The Christian, when he sits down to his repast, should ever remember that he has two guests to entertain, the body and the soul. Let him never so overload the former as to starve, sink and ruin the other; but whether we eat or drink, or whatever we do, let us do all to the glory of God."

The motto of the family of Doddridge was, "Live while you live." On this the excellent and pious Dr. Doddridge wrote the following pointed lines:—

> " ' Live while you live,' the epicure would say,
> 'And seize the pleasures of the present day.'
> ' Live while you live,' the sacred preacher cries,
> ' And give to God each moment as it flies.'
> Lord, in my views let both united be;
> I live in pleasure while I live to Thee."

One Glass more.

> " Stay, mortal, stay! nor heedless thus
> Thy sure destruction seal:
> Within that cup there lurks a curse,
> Which all who drink must feel.
>
> Disease and Death, forever nigh,
> Stand ready at the door,
> And eager wait to hear the cry
> Of ' Give me one glass more.'
>
> Go, view that prison's gloomy cells,
> Their pallid tenants scan;
> Gaze, gaze upon these earthly hells,
> And ask how they began.

Had these a tongue, O man ! thy cheek
  The tale would crimson o'er ;
Had these a tongue, to thee they'd speak,
  And answer, ' One glass more.'

Behold that wretched female form,
  An outcast from her home,
Bleached in affliction's blighting storm,
  And doomed in want to roam :

Behold her ! Ask that prattler dear
  Why mother is so poor ;
She'll whisper in thy startled ear,
  ' 'Twas father's One glass more.'

Stay, mortal, stay ! repent, return ;
  Reflect upon thy fate ;
The poisonous draught indignant spurn—
  Spurn, spurn it, ere too late.

Oh ! fly the ale-house' horrid din,
  Nor linger near the door,
Lest thou, perchance, should sip again
  The treacherous ' One glass more.' "

The Drunkard's Will.

" I, ————, beginning to be enfeebled in body, and fearing I may soon be palsied in mind, and having entered upon that course of intemperance from which I have not resolution to flee, do make and publish this my last will and testament :—

" Having been made in the image of my Creator, capable of rational enjoyment, of imparting happiness to others, and of promoting the glory of God, I know my accountability; yet such is my fondness for sensual gratification, and my utter indisposition to resist temptation, that I give myself entirely to intemperance and its associate vices, and make the following bequests :—My property I give to be dissipated, knowing it will soon fall into the hands of those who furnish me with ardent spirits. My reputation, already tottering on a sandy foundation, I give to destruction. To my beloved wife, who has cheered me thus far through life, I give shame, poverty, sorrow, and a broken heart. To each of my children I bequeath my example, and the inheritance of the shame of their father's character. Finally, I give my body to disease, misery, and early dissolution; and my soul, that can never die, to the disposal of that God whose commands I have broken, and who has warned me by his word, that no drunkard shall inherit the kingdom of heaven."

Drunkard, this is your will.

CHAP. XIII.

NURSING.

It was a common custom in our village, when any poor woman was confined by sickness, to send round to the neighbors who could afford to give such things, and beg wine, beer, or spirits. Some very honest, decent women only desired what they really thought was necessary to support and recruit their strength; but there were others, who made quite a trade of it. It was not what they needed, or thought they needed, but what they could get. No matter to them how much they imposed on the good-nature of those to whom they applied, or how much they injured the cause of charity as to other poor people; they would send to four or five different houses on the same day, and obtain enough to support all their family in intemperance, as well as to endanger their own lives by improper indulgences. These people were sure to be found out in time, and scouted by all the sober and respectable poor people, as well as by their more wealthy neighbors. I have often been struck with the folly of some poor people, in so abusing the kindness of a friend, as that they could not call upon him for aid, in any future time of need. However, these are not the people, nor is this the subject, on which I principally intended to make a few remarks.

There was one family in our village who were very kind, charitable people, and who often received applications of this kind; but they steadily refused to give them a drop of beer, wine, or spirits, without a written statement from the doctor, that it was proper and necessary. Good, plain gruel, any poor woman who needed it, was welcome to, and when it was fit for her, a basin of broth, or a bit of hot meat; but they said they looked upon strong drinks for sick people as a sort of poison. Some of the poor said it was all stinginess; but others were led to think seriously about the matter, and they found the advantage of a change of diet.

My good mother, I have said, occasionally went out to nursing; at first she followed the maxims and customs which had long been established in our village; but when she came to converse with the lady of the family, she found her plans so much more reasonable, that she gradually adopted them all, and often said she was spared many anxious hours on behalf of those women who were wise enough to fall in with them too.

I remember once a decent neighbor of ours, whom my mother had been used to nurse in times of sickness, came to her in great trouble. Several of her children had been ill, and her husband out of work a great part of the winter; so, one way and another, though they were striving, saving people, these things pulled them back sadly. The poor woman could not help weeping, as she observed to my mother, "I never was so badly off before; I have not been able to get things comfortable about me, as I used to do; and such a deal of money as I always have to pay the doctor, what is to become of us, I don't know! I have not been able even to get a bottle of brandy or gin; and it is really miserable to be sick without such needful things in the house."

I believe at that time it had not entered into my mother's mind that such things were otherwise than needful; so, being a kind-hearted body, she bade her poor neighbor be comforted, and promised to mention her wants to a lady, who, she doubted not, would readily assist her. Accordingly she did so; and the lady soon called on the poor woman with a nice bundle of baby-linen, and offered her any proper assistance at the time of her confinement. She was greatly cheered by this seasonable supply, and said, that if she had but got a little brandy in the house, her mind would be quite at ease.

"And why," asked the lady, "are you so anxious about that? What good is it to do you?"

"I don't know for that, Ma'am; but it is what I always did have, and it seems so desolate to be without it."

"Did your doctor order you to take any?"

"No, Ma'am, I can't say that he did; but I always do take it—a little just to comfort and nourish me, and to keep me from taking cold when first I sit up. But I don't get along very well; for I get so feverish, and the doctor is forced to bleed me, and give me cooling physic; and thus I get my strength very slowly, do what I will; and it costs a great deal of money for medicine to strengthen me and get me an appetite; but I don't seem to relish any thing: and then my babies always have the thrush so bad; and that, you know, makes it all the worse for me."

"True," said the lady; "but I can't help thinking that if you were to do without spirits, and without beer caudle, you might do also without bleeding, and physicking, and strengthening medicines, and the thrush for your baby, and much unnecessary suffering for yourself. I assure you, my friend, it is not that I should grudge giving you these things, if I thought they would do you good; but I feel so convinced of the contrary, that I should be guilty of great unkindness in putting it in your power to injure yourself. I do not speak from my own experience merely, but from the testimony of the most eminent medical men. My eldest daughter, who has been lately sick, was attended by one of the most famous doctors in London, who practises chiefly among the nobility; and I can assure you, he never ordered, nor did she ever take, a drop of spirits in any form; and no person could gain her strength faster than she has done. Now let me persuade you, to try if you cannot pursue the same course with advantage. If any circumstance should occur, that the medical man finds it necessary for you to have either wine or spirits, you shall be welcome to whatever our house affords; but if no particular occasion should arise, I really think and hope you would find yourself far better without them."

The lady's kind manner won upon poor neighbor Wilson: she afterwards talked it over with my mother, and both agreed that there seemed to be truth and reason in what she had said: at all events, it was a cheaper plan; it would be a pity to waste money on strong things, if they were not really necessary.

"Ah!" interrupted neighbor Brown, who happened to overhear the conversation, "cheap, indeed, and that's the true meaning of it! Religious folks are always stingy; but if you let a lady talk you out of having a drop of something comfortable when you need it, I say you are a fool for your pains. It is what I won't do, I can tell you. If it can't be got at one place, it can at another. I shall send to the Squire's for what I want, and I know they won't deny me. Their strong beer and a drop of gin or brandy makes the best of caudle."

When the lady afterwards called to see her neighbor, she expressed great pleasure at finding her going on so remarkably well. "Yes, ma'am," she replied, "I am uncommonly well; but I begin now to be almost afraid; for it is just the time I always begin to fall off."

The good lady told her she ought not to indulge gloomy apprehension, but cultivate a spirit of gratitude to God for the great mercies she had already experienced, and humbly and cheerfully commit herself to his gracious care for the future. Then she read her a comfortable portion of scripture, and told her to meditate on that, and to commune with her own heart upon her bed, and be still.

Next day she found her still better; and so she went on steadily, from day to day, and was restored to her family a week or two earlier than had ever been the case before; and she had nearly two pounds less to pay the doctor.

This mode of nursing, by degrees, became pretty general in our neighborhood. Farmer Williams's wife was one of the first to follow it. And when the first farmers' wives were known to follow the new plan, the poor people were more inclined to come into it. One or two still kept to their old notions, and would have their strong beer caudle, and spiced wine; and as my mother used to say, after she had once seen the difference, she was worn out with anxiety when she had to do with those who were bent on such improper indulgences.

I must not omit to mention poor Mrs. Brown, who was so determined to get what she liked one way or other. One day when the physician, who attended them both, called in to see Mrs. Wilson, he looked very gloomy, and mother asked if he was unwell. He told her he was very anxious about a patient, whom he left going on very well, and with a strict injunction to take nothing of a heating kind; but on his next visit, he found her very feverish, in consequence of having taken things very improper in her situation. He wished to bleed her; but she stubbornly refused, from a superstitious idea, that bleeding will save life *once*, and that she was not so ill as to resort to what she considered so desperate a remedy. In a few hours, she was much worse; and though he then insisted on adopting a measure which he considered indispensably necessary, it had not proved successful in removing her fever; and he greatly feared the result. Next morning, mother inquired after Mrs. Brown, for she was the person in question. The doctor shook his head, and feared there was hardly a hope of her recovery. He was unwearied in his attentions; but all in vain. The unhappy woman was soon hurried to the grave, the victim of self-indulgence and obstinacy.

CHAP. XIV.

HEALTH AND SICKNESS.

This is a good place in which to set down a few hints about sickness, which I have gleaned from my good mother, and other friends.

She often observed, that many people make mistakes on this subject, and she took great pains to correct them wherever she had opportunity.

In the first place, she would say, "Do all you can to preserve health; an ounce of prevention is worth a pound of cure. In order that you may be healthy, rise early, live temperately, labor diligently, cultivate a contented spirit, observe cleanliness, use plenty of cold water about your person, admit plenty of fresh air into your houses."

She used to tell a story of a certain great physician, who gave four rules for the preservation of health. When he died, his books were sold: one, which was said to contain very valuable precepts of health, but which the bidders were not permitted to open, sold at a high price. When the purchaser got it home, he was at first disappointed at finding that it contained nothing more than four simple rules; but, on further consideration, he was induced to put the rules in practice; by which means he was restored to a state of health to which he had long been a stranger; and he often spoke of the old physician's book as the cheapest and most valuable purchase he ever made in his life. The rules were these:—
"Keep the head cool. Keep the feet warm. Take a light supper. Rise early."

These simple rules comprehend a vast deal more than may appear at first sight. A word or two on each will show this.

1. "*Keep the head cool.*" All tight bandages on the head are very hurtful, especially to infants. The less of any kind that is worn on the head, by day or by night, the better.

HEALTH AND SICKNESS.

Children whose hair is kept thin, and wno sleep without night-caps, are far less likely to catch infectious diseases than the generality of children.

To "*keep the head cool*," persons must avoid every kind of excess, and maintain moderation in every pursuit, and in every pleasure. The great eater and the great drinker have generally a burning forehead and a cloudy brain. The passionate man, and the intemperate, are strangers to perfect health, as well as to peace of mind. Even too hard study occasions an aching and burning head.

2. "*Keep the feet warm.*" To do this, activity and exercise are necessary, that all the various circulations of the body may be properly carried on. Care must be taken to avoid getting the feet damp, or immediately to remove the effects of such an accident by rubbing the feet till dry and warm, and putting on dry stockings and shoes; or else soaking the feet in warm water and getting into bed. Cold feet always show something amiss in the general health, which ought to be found out, and set to rights. This uncomfortable feeling often proceeds from indigestion, and a disordered state of the stomach and bowels. The same course suggested for keeping the head cool will at the same time tend to keep the feet properly warm, namely, moderation, activity, and calmness of temper. An intemperate, an indolent, or an ill-tempered person, is never really healthy; and, as it is in the power of every one to avoid such vicious habits, and even to resist and break them off when acquired, in that sense and to that degree, every man is the disposer of his own health, and has to answer for trifling with it.

3. "*Take a light supper.*" It is a sign of ill health when people have the strongest relish for food late in the day; and the indulgence of that irregular appetite tends to increase the evil. Formerly it was the fashion, though a very bad one, to eat substantial and often luxurious suppers. There was then a common saying,

"After dinner sit awhile,
After supper walk a mile."

In this homely distich there is much sound wisdom. One moderately hearty meal of animal food daily, is sufficient for nourishment, and conducive to health. After taking it, a short period of comparative repose is desirable, but not the total repose of sleep. After that, several hours of activity, and then a slight repast, such as will not require much exercise of the digestive powers, when the whole system ought to be resigned to complete repose.

Those who eat a hearty supper generally have disturbed, uneasy sleep, and wake at a late hour, languid and drowsy, feeble, sullen, and irritable, with a burning forehead, cold feet, and a disinclination to food and labor.

Some laboring men, however, are obliged to content themselves at mid-day with a slight refreshment, which they can carry with them, and depend on returning home to their principal meal when labor is done. In this case, the meal should be quite ready for them on their return home; and they should not go to bed directly on eating it, but employ themselves for an hour or two on some moderately-active pursuit, which, being of a different nature from their daily labor, will come in as an agreeable variation; such, for instance, as gardening, or carpentering, for the man who has labored through the day in the loom or on the shop-board.

4. "*Rise early.*" Nothing is more conducive to health and excellence of every kind than early rising. All physicians agree in this; and all persons who have attained a good old age, in whatever particulars they might differ from each other, have been distinguished as early risers. Some persons require more sleep than others; but it may be laid down as a general rule, that there is no grown person to whom a period of sleep longer than seven, or, at the very most, eight hours, can be either necessary or beneficial. But a person in health may easily know how much sleep he requires, by going to bed every night at a stated time, and uniformly rising as soon as he awakes, however early that may be. By steadily pursuing this plan for a few days, or at most a few weeks, a habit will be acquired of taking just the rest

that nature requires, and regularly awaking out of one sound and refreshing sleep to new vigor and activity; and when this habit is thoroughly formed, it would be no less disagreeable, than useless and injurious, for such a person, having once beheld the bright morning sun, to turn on his pillow and say, "A little more sleep, a little more slumber, a little more folding of the hands to sleep."

The earlier rest is taken, the more satisfying and beneficial it will be found. "One hour before midnight is worth two hours afterwards." This is a common and a true saying; but it is not to be supposed that two hours in the morning will make up for the loss of one at night. Nothing can be farther from the truth. The loss of night sleep is injurious, but indulgence in day slumbers is still more so. In case of having been disturbed one night, the best way to replace the loss is to go to bed one hour or two earlier, rather than to be later in the morning. Attention to these particulars would do much to preserve health.

"In the historical parts of scripture," says Robinson, "we may observe in general that diligence and early rising are inculcated as a *doctrine;* as, 'Thou shalt diligently keep the commandments'—'Give diligence to make your calling and election sure.' They are exemplified as a *practice;* as, 'Awake, I myself will awake early'—Abraham got up early in the morning—Jacob rose up early—Moses rose early in the morning—Joshua rose early—Samuel rose early—Job rose early in the morning—King Darius rose very early in the morning—Jesus came early in the morning into the temple, and all the people came early to hear him. All these were, probably, early risers by habit; and it is certain most of them were. Moreover, the practice is encouraged by express promise; as, 'I love them that love me, and those that seek me early shall find me.'

"Besides this general view of scripture history, there is a particular and not unedifying view of some remarkable mornings, of which I will just give you a sketch to direct your meditations.

"That was a morning long to be remembered, in which

the angel hastened to Lot, and led him and his family out of Sodom. The sun rose before he entered Zoar; and when Abraham got up early, and looked towards Sodom, he beheld, and, lo! the smoke of the country went up as the smoke of a furnace.

"It was a happy morning in the life of Isaac, when peace and plenty were secured to him and his family by a contract, confirmed by oath, between himself and a neighboring king, to perform which they rose betimes in the morning.

"It was a morning sacred to memory with Jacob and his posterity, when, after his dream of a frame with steps opening a passage to the temple of the King of kings, graced with heavenly officers going up and coming down, to teach him the doctrine of Providence, he rose up early, set him a pillar, and dedicated both the place and himself to God. Nor could time ever raze out of his memory that other morning, when a man wrestled with him until the breaking of day. 'Let me go,' said one, 'for the day breaketh;' 'I will not let thee go,' replied the other, 'except thou bless me.'

"What memorable mornings were those, in which Moses rose up early, stood before Pharaoh, and in the name of Almighty God demanded liberty for his nation! What a night was that, in which the Israelites passed through the sea! and what a morning succeeded, when Moses stretched out his hand, and the tide rolled back with the dawning of the day, and floated the carcasses of the Egyptians to the feet of the people of God, on the shore!

"Early every morning, for forty years, the cloud was taken up, and the manna fell.

"What a busy morning was that on which Gideon suppressed idolatry, at the hazard of his life! What an honorable morning was that to Daniel, when a great king visited him in the lion's den! And, to mention no more, that was a morning sacred to memory throughout all generations, in which Jesus, the King of Israel, was cut off. A belief of these true histories furnishes matter for early meditation, prayer, and praise.

"If any of us have been so unfortunate as to have acquired

the idle habit of lying late in bed, let us get rid of it: nothing is easier. A habit is but a repetition of single acts, and bad habits are to be broken as they were formed, that is, by degrees. An incomparable judge says, 'Habit, like a complex mathematical scheme, flowed originally from a point, which insensibly became a line, which unfortunately became a curve, which finally became a difficulty not easily to be unravelled.'—This difficulty, however, may be unravelled by application and prudence. Let a person, accustomed to sleep till eight in the morning, rise, the first week in April, at a quarter before eight, the second week at half-past seven, and the fourth at seven; let him continue this method till the end of July, subtracting one quarter of an hour from sleep, and he will accomplish the work that at first sight appears so difficult. It is not a stride, it is a succession of short steps, that conveys us from the foot to the top of the mountain. Early rising is a great gain of time; and should the learner, just now supposed, rise, all the harvest month, at four instead of eight, he would make that month equal to five weeks of his former indolent life.

"Early rising is a habit so easily acquired, so advantageous to health, so necessary to the despatch of business, and so important to devotion, that, except in cases of necessity, it cannot be dispensed with by any prudent and diligent man.

"Thanks to the goodness of God, and the fostering hands of our kind parents, this habit is so formed in some of us, that we should think it a cruel punishment to be confined to our beds after the usual hour. Let us prize and preserve this profitable practice, and let us habituate all our children and servants to consider lying in bed after daylight as one of the ills of the aged and the sick, and not as an enjoyment to people in a state of perfect health.

"Early rising is beneficial to health. I am aware that 'to ask what is wholesome, is like asking whether the wind be fair, without specifying to what port we are bound;' for some animals live on poisons. However, it may safely be affirmed, that, in general, lying long and late in bed impairs the health, generates disease, and, in the end, destroys the lives of multitudes. It is an intemperance of the most pernicious kind, having nothing to recommend it, nothing to set against its ten thousand mischievous consequences; for to be asleep is to be dead for the time. This tyrannical habit attacks life in its essential powers; it makes the blood forget its way, and creep lazily along the veins; it relaxes the fibres; unstrings the nerves; evaporates the animal spirits; saddens the soul; dulls the fancy; subdues and stupefies a man to such a degree, that he, the lord of the creation, hath no appetite for any thing in it; loathes labor; yawns for want of thought; trembles at the sight of a spider, and, in the absence of that, at the creatures of his own gloomy imagination."

In addition to these remarks, the following are worth observation. Bed-rooms should be airy, and, if possible, lofty; a low ceiling in a bed-room is very injurious; so also for a bed-room to be crowded with several beds, or with several persons sleeping in them. Windows should be made to open wide, and, if possible, to open from the top. It is unwholesome to sleep under a great quantity of clothes, or to have the curtains closely drawn round the bed.

Every window should be opened as early as possible in the morning, and closed before the damps of evening come on.

Beds should be stripped, and left open some hours, that they may be fresh and wholesome for sleeping in again. Ceilings and walls should be frequently white-washed : this may be done at a very small expense; about two shillings would purchase materials to white-wash several rooms, which any handy man or woman might do in a leisure hour or two. This is particularly necessary when any infectious disorder is in the neighborhood.

Floors should be scoured once a week, or, at least, a damp mop drawn under every bed. Such work should be done early in the day, that it may be thoroughly dry before bedtime.

Many people have a bad habit of continually taking medicine. This weakens the stomach and other digestive organs, and brings them into a habit of never doing their duty without medicine. It also renders medicine the less efficacious, when there is a real occasion for taking it.

It is also a very bad way for persons in general to read medical books. Nervous people are generally most fond of reading them, and they are very apt to fancy themselves the subjects of the diseases treated of, and unnecessarily or injudiciously to dose themselves with the medicines described. Such books are useful only to persons, who have some general knowledge of the principles of medicine, and some judgment in applying or varying general rules to particular cases. Not one in a hundred who dabbles in doctors' books and medicines, possesses a grain of such knowledge; and hence they are far more likely to do harm than good.

Great caution should be used in resorting to any advertised medicine. The more wonderful the cures said to be effected by them, the more strongly are they to be suspected. If these medicines sometimes succeed with peculiar constitutions, and in very desperate cases, it is perhaps because their inventors, who have no character to lose, administer powerful drugs in such quantities as no regular practitioner would venture upon; and one such case will serve to make a great talk about, and to print in hundreds of advertisements; but then they take care never to advertise the far greater number of cases in which the medicine has failed, or in which it has produced, instead of the benefits promised, consequences the most injurious—such as removing a pimple from the face, and bringing on the unhappy subject a deadly palsy.

In purchasing medicines, persons should be careful to procure them from a regular and respectable druggist, who understands what he sells. He should also be requested to write distinctly, on each packet or label, the English name and quantity of the drug it contains. Persons who deal in many other things besides drugs, are very liable to make mistakes in the article they serve, and very frequently they do not purchase drugs of the best quality.

Great care should be taken as to distinctly understanding the dose that is directed to be taken, and that it is accurately weighed or measured accordingly. It is no uncommon thing for ignorant people to advise "*a penny's worth*," "*a little*," or "*a spoonful*," of medicine. However good and suitable the medicine is in itself, it should never be taken on the recommendation of persons so rash and ignorant. A nurse, who was going to attend a gentleman ill with a fever, was advised to take a little nitre, as a good thing to keep off infection. She accordingly purchased "*a penny's worth of nitre*," which was just an ounce, and swallowed the whole quantity, which terminated her life in a very few hours.

Dangerous mistakes are sometimes made in the use of medicines, from similarity in sound or appearance to some other medicine of different qualities. A lady recently lost her life, in consequence of taking a medicine in which *beech-nut oil* was one ingredient, but instead of which she, in mistake, asked for *peach-nut oil*, which is a powerful poison.

Oxalic acid, or spirits of salt, or other poisonous drugs, have often been taken, in mistake, for Epsom, Cheltenham, or Glauber salts. To prevent such a mistake, it is a good way to take a small pinch of the dry salt, and throw it in the fire. If it is the proper medicinal salts, it will melt like snow: but if it is of the other kind, it will spirtle, or send up a blue flame like a match. Besides, the proper salts have a bitter, soapy taste; but the dangerous salts have a sharp, acid, burning taste.

If two kinds of medicine are in use at one time, care should be taken to keep the label fixed on each, and to read it every time of using. For want of this, a whole phial-full has been swallowed, when only a few drops should have been taken; or a medicine has been taken inwardly which was intended for outward application.

Among ignorant people there are a great many unfounded and mischievous notions with respect to sickness.

One stupid saying has been ruinous to many people: it is this—"Stuff a cold, and starve a fever." Now, no person who has a cold is free from some degree of fever; and by eating and drinking improperly, many a mere cold has been forced on to a dangerous and fatal fever.

Another great mistake is that of loading a sick person

with bed-clothes, keeping him in a hot room, and giving him heating things with a view to throw out the disorder. Such a course is sure to aggravate the disease, if not to render it fatal. In some disorders, such as measles, croup, inflammation of the lungs, &c., it is very essential to keep the room in one even degree of warmth: but that should never be warmer than is agreeable to a person in health. In fevers, small-pox, &c., a free current of air is refreshing to the sick person, and tends to lighten the disease, as well as to lessen the danger of infection. The draft of air should pass through the room, but not over the body of the sick. Nothing ventilates a room so well as a handful of fire in the grate.

Some people, when infectious diseases were about in the village, placed great dependence on strong-smelling things, such as camphor, tobacco, and scents, while they were not at all particular in keeping the sick room thoroughly clean, and admitting fresh air. Indeed, some would not venture to change the linen of a sick person through the whole course of the disease. It was no easy matter to break through these old prejudices; but my mother was not to be wearied by one, or two, or half a dozen fruitless attempts: she would still try again, and in this way she was a real blessing to many poor families in the neighborhood. Instead of trusting to scents, which only disguise, but do not destroy what is injurious, she would urge upon those who had the care of the sick, instantly to remove every thing of an offensive kind from their persons and their chambers; also, that they should frequently be refreshed by clean and well-aired linen, and what is removed from them immediately plunged in water, and properly washed as soon as possible.

She always objected to several people being crowded into a sick room, as tending to make the air close, and fatigue the sick person, as well as to aggravate the danger of infection. At the same time, she would urge on those around, the duty of paying proper attention to the sick, and not deserting them, under a timid apprehension of taking the disease. She would say, "Go steadily on, do your duty, use every proper precaution, put your trust in God, and leave the event in his hands." Her endeavors were very useful in causing the sick poor in our village to be much better attended to than had ever been the case before; and, by putting people in a rational way of proceeding, there is no doubt the progress of disease was in many instances cut off.

Another very common prejudice among those who have the care of the sick, is that of avoiding any reference to religious subjects. The Bible, and other good books, must be put out of sight; no religious person must be permitted to visit the sick person, nor prayer be offered in his hearing, lest he should be alarmed with the apprehension of death and eternity. These cruel prejudices have kept good people out of many a sick chamber, where their visits might have been a real blessing; but, as one of my friends used to say, " Does any person die the sooner for being prepared to die ? and is it not of infinitely greater importance, that we be prepared for death, than preserved in life ? Prayer calls in the aid of Him, who can do infinitely more both for body and soul than the kindest and best earthly friend; and danger cannot be averted by being kept out of sight. Now, the sick person is one of three characters, to either of which, the visits of a pious, prudent Christian, the holy word of God, and the throne of grace, must be seasonable. It may be he is a pious person; one who has been accustomed to think of death; one who has felt himself a guilty, perishing sinner, and has fled for refuge to lay hold on the hope set before him in the gospel: he has believed on the Lamb of God, who takes away the sin of the world; the Holy Spirit has been operating on his heart, making him a new creature in Christ Jesus, daily more and more weaned from the world, and fitted for heaven—now to such an one, the Bible, and prayer, and Christian conversation, will afford a delightful solace and refreshment. Some precious promise whispered in his ear, so far from distracting his mind, and aggravating his disease, will be as a cordial to his heart; and, by tranquillizing and cheering his spirit, will tend to aid the efforts of the physician in alleviating his bodily malady. Besides, why should he be checked in those expressions of his feelings, which may be made a great blessing to others? Such a man is not likely to die from fear of death; and whether he live or die, it will be his ardent desire, and his chief happiness, that Christ may be magnified in his body, whether by life or by death.

"But suppose the sick person to be one who has lived in ignorance, carelessness, and neglect of religion; and suppose that *now* some anxious forebodings oppress his mind. 'Death is at hand, and I am not prepared for it! How dreadful I find it to think about death, and judgment, and eternity, which yet I cannot avoid! Is there any hope for a wretch like me? What must I do to be saved?' Now, is it not a most cruel and wicked thing to treat these solemn inquiries as the vagaries of a disordered imagination? to keep back from the poor creature those who would lead him to the Lord Jesus Christ, who is the only way of salvation, the only foundation for a dying sinner's hope; and deny him the use of the appointed means for ministering to a mind diseased?

"Even human reason alone would suggest the propriety of yielding to his wishes, and soothing his mind by satisfying his anxious inquiries, not by evading or stifling them; and the part of common humanity, if those around the sick person are strangers to his alarm, and know not how to meet his feelings, would be to inquire after and give access to those who know how to speak a word in season to him that is distressed. But there is a still higher consideration. Which of the surrounding friends is willing to incur the dreadful guilt of depriving one so dear to them of the means of his soul's everlasting salvation? Which can bear the thought of his perishing in his sins, and his blood being required at their hands?

"But should the person be still in a state of hardened indifference, then the criminality of concealing from him his real state, and suffering him to pass unconsciously into an awful eternity, is dreadfully aggravated indeed! To amuse him with assurances of recovery, and to keep away from him every means of awakening conviction, when it is but too evident that there is but a step between him and death; and, unless he be convinced of sin, and brought to Christ for salvation, but another between him and endless misery! Surely there can be no kindness so false and so cruel as that of concealing truths so infinitely important, however unwelcome: and no circumstances of a sick person, except a state of unconsciousness or delirium, can excuse the suppression of those things that make for his everlasting peace, and which are about to be hid from his eyes."

CHAP. XV.

ACCIDENTS.

In a world like this, where accidents are continually occurring, every person should cultivate such habits of presence of mind, as will enable them to know what to do themselves, instead of depending upon other people.

Early one morning, as a gentleman was at work in his garden, the clergyman's footman came running, in a great fright, and begged to borrow a horse to fetch the doctor to his master, who had taken a dose of wrong medicine, and was in a most dangerous state. Two phials of nearly the same size and color had been sent over night: one was a draught to be taken early in the morning; the other contained a composing medicine, of which only a few drops were to be taken at night. The servant who administered the medicine, either could not read, or neglected to read the label, and gave the wrong medicine, the whole of which his master swallowed, before the mistake was perceived; and as no one in the house knew what should be done, the only resource was to send for the doctor : as he lived three miles off, some time must needs elapse before he could arrive. The gentleman readily lent the horse, and then hastened himself to the parsonage. He found the clergyman sinking into a stupor, and perceived that in a very short time he would be too far gone to take any thing. So, not having a proper emetic at hand, he got a large spoonful of flour of mustard, which he mixed in a glass of vinegar, and then suddenly dashed two or three basins of cold water at the patient's head. This roused him a little, and he was persuaded to swallow the mustard and vinegar, which soon made him very sick; and then the principal danger was over. When the doctor came, he, of course, administered the proper medicines; but he said the cure would have been hopeless, if nothing had been attempted before he arrived.

In like manner, presence of mind was once the means of saving the life of a poor man, who fell over a hatchet, and cut his leg in a dreadful manner. It burst out a bleeding at such a rate, as if all the blood would flow out of his body in a few minutes; but a gentleman, who was standing by, took a fold of linen, dipped it in vinegar, bound it round the wound, and then tied his handkerchief firmly over it, taking care to keep the edges of the cut closely together. Then he had the man carefully lifted into a cart, and so placed that the foot was higher than the knee, and so he was carried away to a surgeon. If the blood had been left flowing, the poor man would have bled to death before he could have been got to the surgeon. It is such a good thing to know what ought to be done, and to think of it at the proper time!

In case of an accident by water, the greatest security is in lying still on the back till assistance can arrive; and by struggling in their fright, people only hasten their sinking, and greatly increase the difficulty and uncertainty of rescuing them. I once read a very pretty letter I received from a young lady at a distance, thanking a gentleman for having taught her this lesson, and saying that, through the mercy of

God in preserving to her presence of mind to act upon it, her life had been saved when she was upset in a boat on the Thames, where the water was twenty feet deep. She caught hold of a pole that was thrown to her; but as the stream was very strong, she was whirled down it at a very rapid rate. With great difficulty she managed to keep her face out of water; for her bonnet filled, slipped off her head, hung, and became a terrible weight round her neck: but she knew that every means of assistance would be afforded her, and that her only hope was in keeping herself quiet and composed. The goodness of the Almighty enabled her to do this; and, after floating about twenty minutes on her back, she was taken out and restored to her friends, who had witnessed the accident, and altogether despaired of her life.

A poor lad was once fishing on the towing-path of a canal: some barge horses came up, and the boy, not getting out of the way in time, was carried by the barge rope into the stream. It was some minutes before he could be got out, and the bystanders concluded he was gone past all hope. Then some were for holding the body up by the heels to let the water run out, and some wanted to roll it on a cask, or to rub it with salt; but a gentleman present had some rules, printed on a card, which, he said, came from the Royal Humane Society, in London, set up on purpose to find out and practise the best method of doing things on these trying occasions; and these rules he strictly followed. He caused the lad to be placed in a warm bed, and had him gently rubbed with warm cloths and flannels, especially on the belly and chest: when, by these means, the body was thoroughly dry, and somewhat warmed, he had it put into a warm bath for five minutes. If there had not been hot water at hand, he said that brewers' grains would answer the same purpose, or hot sand, or ashes out of a baker's oven, or even hot bricks, or bladders filled with hot water, applied to the feet, hands and armpits; or flannels wrung out of hot water, and changed as they begin to cool. It is a good maxim, "If you have not got at hand the very thing you want, don't waste the time in saying, 'What a pity!' but think promptly of the next best thing that is at hand." After the warm bath, the body was put again into the bed, thoroughly heated. All the time of thus trying to restore warmth to the body, the bellows were applied to one nostril, the other nostril and the mouth being kept close shut, and a gentle pressure was made on the chest; thus the lungs were made to let out and take in the air, as they do in natural breathing. After a long time, and when almost every body gave it up for a lost case, there appeared some signs of breathing. The nostrils were then gently touched with a feather dipped in sal volatile; this made the poor fellow sneeze; the rubbing was then continued some time longer, and as soon as the lad could swallow, they gave him a little warm wine, by a spoonful at a time, and continued to do this for some hours, till a fine perspiration came on, and the lad fell into a comfortable sleep. All this took place before the doctor arrived, for he lived three miles off, and, when sent for, he was gone out in one direction, and his assistant in another : so, if nothing had been done till their arrival, there would have been nothing to do but prepare for a funeral, instead of restoring the poor lad alive to his grateful parents. I remember the same person said, that, if no success had attended his efforts, he would not have ceased making them for five or six hours, for that persons have been restored after that length of time; and he thought that many had been cast away for want of perseverance in the use of means.

If a chimney is on fire, instead of throwing open the doors, running about alarming the neighborhood, and destroying the furniture, close all the doors, keep the house as quiet as possible, and carefully and instantly put out the fire in the grate, and then that in the chimney will soon go out, or burn itself out without injury or danger.

If a person's clothes catch fire, how foolish it is to run

screaming into the air! Instead of that, if the person, or those around, had presence of mind to wrap him closely up in a carpet, blanket, or thick quilt, or even to roll him on the floor, the flames might be easily subdued.

There was once a house on fire in our village, and as it happened in the dead of the night, and most of the people were frightened out of their wits, in all likelihood several lives would have been lost, if it had not been for one person's presence of mind and activity. When he arrived at the spot, all was terror and confusion, the people running against one another, and pouring the water over themselves and each other. But it was just as if an officer made his appearance and gave the word of command. He arranged all the people, gave them something to do, and charged each to stand to his post. Instead of letting the men run backwards and forwards to the river for water, he made them all stand in a line, to hand the full buckets from one to another, and a line of women and boys to hand back the empty buckets. Meanwhile he and his man-servant got the family safely out of window, including a poor old woman, who was bed-ridden, and who, as every body concluded, must perish in the flames. The house was not very high, to be sure, but the danger was great, on account of the thatched roof; and had not some one been at hand, to take an active part, and to direct others, the family would have lost their lives, and the flames have spread much farther.

After that affair, the same gentleman taught the young men a number of clever contrivances; how to fasten sheets together, and to make knots that will not slip, for the purpose of persons letting themselves down from a window. He also offered a little reward to any one who should invent any likely method of preventing mischief, and especially of saving life in case of any future alarm. This set us all to thinking; and perhaps gave us all some notion of being a help, rather than a hinderance, in time of alarm. I shall close my hints on this subject with a maxim, which a friend told us all to commit to memory: "Let nothing be thought trifling, which may one day save your own life, or that of a fellow-creature."

CHAP. XVI.

LOOKING FOR THINGS IN THE WRONG PLACE.

THERE was in our neighborhood a poor, half-witted fellow, who had a fine ear for music, and got his living by going for many miles round to the houses of the gentry to tune their musical instruments. One day, when he was tuning a piano-forte, he dropped or mislaid one of the keys. Without troubling himself to look for it in the place where he had lost it, away he posted to Farmer Williams's, nearly a mile off, and, without saying a word to any one, raked out the kitchen fire, and began hunting very carefully among the cinders. Mrs. Williams, hearing a strange noise in the kitchen, came to inquire what was going on. Silly Sam, as they called him, very coolly replied, that he was only looking for an ivory key which he had just lost in Squire Sutton's drawing room.

We all laughed at the poor silly man's useless labor; but it does not belong to idiots alone to look for things in the wrong place. Dick Rogers has been more than ten years looking for a fortune; but his countenance, his dress, and his dwelling, all say that he has not found it: a good reason why: he has been wishing that he might find a pot of money in his garden, or that some rich person would take a fancy to him, and make him his heir; or that some fine lady would fall in love with him, and marry him. Poor Dick! he has been looking for riches in the wrong place: he would have stood a much better chance, if, like his old fellow-apprentice, he had sought them in the sweat of his own brow, and the labor of his own hands. He is likely to go hungry, who lies gaping for windfalls. " Watching for riches consumes the flesh, and the care thereof drives away sleep ;" but " the hand of the diligent makes rich," and " the sleep of the laboring man is sweet."—Then I could point you to more than one young woman, who is looking for admiration in the wrong place. They dress themselves up in finery, and go flaunting about, and giving themselves airs of consequence. But do they find what they seek : no more than this poor idiot found the pianoforte key in Farmer Williams's kitchen. A gentleman does not admire them ; for he sees plainly enough that they are not ladies. A poor man does not admire them; for he sees, from their very outside appearance, that they would bring misery and ruin to a poor man's cottage ; and every man of sense, instead of admiring, despises vanity and affectation. Indeed, it may be said, that wherever admiration is looked for, it is in the wrong place : the likeliest way to find it, is not to look for it at all ; but to think nothing about it, while we steadily go on doing our duty : then admiration comes unsought, like the shadow which flees the pursuer, but follows those who go right on their way. " Favor is deceitful, and beauty is vain ; but a woman that fears the Lord, she shall be praised : give her of the fruit of her hand, and let her own works praise her in the gates."

King Solomon complained that he found not one virtuous woman, on whom dependence might be placed ; it would have been strange indeed if he had, while he looked in the wrong place. He sought among a crowd of worthless beauties, not in the domestic retirement of conjugal felicity.

Those young people look for enjoyment in the wrong place, who seek it in a selfish, perverse following of their own way, and throwing off parental restraints ; and all who expect happiness in the indulgence of evil tempers and vicious propensities will find themselves grievously mistaken.

Even of those who are actuated by better motives and principles, it has been well said, " Christians are to blame : first, for seeking for that in themselves, which can only be found in Christ, namely, righteousness and strength, stability, fulness and perfection; secondly, for seeking that in the law, which can only be found in the gospel—pardon, consolation, peace, and hope; and, thirdly, for seeking that upon earth, which can only be enjoyed in heaven—a settled home, and perfect happiness."

CHAP. XVII.

GOOD THOUGHTS IN THE MIDST OF BUSINESS.

It is one of the great faults of human nature, to suppose that attention to one duty is an excuse for neglecting another. People who have their families or their business to attend to, are very apt to say, "I am so busy, I have no time to think about religion." Now, sure enough, worldly business has a tendency to put good thoughts out of the mind; and yet, if we try sincerely, we may generally find room to think of something good, without driving out necessary attention to our common duties; indeed, full employment is a fine remedy against idle and mischievous thoughts, and one evil thought hinders religion more than ten busy thoughts. Some good old writer says, "The grand secret to prevent bad thoughts, is to have plenty of employment; an empty house is every body's property; all the vagrants in the country will take up their quarters in it: always, therefore, have something to do, and then you will always have something to think of." Such were the remarks of a good man to one of his neighbors, who said she never had a minute to look into a good book, or, indeed, to bestow a thought upon religion. "Besides," he observed, "when employed in that with which we have by habit become very familiar, we may do it well, and quickly, without giving it all our thoughts. A weaver in his loom, a carpenter on his bench, a mother with her babe in her arms, or while sewing or knitting, often sing a song without hindering their work, or diverting their attention from it. Now, the words of that song might as well e:-

press sense as nonsense; had much better be the language of heartfelt devotion, than of profanity or indecency. I knew a good shepherd," continued he, "who said he had always learned by heart a verse of scripture at breakfast time, which served him to meditate upon through the day; and so rich was the treasure of scripture thus laid up in his mind, in the course of a long life, that the neighbors used to call him a walking Bible. I suppose you could scarcely name a passage of scripture but he could take it up, and go on with the connection, and that in such a way as proved that he not only recollected the words of scripture, but relished its sweetness. The word of Christ dwelt in him richly in all wisdom; it was to him the joy and rejoicing of his heart, and it seasoned his conversation with the salt of heavenly wisdom, and rendered it profitable to those who heard it. In like manner, I knew a pious weaver, who used to have a hymn-book or a Testament lying open on his loom, which afforded him many a refreshing thought. A poor shoemaker, I have often with pleasure observed hearing his children their catechism and hymns, while sewing away at his last; and a mother of a family always kept in her pocket 'Mason's Select Remains,' or some other little book of the same kind, which she could look at a minute or two while she was giving her babe the breast, or lulling it to sleep. These examples show what may be done by trying; and, at least, no one should rest satisfied in having no time for good thoughts, who ever finds time to admit a thought of vanity and folly. Those who sincerely try will find it much easier than they imagined, and still more refreshing and delightful than easy, to raise a thought to God and heavenly things, while the hands are busy for earth. Even if we are surrounded with bustle and clamor, it is not quite impossible to raise a secret thought in prayer, like Nehemiah, when, handing the cup to the king at the royal banquet, and his heart overcharged with care and distress—'So I prayed to the God of heaven;'—or, like Zaccheus, we may climb the sycamore tree, and get a sight of Jesus. Prayer can find its way to God above the heads of the crowd, and none but the holy soul itself see or know what is going forward. A penitent, believing heart is always in a fit place and frame for prayer; and a believing prayer is sure to turn the promises of God into performances. The mind of man is never so eagerly disposed to pray, but God is still more ready to give; and those who know the way to the throne of grace, will often say, with Melancthon, 'Trouble and perplexity compel me to pray; and prayer drives away perplexity and trouble.'"

CHAP. XVIII.

WHERE THERE IS A WILL, THERE IS A WAY.

A GENTLEMAN once had a present from abroad of several flasks of fine Florence oil. He placed them in a cellar to which no one had access beside himself. One day, to his great surprise, he observed that two of the flasks were empty. The next day, he found another flask empty, and was still more perplexed to account for it. He could not for a moment think that any person on the premises had contrived secret means to get at the cellar; and lest such a surmise should unjustly be awakened in his mind, he resolved secretly to watch in the cellar. I forget by what means he kept a light, but I am certain as to the fact, that after his remaining in the cellar more than an hour, three rats issued from a hole in the corner, and proceeded to the next flask. One rat stood upon his hind legs, and with his fore feet held the flask steady. The second sprang on the shoulders of the first, by which means he could reach the top of the flask. With his teeth he very carefully drew out the cork, by means of a bit of cotton twisted round it; then, dipping in his long tail, he presented it to the third rat to lick. They then changed places, as regularly as a set of soldiers relieving guard, and continued to do so till the flask was empty, each rat having had a fair proportion of the spoil. They then quitted the cellar. I have often heard this gentleman mention this singular fact. He always related it, if any one, in a hopeless, indolent tone, said of any thing that ought to be done, "I can't do it. It is of no use to try." He would say, "If you had but as much heart for your duty as the rats had for the oil, you would neither want time nor ability to do it. How is it that Jem Price always looks decent and respectable, has a good coat for Sundays, and a mite to put in the savings' bank every Saturday, while his next door neighbor, who takes the same wages, and has not so large a family, goes like a beggar and a vagabond, and finds it impossible to make both ends meet? Just because Price has set his mind upon being decent and thrifty, and 'where there is a will, there is a way.' No doubt he bestirs himself when his neighbor lies idle, and denies himself while his neighbor lives in swinish self-indulgence; but then success and satisfaction attend his endeavors, and he finds that, under the blessing of God, nothing is impossible to labor and patience.

"How is it that Mary Jones keeps her children so clean and decent, when every body knows that she must have many a hard pinch to get a bit of bread, now work is scarce, and her husband has had a very severe illness, and she herself also is but sickly? If you give her an old thing for the children, you see it, month after month, tidily patched, and always clean. It is astonishing how she manages. Those little, dirty, ragged beings at the next door have three times the money spent on them, and yet one should be afraid to come within three yards of them, for fear of being poisoned with their dirt, while Mary Jones's children are as clean as the children of a lord. What can make the difference? Just this—Mary Jones cannot live in dirt: she says, the victuals, if ever so little, do the children twice the good if they have but a clean skin; and though, poor woman, she has not wherewithal to change them, she sends them to bed betimes, and washes their clothes, and presses them smooth with a rolling-pin, for want of a fire to heat irons, and gets them tidily mended to go to school the next day. Whatever hardships she endures, she must and will be clean, and will see her children clean about her; and 'where there is a will, there is a way.' Her neighbor, with better means, has not a *will*, and that is the reason she never finds out a *way*.

"How is it that John Richards, with his numerous young family, contrives also to keep his aged mother in comfort, and will not suffer her to be a burden on the parish, while Thomas Smith cannot spare a shilling to help his mother, but lets her live in the parish workhouse, and does not even allow her a trifle for tea and sugar? Why, we must come to the old answer,—' Where there is a will, there is a way.' John feels grateful to his mother for her kindness to him in childhood; and he says it would break his heart to see her want for comforts in her old age, or have to look to the parish for them. 'No,' says he,—and his wife heartily joins in the sentiment,— 'if it please God to grant us health to work for her, she shall never want: it is but working an hour earlier and later, and sparing a few things, which we, who are strong and healthy, can do very well without, and the dear old woman is made comfortable for her last days, and many a blessing comes upon us and ours, through her prayers and holy sayings.' When the heart is thoroughly set upon duty, God gives ability and opportunity for the performance. One thing in which John had been used to indulge himself was a pipe of tobacco and a glass of gin and water, most evenings. He never took more than one, but he had been long used to it, and it seemed as if he could not do without it. When twins were added to his family of little ones, he was musing how they should be able to get along and do as they had done for his mother. They could not save in rent, or firing, or bread, or shoe-leather. 'But,' thought John, 'I might spare my pipe and gin and water, which cost me the best part of two shillings a week; it is but trying.' He said nothing of his resolution; but, from that day, he left it off, and has found not only that he *could* do without, but that he has ever since been richer, and healthier, and happier every way. Self-denial not only puts in a man's power the means of doing good, and accomplishing what seemed almost impossible, but it is its own reward in real satisfaction of mind and independence of outward circumstances.

"Can any one tell how Sam Driver got his learning? He was a poor lad, who had to work hard for his daily bread, and nothing to spare for going to school; but, somehow or other, he has got more learning than the schoolmaster himself, and a room full of books, about stars, and air-pumps, and foreign languages; and he understands them all. Why, Sam had set his heart on learning: there is the secret of it; and he denied himself, to save a penny or two pence a week, to buy books; and he spent every moment of his leisure in poring over them; and, if he met a friend who could instruct him, he never failed to propose some questions, or lay before him some difficulty; and, if he was baffled once, twice, or thrice, in any pursuit, he tried again and again, till he surmounted the difficulty. It was a favorite saying of his, 'Whatever man has done, man may do.' The further he advanced, the more easy seemed his progress. For many years he has been enabled to instruct others by his writings and experiments; and, while he gratefully acknowledges the goodness of God, in giving both ability and success, he stands as a fair example, that 'where there is a will, there is a way.'

"How is it that Ned Turner and his wife are seen, every Sunday morning, taking their whole family to the house of God, and spending every part of the day in holy leisure, as much as if they had servants to do their work, while Waters and his wife tell us they are obliged to drudge hard all day long, and can't see the inside of a church from one year's end to another? The thing is this: Turner and his wife know the value of the Sabbath, and their hearts are set upon enjoying and improving it. Many contrivances are employed through the week, to enable them on the Sabbath to lay aside all manner of work; but their success and enjoyment prove that 'where there is a will, there is a way.'

"May it not be added, 'Why is it that some persons are found to excuse themselves in sin and neglect of religion, by saying they cannot change their own hearts; they cannot possess themselves with grace; they cannot even pray to God acceptably, unless he give them his Holy Spirit?' All this is true; but what does it prove? Not that they are excusable in their neglect, or that they will escape the punishment due on account of it, but that they have no real desire after those unspeakable blessings, which they profess themselves unable to obtain. If they really felt themselves lost and undone without access to the pardoning mercy and gracious favor of God, through Jesus Christ, they would give themselves no rest until they attained it. They would use every appointed means of grace, as though all depended on their own diligence; and they would cry mightily for that aid, without which their endeavors must prove ineffectual. Salvation is not to be attained by a few faint, lazy wishes, but by an *agonizing* effort to enter in at the straight gate; by earnest, importunate, persevering cries at the footstool of mercy, ' Lord, save, or I perish! I cannot let thee go, unless thou bless me.' "

CHAP. XIX.

CORRECTING MISTAKES.

Some people find it a very hard thing to say, " I was mistaken," and will persist in error, rather than give up a point, or alter a practice, even when convinced that they were wrong. This is a very foolish sort of pride. The wisest of men are most deeply convinced of their own ignorance and liability to err; consequently, they are the most humble and candid. He who owns himself to have been in an error, only proves himself wiser than he was before; but, " Seest thou a man wise in his own conceit? There is more hope of a fool than of him."

" My whole life," said a certain good man, " has been

spent in discovering my own ignorance and mistakes, and in endeavoring to correct them; and now that I am an old man, instead of finding more reason than formerly to trust myself, I am, every day, more and more convinced of the necessity of praying for constant guidance, instruction, and correction from God. This is my daily prayer: 'Search me, O God, and know my heart; try me, and know my thoughts, and see if there be any wicked way in me, and lead me in the way everlasting.' I hope and trust I shall not be found mistaken at last!"

CHAP. XX.

CONQUEST OF EVIL TEMPERS.

People are born into the world with a difference of temper; but then they are accountable for the management of their tempers. Those who possess a gentle, even temper, should reckon it among their mercies; they should consider it also as laying a strong claim on them to be kind and forbearing to those around them; and, as much as in them lies, to take away the occasions of peevishness and irritability from those who may not, in this respect, be so highly favored as themselves.

It has been sometimes observed, that good-tempered people are apt to be forgetful; and hence they sometimes very unintentionally give provocation to others. A very easy, good-tempered girl has been heard to say, "Master was in *such* a passion, only because I did not hang his great coat on the right hook," or, "Mistress was *so* angry, only because I did not put the bread in the right basket. They are such bad-tempered people, there is no such thing as living with them." Now, even admitting that the master or the mistress might discover more irritation than the occasion warranted, the good-tempered servant should be reminded, that masters and mistresses have a right, not only to say what work shall be done, but in what manner; and if they choose to give directions in the minutest particulars, those directions should be obeyed. If a master says, "On this hook I wish my coat to be hung," the servant can hardly clear herself of disobedience, who, even thoughtlessly, hangs it on another. If she did not think, she ought to have thought. Besides, very serious inconvenience is often occasioned by inattention to these little things. To a thoughtless house-maid, it may seem of very little consequence, when she has dusted a book, whether she lays it down shut or open in the place she found it; or whether she replaces a lot of papers on the desk in the same order as she found them, or turns them topsy-turvy. But either of these exploits may, perhaps, give the studious master hours of disappointment and perplexity. Besides, more irritation of temper in families arises from these petty vexations than from more serious and wilful faults. Before, then, the easy-tempered person reproaches him who is angry, with too great irritability, it may be worth considering whether part of the sin does not lie at the door of him who thoughtlessly gives the provocation.

Every one has something to do in the management of his temper; and those who are themselves most highly favored, should consider it part of their task to remove occasions of irritation out of the way of others.

But some persons are conscious of having a naturally bad temper. They are peevish, or passionate, or sullen, or resentful. The person who is the subject of these dispositions must be aware of it. What, then, is his duty? I will just set down a few hints of advice, given by a friend to one who was very near and dear to me, and who found them very beneficial.

"If you are the subject of ill temper, in the first place, *never justify it* by saying, 'It is my natural disposition, and I cannot help it;' or, 'It was enough to provoke any body. Nobody can blame me for being in a passion;' or, 'I don't harbor malice; but I can never forget the offence.' All these are but false excuses for a cherished evil.

"In the next place, *constantly resist* the risings of an evil temper; turn away from the occasions of it; and check its first emotions within. It is much easier to refrain from uttering the first angry word, than to stop short at the second or the third. 'The beginning of strife is as when one letteth out water; therefore, leave off contention before it be meddled with.'

"But be careful to *resist on Christian principles.* To give way to evil tempers and passions, is not only foolish, and disgraceful, and injurious; it is also *sinful.* Too many people who would look upon theft, or drunkenness, as a sin against God, forget that ill temper and unkindness are equally so; and hence they neglect to control their tempers. But he who views evil tempers in their proper light, will say, before he ventures to indulge them, 'How can I do this great wickedness, and sin against my God?'

"The Christian has a never-failing rule for the government of his temper, in that prescription, 'Whatsoever ye would that men should do unto you, do ye even so unto them.' Here mark the difference between the world's maxims and Christ's maxims. The world says, 'Do to others as they do to you;' Christ says, 'Do to them as you would *wish* them to do to you.' If we never say nor do to others worse than we would wish them to say or do to us, we are not likely to say or do much amiss.

"Cultivate a spirit of Christian *humility.* This is a fine cure for evil tempers. Pride is always the companion, generally the origin, of petulance and passion: 'Only by pride cometh contention.' To think that any thing should stand in *my* way! that any one should presume to oppose *me!* Such is the haughty feeling of the angry man; but where Christian humility prevails, the feeling is, 'What an insignificant, unworthy creature I am! and yet from how many deserved miseries am I spared! how many undeserved mercies am I permitted to enjoy! Surely, I have enough to keep me contented and easy, and to reconcile me to any little inconveniences I may meet with.'

"Look to the *example of Christ*, who endured the contradiction of sinners against himself, Heb. xii. 3; who, when he was reviled, reviled not again, 1 Pet. ii. 23; who forbore to resent injuries, Luke ix. 53—56; who pitied his persecutors, Luke xix. 41; prayed for his murderers, Luke xxiii. 34; and has left us an example that we should follow in his steps, 1 Pet. ii. 21.

"Seek the *influences of the Holy Spirit.* The indulgence of clamor, wrath, envy, evil speaking, grieves the Spirit of God, and drives him away. But if the Holy Spirit's aid is humbly and constantly sought, he will dwell in the soul, and subdue those tempers and feelings which are offensive in his sight."

The influence of Christian principles is not more strikingly seen in any particular than in the conquest of evil tempers. I remember hearing some remarks made about several persons who, nearly at the same time, took up a profession of religion. Some one present observed, "What a striking change appears in Martha ———! she who used to be such a flaunting, dressy girl, has had her hair cut close, and will not even wear a bow in her bonnet." "Well, well," said a mother present, "I hope the change is not all outside." "And Susan ———, she who was always gadding about and taking her pleasure on a Sunday, now attends three or four public services every Sunday, and several more during the week." "Well, I wish it may prove abiding; far be it from me to say it will not; but, for my own part, I have much greater confidence in the far less glaring profession of Betsy ———, from the testimony of her mother, that, since she has attended to religion, *she strives to conquer her temper*, which was a source of continual uneasiness in the family." Many years have passed since these remarks were made; and I have seen Martha and Susan return to their finery, vanity and folly; but Betsy has gone steadily on, exhibiting the growing triumphs of divine grace over a naturally violent and stubborn temper.

I remember hearing a story of Socrates, who was one of the greatest philosophers among the heathens, and who was celebrated for mildness, patience, and evenness of temper. Few men had greater trials than he, both from the perverseness of his wife, and the ingratitude of his country; yet he was never seen with a cloud on his brow.

A certain physiognomist (or one who professes to judge of a person's natural temper and disposition by the features of his countenance) was requested to give his opinion of the character of Socrates. Having examined the lines of his countenance, he hesitated in giving an opinion, "For," said he, "your established character gives the lie to my science." He was urged to speak his mind freely, and declared that the countenance of Socrates indicated much natural peevishness, irritability, and stubbornness. The friends of the philosopher reproached the physiognomist with ignorance and mistake; but Socrates himself declared that his native temper fully corresponded with the description given, and that it was only by dint of severe discipline he had gained such an ascendency over it, and was enabled to maintain such a degree of mildness and forbearance; a proof that *something* may be done with the worst of tempers by proper management: and if a mere heathen could do this, what may not be expected from those who profess to be influenced and animated by the precepts, principles and motives of Christianity?

Both the good-tempered and the ill-tempered may find their advantage in committing to memory the following precepts of holy writ:—

"The discretion of a man deferreth his anger, and it is his glory to pass by a transgression."

"He that is soon angry dealeth foolishly."

"He that is slow to wrath is of great understanding; but he that is of a hasty spirit exalteth folly."

"A soft answer turneth away wrath; but grievous words stir up anger."

"He that hath no rule over his own spirit, is like a city broken down, and without walls."

"He that is slow to anger is better than the mighty; and he that ruleth his spirit, than he that taketh a city."

"Blessed are the meek, for they shall inherit the earth."

"Let the same mind be in you that was also in Christ Jesus."

"Those that are strong ought to bear the infirmities of the weak, and not to please themselves. Let every one of us please his neighbor for his good to edification."

"Put on, therefore, as the elect of God, holy and beloved, bowels of mercies, kindness, humbleness of mind, meekness, long-suffering, forbearing one another, and forgiving one another; if any man have a quarrel against any, even as Christ forgave you, so also do ye."

CHAP. XXI.

ILL-GOTTEN GOODS.

"ILL-GOTTEN goods never prosper," is a saying that has stood the test of ages. "A knave may get more than an honest man for a day, but the honest man gets most by the year." "Wealth gotten by vanity (that is, *injustice, fraud*) shall be diminished; but he that gathereth by labor shall increase." "He that by usury and unjust gain increaseth his substance, he shall gather it for him that will pity the poor." "Wo to him that buildeth his house by unrighteousness, and his chambers by wrong; that useth his neighbor's service without wages, and giveth him not for his work." Many, many times have these awful sayings been verified. Ah! there was poor old Farmer Hunter—I say *poor*, and so he was; though he was the richest man for miles round, he was far more an object of pity than of envy. It was he who used to gripe and grind the poor; who dealt hardly with many an honest little farmer, and brought him to ruin. There was not a mean trick of which he would not be guilty, to keep down the price of labor, or to keep up the price of corn, to overreach in buying and selling, in weight and in measure; and how did it succeed? Why, he got together a great property; pretty nearly the whole parish fell into his hands. He had more sheep and cattle than any farmer for forty miles round, besides thousands and thousands of money in the bank; but, poor old man, he had no enjoyment of his riches. He grudged himself every thing he ate or wore, and was always afraid somebody was coming to dispute his right, or take away his money, and that he should die in the workhouse. He had only one son, who was an honest man enough, and much respected in the neighborhood, but he died in early life, and left two little lads who were brought up for gentlemen, to inherit all their old grandfather's property. They came into it young, and contrived to spend it much faster than the old gentleman gathered it; for, before either of them attained the age of forty, houses, and lands, and money, were all gone; and they were far worse off than an honest day-laborer who had never known higher life. It seemed most astonishing where it could all have flown; and though it was often said with very improper levity, it was perhaps said with too much truth, that " Satan helped to get the money, and helped to spend it too." Ah! those who heap together unjust gains, don't consider how much they put themselves and their children under the snare of the devil, to be led captive by him at his will.

Old Madam West, in the next village to ours, lived upon her property, much respected both by rich and poor. She had five nephews and nieces, whom she had partly brought up, and among whom the property of her late husband was to be divided at her death. And it was her full intention to do the same with what was at her own disposal. The young people were very kind and affectionate among themselves; and not one of them, I believe, had a thought about being a favorite more than the rest, or a wish to gain any thing at the expense of the others, until one of the young men married a crafty, designing woman, who left no artifice untried to work into the old lady's favor. By her artful tricks, she at last won upon her to make a will, leaving to that branch of the family considerably more than the rest; indeed, all that was in her power to will away, consisting chiefly of a large quantity of valuable household furniture and plate, wearing apparel, and ready money.

The other branches of the family had no idea of the ungenerous trick that had been played upon them. But shortly after, this crafty woman returned home, (for she lived in a town some miles distant,) Madam West had the rest of her nephews and nieces to dinner with her, and going to her bureau, she fetched out the said will, and threw it in the fire. "There," said she, "now my mind will be at rest, and the property be share and share alike among you all, as your poor dear uncle intended, and as I always intended myself; but somehow that artful woman came round me, and persuaded me to do a wrong thing before I was aware." After a very few months had elapsed, the old lady died rather suddenly, and then the full artifice came to light. Another will was produced, to the same purport as that she had destroyed; for, suspecting the possibility that, when left to herself, she might repent and revoke so unjust a deed, her signature had been obtained twice, under the pretence of its being only one deed, while in fact it was two, one of which was left in her hands, to amuse her with the idea that the property was still in her own disposal; but the other of which was carefully concealed by the designing party, and in due time brought forward to establish their unrighteous claims. The rest of the family were indignant at the fraud by which they had been so shamefully injured, and grieved at the interruption of harmony in a family that had hitherto been united. They, however, resolved rather to bear injury than to engage in contention. But William and his wife had little reason to congratulate themselves on their unjust gains. Their own feelings were best known to themselves; but they had lost the countenance and assistance of the rest of the family, all of whom were more or less able to help them. The handsome old furniture was quite unsuitable to their little cottage, indeed, crowded it up as mere useless lumber. Confidence at home was also lost; for, though William, through selfish motives, had been induced to concur in his wife's act and deed, he naturally concluded that she who had acted so treacherously by others, was not very likely to be faithful to him; and from that time, though they lived together many years, it may be fairly said, they never had another happy hour together, nor had they any enjoyment of their ill-gotten goods. During their life, the money was hoarded, and the plate hid, as thet which they were ashamed to use or to look upon; and, after their death, old Madam West's rich clothes and thick blankets were found consumed by moths, without having been worn, used, or even unpacked. The children, who came into possession of the property, soon squandered the money, sold or pawned the plate, parted with the furniture, one thing after another, and came into the depth of poverty. Of all the old lady's furniture, the little that remained in the family was that which the injured branches were enabled to buy, out of charity to the unjust possessors, in their times of distress. It is a dreadful thing to have riches corrupted, and garments motheaten, as by the secret curse of God on that which is unjustly gained.

CHAP. XXII.

REMOVALS.

My eldest brother, a steady, industrious young man, had been married three or four years, and had got things a little comfortable about him, when he was strongly tempted to move into a house, that had stood some time empty in a neighboring town, and which was offered him, as he thought, on very advantageous terms. He had pretty much set his mind upon it, when he came to consult father and mother on the subject. They scarcely knew what to say, lest they should advise him against his real interest. For their parts, they did not much like the notion of moving; but then they considered that they were elderly, and, as it were, rooted in the soil, and had not the spirit to try new openings and new enterprises which young people might try, and succeed very well. At last they advised him to consult with a friend, who was very well known as a gentleman of great wisdom and experience. To this proposal he readily agreed. The gentleman asked my brother what reason he had for wishing to leave his present abode. Was he likely to be turned out; or was it out of repair, or unhealthy, or inconvenient?—No; the place was in very decent repair, and suited the family very well; and as he had always paid his rent, he had no reason to think his landlord would turn him out. "Then," said he, "if you ask my advice, stay where you are. There must be at least three good reasons for moving to weigh against one for staying." But the house he proposed taking was a larger, smarter-looking house, and no higher in the rent. "Then you must add to the rent the expense of removing your family and goods; here and there an odd bit of repair which you will find necessary; the wear and tear of furniture in taking down and putting up again; the chance of some things being too large and others too small for the places where they are to stand; and the time you will be put to inconvenience before you will have got your garden to grow, and your family settled in your new abode." "Very true, sir; I hardly know what to do; but they say there is a great chance of getting on in business there: the landlord has promised to get me customers." "Have you not got good employ here?"—"Pretty fair, sir; we make a pretty good shift to live, and lay by a trifle." "Then would it not be very unwise to give up a present certainty, though moderate, for the sake of a distant uncertainty, which may chance to be better, as you say, but which may chance to be good for nothing at all? It is for the interest of the man who has the house to dispose of to represent every thing in the best light he can; but you ought to allow a considerable set-off from his statements. He may do what he can to serve you, and that may be little or much; or he may forget his promise, and leave you to take care of yourself. At any rate, you will have much up-hill work before you can establish a good connection, like that you leave. Remember the old saying, 'A bird in the hand is worth two in the bush; and those in Poor Richard's famous Almanac,

> "I never saw an oft-removed tree,
> Nor yet an oft-removed family,
> That throve so well as those that settled be"—

and 'Three removes are as bad as a fire.' There is another thing which ought not to be overlooked. How will the removal affect your best interests? Your present abode is very near the house of God, which is no small convenience to the mother of a young family; you are well known to the minister, and kindly cared for by him; your pious parents reside here, and might often warn you of any evil or danger which you did not suspect; you have steady Christian friends here, and are engaged with them in endeavoring to do good. Now, I don't say that there are not good people in another place, or that you would not do good and get good there; but removing into a new connection is too often the occasion of breaking off some profitable friendship or some beneficial habit, which might not be readily replaced in a new situation. Let all these things be well weighed in your own mind, and sincerely prayed over before you come to a decision; for I hope you know the value of that precept, 'In all thy ways acknowledge Him, and he shall direct thy paths.'"

My brother was wise enough to listen to this wholesome advice. He soon made up his mind to remain where he was; and he never had reason to repent it.

CHAP. XXIII.

PROVIDENCE.

Some people sadly forget that they are constantly dependent on Providence. If things prosper with them, they take all the credit to their own skill and diligence, and, as the scripture says, "burn incense to their own net and their own drag;" or else they stupidly ascribe it to good luck. Others speak of Providence with a trifling levity very unbecoming the subject. In the most thoughtless manner such persons will say, 'Please God, I'll do so and so," or "God bless you," and other similar expressions, which never ought to be uttered but with seriousness and reverence. A person, going out, very irreverently and foolishly said, "I don't know whether or not it will rain, but I will trust to Providence to send me an umbrella." Others, again, presumptuously talk of putting their trust in Providence, while they neglect to use the means which Providence has appointed. They involve themselves in difficulties by their extravagance or imprudence, and trust to Providence to get them out; or they neglect to make provision for a time of need, in the hope that Providence will send them a supply. Such conduct is not trusting, but tempting Providence; and such hopes, sooner or later, make ashamed.

The following maxims on Providence are well worth committing to memory. "The lot is cast into the lap, but the whole disposal thereof is of the Lord." "Commit thy works unto the Lord, and thy thought shall be established." "In all thy ways acknowledge Him, and He will direct thy paths."

"Without God's providence nothing falls out in the world; without his commission nothing stirs; without his blessing nothing prospers." This saying, properly understood, believed, and acted on, would tend to keep our minds quiet under the many things that occur to ruffle them, and would encourage a habit of constant prayer, since nothing can hurt *him* who has God for his friend,—nothing can, finally, be a blessing to him who has God for his enemy.

"The blessing of God, it maketh rich, and he addeth no sorrow with it."

Success is God's blessing on a good cause, his curse on a bad one.

God's word and his providences mutually expound each other. "Providences are sometimes dark texts, that want an expositor." Then comes scripture to explain; "As many as I love I rebuke and chasten." "All things work together for good to them that love God."

"God's providences fulfil his promises." Though they sometimes seem to cross, in reality they are in perfect harmony. Jacob said in haste, All these things are against me; but a few days proved that all these things were working together for his good,—to restore to him his long-lost son, to provide for the welfare of himself and his family, and to bring about the fulfilment of God's promises concerning his posterity.

"Count every day, as well as you can, the providences of God towards you on that day." This will excite holy wonder and gratitude, deep humility, holy circumspection, and cheerful confidence.

> "Lord, when I count thy mercies o'er,
> They strike me with surprise!
> Not all the sands that spread the shore
> To equal number rise."

"He that carefully considers the providence of God shall never want a providence to consider and admire."

"Whoso is wise, and he shall understand these things? prudent, and he shall know them? For the ways of the Lord are right, and the just shall walk in them; but the transgressors shall fall therein."

CHAP. XXIV.

PEACE AND FORGIVENESS.

I have often tried to reckon in how many ways a good man may be a blessing to the neighborhood in which he dwells; and I am continually adding to the list. My mind, at such times, is sure to revert to some of my early and venerated friends, whose whole character exemplified that saying of the wise man, "The fruit of the righteous is a tree of life." One particular in which they were very useful, was in promoting a spirit of peace and forgiveness among the neighbors, who were too apt to indulge a litigious or a malicious spirit. "Blessed are the peace-makers, for they shall be called the children of God;" and truly enviable is that person whose endeavors, under the divine blessing, prove the means of banishing a spirit of contention and discord, and promoting that harmony and peace by which earth may be made in some degree to resemble heaven.

Let me set down a few rules for living in peace.

"Mind your own business." Half the quarrels among neighbors arise from idle curiosity, impertinent meddling, and foolish talking about the affairs of others.

"Keep your tongue from evil." If you cannot speak well of a neighbor, speak no evil. Never be afraid of the tongue growing rusty for want of use: give it no work but what is really profitable: keep it constantly under the direction of the law of wisdom, and the law of kindness; and *they* must be quarrelsome people indeed that will quarrel with you. If a spark from their ill temper should fall, it will soon go out for want of fuel. It is the second blow makes the fray. A peaceful man is not likely to strike the first blow: let him resolve not to strike the second, and the matter will soon end.

"Do not contend for every trifle, whether it be matter of right or opinion." There is great dignity and magnanimity in yielding a just right, rather than indulging contention;

and as to matters of opinion, nothing can be more foolish than to wish other people to see with our eyes, or to desire a law that all the clocks in the parish should strike at the same moment with ours. If we think that others are wrong, we may with meekness instruct those that oppose themselves. If called upon to defend our principles or our practice, our contest should be for truth, not for victory; and truth is best sought in the spirit of peace.

"If others neglect their duty to you, be sure that you perform yours to them." The rule is, "Do to them (not as they *do* to you, but) as *you would desire them to do* to you." To return railing for railing, is to return sin for sin.

"If you have an enemy, make him see and feel that you love him." Love in return for hatred, and good for evil, penetrates like oil in the bones; it subdues without striking a blow.

"Beg of God for universal charity." Whenever you pray for yourself, pray for all mankind; especially remembering those who have done you evil, or attempted to do it. Pray for grace to forgive them from your heart, and beg of God for Christ's sake to forgive them too. Remember Him who prayed for his cruel murderers, "Father, forgive them, for they know not what they do."

"Be humble." Have no lofty claims, no high conceits Think how insignificant, undeserving and guilty you are; then you will be slow to perceive or take offence, prompt in forgiving and forgetting, and incapable of revenge. When any injure you, think, "If I did not deserve this particular injury at the hand of my neighbor, I deserve far worse at the hand of God." Forget the faults of others, and remember your own. Forgive any body rather than yourself.

"By faith wait for the providence of God." Be not hasty in vindicating yourself, but commit your cause to Him that judgeth righteously; and in due time he will bring forth your righteousness as the light, and your judgment as the noonday. "Say not thou, I will recompense evil; but wait on the Lord, and he shall save thee." Our remembering an injury often does us more harm than our receiving it.

PEACE AND FORGIVENESS.

"God permits a Christian to be wronged that he may exercise his patience. He commands him to forgive the wrong that he may exercise his charity."

He that overcomes evil with good, overcomes three at once, namely, the devil, his adversary, and himself; and the self-conqueror is the greatest of all conquerors.

By taking revenge a man may be even with his enemy; but by rendering good for evil he is superior.

> "I will be even with my bitterest foe,"
> Revenge exclaims, and then returns the blow.
> "I'll be superior," should the Christian say,
> "And kind forgiveness readily display."

Lines on Bishop Boulter.

> "Some write their wrongs in marble—he, more just,
> Stooped down serene, and wrote them in the dust;
> Trod under foot the sport of every wind,
> Swept from the earth and blotted from his mind.
> There, buried in the dust, he bade them lie;
> And grieved they could not 'scape th' Almighty's eye."

Archbishop Cranmer was so remarkable for returning good for evil, that it was commonly said, "Do him an ill turn, and you make him your friend forever."

I know a gentleman who had a fine garden, in which he took great delight. It was surrounded by the cottages of his tenants and laborers, to whom he justly looked as to the protectors of his property, and felt secure, inasmuch as no person could approach his premises but through theirs. He had for some days watched the progress of a fine bed of tulips. "To-morrow," said he, "they will be in full perfection;" and he invited a company of friends to witness the display of their beauties. In the morning he hastened to the spot; but, to his utter astonishment, the whole bed was a scene of shrivelled desolation. Some unaccountable influence had withered every stem, and each flower lay prostrate and fading on the ground.

A short time afterwards, a bed of ranunculus shared the same fate; and in succession several other choice and favorite productions. At length the gentleman became persuaded that the destruction did not proceed from any natural cause, such as blight or lightning, but that it must have been occasioned by the intentional mischief of some treacherous and malignant individual, who had access to the grounds. He resolved, therefore, to watch, and engaged a friend to accompany him for that purpose. After remaining in their station some time, they saw a person come out of one of the cottages, and apply some destructive preparation to the roots of such flowers as were advancing to blossom. The gentleman at once recognized him as a workman whom, a few weeks before, he had had occasion to reprove, and who thus malignantly gratified his resentment. His friend strongly urged that the offender should be prosecuted, and offered to bear witness against him. But the proprietor replied, "No; I am much obliged by your kindness in remaining with me; I have ascertained the author of the mischief, and am satisfied; I must use another method of dealing with him."

In the morning, the gentleman ordered his servant to purchase a fine joint of meat, and carry it to the cottage of this man, desiring he would enjoy it with his family. This treatment, so contrary to his deserts and expectations, proved the means of effectually humbling and softening the stubborn and malignant heart. The offender presented himself before his injured master, freely confessed his guilt, implored forgiveness, and proved, from that day forward, a most faithful, diligent, and devoted servant. "If thine enemy hunger, feed him; if he thirst, give him drink; for in so doing thou shalt heap coals of fire on his head: and be not overcome of evil, but overcome evil with good."

Among the lot of furniture which William West, who was mentioned in the 21st chapter, inherited from his old aunt, was an easy chair: it had been good in its day, but was dropping to pieces, and stood about as mere lumber. This was many years after the old lady's death, and the rest of the family had forgiven William, though, perhaps, he never forgave himself. One of his nieces happened to be in want of such an article, and offered to purchase it of him. He readily consented, on condition of borrowing the chair in case he should be ill. The full value was given for the chair, and twice that sum expended on repairing and new covering it. When this was done, it presented a very respectable appearance. After some years, the old gentleman fell ill. His niece, unsolicited, offered the use of the easy chair, and did whatever else could contribute to his comfort. He expressed much gratitude for her kindness, and, what to her was far more pleasing, expressed anxious concern, where he had formerly displayed careless indifference. He died, praying, "God be merciful to me a sinner!"

When the funeral was over, the chair was of course claimed by its rightful owner, but unjustly withheld by the children, whose mother had set them an example of loving unjust gain. Such ingratitude and dishonesty was very provoking to the injured parties, who, for a moment, indulged a thought of enforcing the restitution of their property. But, on consulting their father, his more judicious counsel prevented such a step. He said, "You have nothing to expect from them: as selfish, worldly people, they have acted in character. But you must act in character as Christians: much is expected from you, and much is due to your profession and your principles. If you submit in silence to injury, you will lodge in the bosom of the aggressors a reproof keener than the most angry invectives, or the most expensive lawsuit. Suppose that, instead of resenting their injustice in withholding the chair, you were to give them the best cover, which you tell me you still have in your possession, you would ride a horse sixteen hands high."

This proved to be almost the last counsel of a venerated parent; for, though then in health, he died a few days afterwards. The advice was followed by his children; the chair-cover was packed up, and sent without remark. No expression of gratitude was returned at the time; perhaps shame suppressed it. In a short time, the easy chair, like the rest of the furniture, went to a broker's for a few shillings; but years afterwards, the parties, from whom it was unjustly wrested, had the satisfaction of knowing that their conduct had been the means of impressing this conviction on the minds of this selfish family: "There must be something in their religion, because it enables them to return good for evil."

We will give one more example, which illustrates this subject. When the indefatigable traveller, Bruce, was in Abyssinia, one of the governors, according to the custom of the country, sent him twelve horses, saddled and bridled, desiring him to fix on one for his own use. The groom urged Bruce to mount one of them, assuring him it was a most excellent animal, and very quiet and safe to ride. It proved that the horse was extremely vicious, of which the man was well aware, and apparently had selected him with a malicious intention. The traveller, however, was well skilled in horsemanship. After a severe contest, he successfully curbed the unruly animal, completely exhausted him, and descended unhurt. The governor expressed the greatest surprise and concern at the transaction, and most solemnly protested his entire innocence of any design in it, adding, that the groom was already in irons, and before many hours passed would be put to death. "Sir," said Bruce, "as this man has attempted my life, according to the laws of the country, it is I that should name his punishment." "It is very true," replied the governor; "take him and cut him in a thousand pieces, if you please, and give his body to the kites." "Are you really sincere in what you say?" asked Bruce; "and will you have no after excuses?" He swore solemnly that he would not. "Then," said Bruce, "I am a Christian; the way my religion teaches me to punish my enemies, is, by doing good for evil; and, therefore, I keep you to the oath you have sworn. I desire you to set this man at liberty, and put him in the place he held before; for he has not been undutiful to you." Every one present seemed pleased with these sentiments; one of the attendants could not contain himself, but, turning to the governor, said, "Did not I tell you what my brother thought about this man? He was just the same all through Tigré." The governor, in a low voice, very justly replied, " A man that behaves as he does, may go through any country."

CHAP. XXV.

KINDNESS AMONG NEIGHBORS.

It is a pleasant thing to have the character of a good neighbor. Who is it that deserves it? Not the idle gossip, who, for want of useful employment at home, goes to spend an hour in one neighbor's house, and an hour in another's, assisting the idle in squandering the time they already despise, and robbing the industrious of a precious jewel, of which they (the industrious, not the visitor) know the value. Such neighbors have often extorted from those on whom they bestow their senseless visits, the pathetic exclamation, " Parish taxes and assessed taxes press heavily enough; but the hardest tax of all is that which the forms of society authorize the idle to levy on the well-employed, by interrupting their engagements and defeating their purposes." Well has the wise man said, "Withdraw thy foot from thy neighbor's house, lest he be weary of thee, and hate thee," Prov. xxv. 17. Still less is the character of a good neighbor due to those who ingratiate themselves into families, and become possessed of their secrets, or draw from them remarks on others, and then go elsewhere and make mischief of what they have heard.

Those are not good neighbors who lead each other into pleasures and expenses which are unprofitable in themselves, or which the circumstances of the parties do not justify. There are many families living in frugal comfort, to whom the expense of a dinner or tea-party would be a serious inconvenience; yet such inconvenience is frequently entailed by thoughtless, though perhaps well-meaning neighbors, who press them to accept of entertainments, which seem to lay them under a sort of obligation to invite in return.

A good neighbor is, first, *harmless and peaceable*. He will not intentionally annoy or injure another. No noisome dunghill, no unseasonable noises, are permitted on his premises, to endanger the health or disturb the repose of the neighborhood.

The children of such a family are not permitted to throw stones into a neighbor's garden, to hurt his cat, or to worry his poultry; or to slip the fastenings of his window-shutters, and suffer them to escape and break the glass. These, and numerous other feats, performed by rude and ill-trained children, for the annoyance of the neighborhood, are never tolerated in the family of the good neighbor. Should any inconvenience have been inadvertently occasioned by him or his, it is no sooner mentioned than cheerfully removed or repaired.

The good neighbor is *kind and accommodating*. It gives him pleasure to promote the comfort and welfare of those around him. If persons are of the same trade, no mean jealousies are indulged, no petty tricks practised against them; but the proper feeling is cherished—" I wish to do well for myself, and I wish well to my neighbor; the world is wide enough for us both." Among neighbors of the poorer class, a good or an ill disposition is manifested in the manner in which they regard the conduct of their wealthy neighbors towards each other. Some poor people rejoice in the kindness shown to a neighbor, and gladly embrace an opportunity of speaking favorably of his character, or representing his need to those who can assist him : while others are spiteful enough to regard the good done to a neighbor as an injury done to themselves, both by the person who confers and the person who receives the benefit.

Good neighbors, especially among the industrious poor, frequently have it in their power to protect each other's children and property during the absence of the parents. They may also materially assist each other in enjoying the public services of religion, by alternately taking charge of each other's infants and household affairs during the hours of worship.

In time of sickness, the kind offices of a good neighbor are peculiarly valuable. "Better is a neighbor that is at hand, than a brother that is afar off." The kindness of *such* a neighbor has been thus vividly and beautifully described: "Oh, I love the soul that must and will do good; the kind creature who runs to the sick bed, I might rather say, bedstead, of a poor neighbor; wipes away the moisture of a fever, smooths the clothes, beats up the pillow, fills the pitcher, sets it within reach; administers only a cup of cold water, but in the true spirit of a disciple of Christ, and becomes a fellow-worker with Christ, in the administration of happiness to mankind. Peace be with that good soul! She must come in due time into the condition of her neighbor; and then, may the Lord strengthen her on the bed of languishing, and, by some kind hand like her own, make all her bed in her sickness."

The good neighbor will avoid a meddlesome, obtrusive interference, yet will not hesitate to point out, in a kind and gentle manner, any mistake into which a neighbor may have fallen, or any advantage he may have overlooked, by which the interests of himself and family may be promoted.

Especially, the good neighbor will not fail to use the influence given him, by kindness in common things, to persuade those for whom he is interested, to frequent the worship of God in his sanctuary; to maintain family prayer; and to attend to the moral and religious education of their children. The conduct of a consistent Christian family is a kind of living invitation to those around; "Come with us, and we will do you good, for God hath spoken good concerning Israel;" and not unfrequently has the reply been heard, "We will go with you, for we perceive that God is with you." Although I have not, in this chapter, mentioned the names of my venerable friends, my mind looks back to many families, to whom their neighborhood was thus made a blessing, and to many others, on whom they impressed the duty, and whom they awakened to the practicability and the pleasure of being good and useful neighbors. I shall add some of their maxims, gleaned from scripture and other sources.

Maxims on Friendship and Company.

"Too much familiarity breeds contempt."

"Suspect extraordinary and groundless civilities."

"Suspect a tale-bearer; and never trust him with thy secrets who is fond of entertaining thee with those of another person. No wise man will put good liquor in a leaky vessel."

"By the company a man keeps, you may know what he is, or, at least, what he shortly will be."

"He that walketh with wise men shall be wise; but a companion of fools shall be destroyed."

"No man can be provident of his time, that is not prudent in the choice of his company."

"Make no friendship with an angry man; and with a furious man thou shalt not go, lest thou learn of his ways, and get a snare to thy soul."

"Be not among wine-bibbers, among riotous eaters of flesh; for the drunkard and the glutton shall come to poverty."

"Beware of a reconciled enemy and an untried friend."

"Thine own friend, and thy father's friend, forsake not."

"Prosperity gains friends; adversity tries them."

"Confidence in an unfaithful man, in time of trouble, is like a broken tooth, and a foot out of joint."

"A friend in need is a friend indeed."

"The best mirror is an old friend."

"Faithful are the wounds of a friend; but the kisses of an enemy are deceitful."

"Iron sharpeneth iron; so a man the countenance of his friend."

"Ointment and perfume rejoice the heart; so doth the sweetness of a man his friend, by hearty counsel."

"The best friendship is that which is cemented by love to

Christ, the best of Friends. Those who are thus united, will, like David and Jonathan, strengthen each other's hands in God; and the friendship begun on earth will be carried on and perfected in heaven."

CHAP. XXVI.

SELF-DENIAL.

It is no uncommon thing for people to go to some benevolent, influential man in their vicinity, with heavy complaints of uneasiness in their families and their circumstances. If things were but so and so, different from what they are, how much happier they should be! "I'll tell you what," said a gentleman once, who heard complaints of this kind, "there is a much shorter way to happiness than getting your circumstances and connections altered. It is this,—you must cultivate a spirit of self-denial. What is the great cause of misery in the heart, and in the family? The worship of that great idol, self-will. What is the readiest way to happiness? For a man to deny himself, take up his cross, and follow Christ daily. Could we but deny ourselves in our own wisdom and will, we should never more know a restless hour.

Sometimes our minds are set upon that which is in itself evil. We are restless for the attainment of it, and it would seem a great act of self-denial to debar ourselves of it; but there is nothing sinful to which we can be tempted, but we shall find greater comfort in resisting than in indulging it.

"To conquer a lust is greater than to conquer a kingdom. He who follows Christ in the path of self-denial, will dwell with him in the world of glory; and who would not deny himself for a time, that he may enjoy himself forever?"

CHAP. XXVII.

USEFULNESS.

My mother once said to a rich acquaintance, "Sir, there is only one thing I envy you, and that is your usefulness. What a deal of good may be done by one person, who has good learning, good property, and a good will!" "My friend," replied he, "that God has in any degree made me useful to my fellow-creatures, is, indeed, one prime enjoyment of my life; but you need not envy me a pleasure that is so freely open to yourself. You speak of learning and property: it is true, they are both means of usefulness; but let me tell you, that good-will is far more essential than either."

"Can you tell me, sir, any way in which such a poor creature as I can be useful?"

"Yes, many ways; but, if you have the sincere desire, as I believe you have, you will be sure to find out occasions. Do you never exert yourself to do good to your fellow-creatures in their bodies and in their souls? never do a kind action, or give a useful hint? Have you never been successful in warning any one against error or danger into which they were falling; or spoken a word to a young person which may be remembered through life?"

"'Tis little, sir, that I can say worth remembering: and yet I wish to say and do what I can; and you know God can give his blessing to the weakest."

"Well, if you say and do what you can, you will be useful; remember what seems at the time a very small degree of usefulness may be the seed of a great deal. There is a good saying, 'A whetstone, though it cannot cut, may sharpen a knife; a taper may light a torch.' To encourage you in trying to do good, I will mention an anecdote of a poor, but pious, shoemaker. Meeting a young gentleman just going to the university, to study with a view to the ministry, he thus addressed him: 'Then, sir, I hope you will study your Bible, that you may be qualified for feeding the sheep of Christ with the bread of eternal life.' A divine blessing attended this hint, and impressed it on the mind of the student. He never forgot it while he lived, and he lived to be an able, faithful, and successful minister* of the gospel."

Timothy, that eminent young evangelist, who was honored as the companion of the apostle Paul, was distinguished for his knowledge of the holy scriptures. And how did he acquire it? By the early instructions of his pious mother and grandmother. Here was the whetstone sharpening the knife, and the taper lighting the torch; and who shall say that the pious parents who trained the young minister were less useful than the minister himself?

There is another way in which Christians may be useful, even when under the most trying feelings of uselessness and helplessness,—by patiently suffering the will of God. The calmness and cheerfulness of a bed-ridden Christian have been made the means of carrying conviction to the heart shut against all the eloquence and appeals of the pulpit.

An eminent Scotch divine† visiting a poor crippled woman, she thus addressed him: "O, sir, I am just lying here, a poor useless creature." "Think you so?" said the minister. "I think," added she, "that if I were away to heaven, I should be of some use to glorify God without sin." "Indeed," replied the good man, "I think you are glorifying God now, by resignation and submission to his will, and that in the face of many difficulties, and under many distresses. In heaven the saints have not your burdens to groan under. Your praise, burdened as you are, is more wonderful to me, and, I trust, acceptable to God."

The great secret of Christian usefulness is to be awake to opportunities, and intent on doing what we can, rather than bewailing that it is in our power to do so little; and, in this respect, he who faithfully improves the one talent, bids fair to be intrusted with the five or the ten.

---

* Rev. Thomas Robinson.   † Rev. Ralph Erskine.

I must not omit to tell you of one instance more, showing how a person in an humble station of life may be honorable and useful, and greatly promote the usefulness of those above him.

Philip Melancthon was one of the reformers, those great and good men who were instrumental in bringing about the reformation from popery. He labored, by his conversation and his writings, to enlighten the minds of men; and his kind and amiable disposition and manners did much to win their hearts and engage their attention. Among the many Christian virtues that adorned his character, Melancthon was highly esteemed for his great generosity. Indeed, his friends were astonished at his liberality, and wondered how, with his small means, he could afford to give so much in charity. It appears to have been principally owing to the care and good management of an excellent and faithful servant named John, a native of Sweden. The whole duty of provisioning the family was intrusted to this domestic, whose care, assiduity and prudence amply justified the unbounded confidence reposed in him. He made the concerns of the family his own, avoiding all needless expenditure, and watching with a jealous eye his master's property. He was also the first instructer of the children during their infancy. John grew old in his master's service, and expired in his house, amidst the affectionate regrets of the whole family. During a service of thirty-four years, how much usefulness was effected by honest John, and by his master through his instrumentality! Melancthon invited the students of the university to attend the funeral of his faithful servant, delivered an oration over his grave, and composed a Latin epitaph for his tombstone, of which the following is a translation:—

> " Here, at a distance from his native land,
> Came honest John, at Philip's first command,
> Companion of his exile, doubly dear,
> Who in a servant found a friend sincere;
> And more than friend—a man of faith and prayer,
> Assiduous soother of his master's care.
> Here to the worms his lifeless body 's given,
> But his immortal soul sees God in heaven."

This is, perhaps, as good a place as any to add another epitaph on a faithful servant, copied from a village church in Leicestershire.

> "Reader,
> Respect the memory of
> Sarah Jackson,
> An invaluable servant, a sincere Christian;
> Distinguished beyond wealth and titles
> By the dignity of worth.
> Let her remind you, that an humble station may exercise
> The highest virtues;
> And that a well-earned pittance of earthly wages
> May prove the richest treasure in heaven.
> She lived, during twenty-seven years,
> In the family of the Rev. Spencer Madan,
> By whom this marble is affectionately inscribed,
> In token of respect, esteem, and gratitude.
>
> "A servant—no—an unassuming friend
> Sinks to the tomb in Sally's mournful end!
> Peace, honest Sally, to a soul that knew
> No deed unfaithful, and no word untrue!
>
> "Thrice happy they, whose mortal labors done,
> May lead, like thine, from service to a throne.
> —Go, claim the promise of thy chosen part,
> In zeal a Martha, with a Mary's heart."

"Masters and mistresses must have devices how to do good to their domestics; how to make them the servants of Christ and the children of God. God, whom you must remember to be 'your Master in heaven,' has brought them to you, and placed them under your care. 'Who can tell' for what good he has brought them? What if they should be the elect of God, fetched from different parts, and brought into your family on *purpose*, that, by means of their situation, they may be brought home to the Shepherd of souls? O that the souls of our servants were more regarded by us; that we might give a better demonstration that we despise not our own souls, by doing what we can for the souls of our servants! How can we pretend to Christianity when we do so little to *Christianize* our servants?—Verily, you *must* give an account to God concerning them. If their souls should be lost through your negligence, what answer can you make to 'God the Judge of all?' Methinks, common principles of gratitude should incline you to study the happiness of those, by whose labors your lives are so much accommodated. Certainly, they would be the better servants to you, more faithful, honest, industrious, and submissive, for your bringing them into the service of your common Lord."

I somewhere met with a paper under this title, the '*Resolution of a Master;*' which pleased me so much that I transcribed it.

"I would always remember, that my domestics are, in some sense, my children; and by taking care that they want nothing which may be good for them, I would make them as my children; and as far as the methods of instilling piety into the mind, which I use with my children, may be properly and prudently used with them, they shall be partakers in them. Nor will I leave them ignorant of any thing, wherein I may instruct them to be useful to their generation.

"I will see that my domestics be furnished with Bibles, and be able and careful to read the lively oracles. I will put Bibles and other good and proper books into their hands; will allow them *time* to *read*, and assure myself that they do not misspend *this time*. If I discover any wicked books in their hands, I will take away from them those pestilential instruments of wickedness. They shall also write as well as read, if I may be able to bring them to it. And I will appoint them now and then such things to write, as may be for their greatest advantage.

"I will be very inquisitive and solicitous about the company chosen by my servants; and with all possible earnestness will rescue them from the snares of evil company, and forbid their being the 'companions of fools.'

"Such of them as may be capable of the task, I will employ to teach lessons of piety to my children, and will recompense them for so doing. But I would, with particular care, contrive them to be such lessons as may be for their own edification too.

"I will sometimes call them alone, talk to them about the state of their souls; tell them how to close with their only Saviour; charge them to do so, and 'lay hold on eternal life;' and show them, very particularly, how they may render all they do for *me* a service to the *glorious Lord;* how they may do all from the principle of obedience *to him*, and become entitled to the 'reward of the heavenly inheritance.'"

CHAP. XXVIII.

COURTSHIP AND MARRIAGE.

ON these subjects much advice is given, and very little taken. If asked at all, it is generally not until the mind is made up, the affections engaged, and perhaps the honor pledged.

There was one gentleman and lady in our village, who were commonly consulted on this business by all the prudent young people in the neighborhood. The first question they generally asked was, "Have you consulted your parents, and what do they think of it? for you cannot expect happiness if you marry without the full consent of your own parents and the parents of your intended partner." Very commonly the answer was, "I have spoken to my parents, and they advised me to consult you." These people had a way of making young persons themselves see and own if there was any thing imprudent or wrong, so as to induce them to give up the matter of their own accord, which was easier than for the parents directly to forbid it.

My brother Richard, I remember, was in a terrible hurry to get married before he was out of his apprenticeship. Father and mother did all they could to persuade him to wait a while, and it was well for him, that they succeeded. The gentleman, too, of whom I have just spoken, talked kindly to him on the subject. "Don't be too hasty, young man; 'tis easy to marry in haste, and repent at leisure. I would advise you not to think of marrying till you are settled in a fair way of getting a living. You don't wish to be a burden to your parents, but to be able to provide for yourself, and those dependent on you; and for some years to come it will be much better for you to have one plough going than two cradles. You may think that love and a *little* will be quite enough, but let me tell you, love and *nothing* will be but sorry fare; and, 'When poverty comes in at the door, love flies out at the window.' You think, perhaps, that no such thing can happen to you: then let me tell you, that, if you think your love strong enough to bear poverty after marriage, you had better try its strength in waiting beforehand. If you do really love one another, I think you will find it easy and pleasant to work and save, that you may have something about you to make your home comfortable, when it is prudent for you to marry." My brother promised to wait a year or two, and set about in good earnest every leisure hour he had, to work and save for future comfort. But in less than three months' time, he came again to his friend in great trouble, and told him that Fanny was getting very shy of him, and had been seen walking with the 'squire's groom, and now what was to be done?

"By all means let her go," he replied, "and reckon it a very good miss for you. If she is tired of waiting, let her go on without you; and when she is gone, comfort yourself with remembering that there are as good fish left in the sea as ever were caught out of it."

This seemed hard doctrine at the time, and Dick was half inclined to break his promise, and go after Fanny with an offer to marry directly; but prudence prevailed.

After flirting about with three or four different young men, Fanny at last married William Stephens, the sawyer, and a poor, dressy dawdle of a wife she made him. As for Richard, he soon found that he could do vastly well without her; and,

I believe, he forgot all about marrying for four or five years, until he met with a steady, respectable young woman, whom all his friends approved, and who turned out an excellent partner to him, and a good mother to his children. When he looked at his decent, tidy wife, his well-furnished cottage, and his clean, well-managed children, and contrasted them with those of his neighbor Stephens, he sometimes went across the house humming the old ditty,

> "Sic a wife as Willie had!
> I wadna gie a button for her."

A second question which these friends used to ask the young people who came to consult them, was this: "What is it in the person of whom you speak, that makes you think you should love him (or her) better than all the world beside? You ought to be able to do this; for it is a very foolish action either to marry without love, or to love without reason. Is it *beauty*? Beauty is only skin deep, and sometimes covers a heart deformed by vice and ill temper. Beauty is a poor thing, unless it accompanies something far better than itself, and that will long outlive it. To marry only for beauty, would be like buying a house for the nosegays in the windows. 'Favor is deceitful, and beauty is vain, but a woman that feareth the Lord, she shall be praised,' and chosen too by the wise man who seeks a helpmate. Would you marry for *money*? 'In seeking after a comfortable yoke-fellow, good conditions are more to be sought for than a great dowry.' 'Better have a fortune *in* a wife than a fortune *with* a wife.'

"Is it for *genteel, attractive manners and polite accomplishments*? Don't be imposed upon: 'all is not gold that glitters.' Beauty, and property, and pleasing manners, and polite accomplishments, are all very good make-weights to a bargain that is good independently of them, but would made a wretchedly bad bargain of themselves. In marrying, you want not only what will look well, and excite admiration when all goes on smoothly, but you want what will afford real comfort and support in the time of adversity."

Then they would ask, "How does the party behave in present relations? Is he (or she) remarked as a dutiful, affectionate, attentive child; a kind brother or sister? for never yet was it found that the disobedient, rebellious son, or the pert, undutiful daughter, was fitted to make an affectionate, faithful, valuable husband or wife."

Then again, "Is the intended party of age, temper and habits suitable to your own? for people may be very good in themselves who are not suitable to each other; and two people who have been used to different ways of living, must have an uncommon share of good temper and forbearance, if ever they make each other happy in the married life. Remember, 'Marriage with peace and piety is this world's paradise; with strife and disagreement, it is this life's purgatory.'

"Is the person humble, industrious, and contented? If not, your present lot will not satisfy her; still less will she be willing to descend to a lower state, if such should be the appointment of Providence.

"And then, how is it as to *the one thing needful?* Whatever you do, don't let this be overlooked. Without true religion, you lose the best sweetness and relish of prosperity, and you have no provision whatever for meeting trials and afflictions: besides, if you could live together a century in the tenderest affection, and the most unmingled comfort, what a dreadful thing to think of death coming and separating you forever! Be sure, then, you remember the scripture rule, 'only in the Lord;' and expect not the blessing of God if you violate it. Ask the blessing of God on all your engagements. 'A prudent wife is of the Lord.' 'In all your ways acknowledge Him, and He will direct your paths.'

"When all these matters are satisfactorily settled, and your choice is fixed, be steady and faithful. Never act with levity, or say or do a thing that would give each other pain. Be very prudent and circumspect in your intercourse with each other. In this respect, your future comfort and confidence are at stake, as well as your fair character in the world. Let nothing that occurs now, furnish matter for reproach or regret at any future time."

To young married people, our friends would say, "Let your conduct be such as to render easy the duties of the other party. A wife is commanded to *reverence* her husband. Let his conduct be wise and holy, and then it will command reverence. 'Husbands, *love* your wives;' then wives should be truly amiable; a man can hardly love a vixen or a slattern. If a wife wishes to keep her husband at home, she must make home comfortable to him : in order to this, she must be, as the apostle says, ' discreet, chaste, a keeper at home.' A giddy, gadding wife is sure to make a dissatisfied, if not a dissolute husband. Seek to promote each other's comforts; so will you best secure your own.

"Let there be no secrets, and no separate interests. Do nothing that requires concealment, and never act in such a way as to provoke it. Many a partner, of a generous and open disposition, has been driven to practise concealment by the extravagance or unkindness of the associate."

To husbands they said—" Treat your wife always with respect. It will procure respect to you not only from her, but from all who observe it. 'Never use a slighting expression to her even in jest, for slights in jest, after frequent bandyings, are apt to end in angry earnest.'" To both :—" Remember the design of your union, to promote each other's honor, comfort and usefulness in this life, and preparation for a better. You are to walk together as fellow-travellers throughs the paths of time, whether smooth or rugged ; and as fellow-heirs of the grace of life, helping each other by prayer, counsel, sympathy and forbearance.

"Always keep in view the termination of your union,— '*till death us do part.*' This will keep you sober and moderate in your worldly enjoyments and expectations, and at the same time will preserve you from such conduct as would embitter the parting moment, or add an unnecessary pang to the grief of the survivor."

It was no uncommon thing for persons to carry to our

good friends complaints against bad husbands or bad wives. Such complainants generally met the reply : " Go back, then, and be thyself a better wife, (or husband,) and see if that do not prevail with him (or her) to be a better husband (or wife.") Another sound piece of advice often given them was this : " Whenever differences arise, endeavor to persuade yourself that they must have arisen from some mistake or misunderstanding of *your own;* never suppose the other party in fault, or that any thing unkind *could* have been intended, but charge all the blame on yourself, and make it *your* business to promote reconciliation and preserve peace. This will at once mellow your own spirit, and win the other party to reconciliation and love." I remember being greatly pleased with a fable which I once read. It was something like this :—The sun and the north wind were trying which could soonest make a traveller part with his loose coat. The wind began, and, storming with all its force, tumbled and tossed the coat about the poor man's ears, but to no purpose ; for the stronger it blew, the man held and wrapt his coat the closer about him. When the wind was weary, the sun began, and played his cheerful beams so successfully, that he soon melted the traveller into a kindly warmth, and made his coat not only useless, but troublesome to him, and so he quickly threw it off. The moral is plain and easy ; and all married people, in particular, would do well to remember, that when storming and raging are ineffectual to gain their ends, kindness and good-nature will seldom or never fail of success.

Another good rule is this :—Let husband and wife never be angry at the same time : by this means family feuds and discord will neither come often, nor continue long.

By way of reconciling married people to their own peculiar lot, our friends would say, " If marriages are appointed in heaven before they are solemnized on earth, then, though a Christian might have had a richer, better, or more sweet-tempered yoke-fellow, yet probably not a *fitter;* therefore, though nuptial love and other duties be not performed to you, yet do your part, in obedience to God, and you will assuredly find comfort in the end, whatever crosses you may meet with in the way."

I may add, that by the counsels of these judicious friends, many connections were prevented which were likely only to end in sorrow and ruin; many were formed to the satisfaction and real enjoyment of the parties; and many persons were brought to a more correct and faithful discharge of their duties, and, consequently, to a higher degree of happiness in the conjugal relation.

CHAP. XXIX.

CARE OF CHILDREN.

WE occasionally find a lady, who is the kind friend of all the young mothers in the village. I was once acquainted with such a lady, and I can speak of her friendly advice with great gratitude, and have reason to know that many others can do the same. I have often thought that by attention to her good rules, the lives of many children were saved; and by being properly trained, many have become real comforts to their parents, and useful members of society. I am sure that many lives are sacrificed to bad management in infancy; and others have grown up, under parental neglect and bad example, such vicious characters, that it might truly be said of them, "It had been better for them if they had never been born." Parents ought seriously to consider that they are to their children either their best friends or their worst enemies; and a solemn reckoning will be made at the last great day. What an awful meeting will that be for ungodly parents and ungodly children! What a blessed meeting for pious parents and grateful, happy children, whose feet they have early directed into the way of peace! How true and how weighty are those sayings of holy writ, "Train up a child in the way he should go, and when he is old he will not depart from it;" but " a child left to himself bringeth his mother to shame!"

I remember this lady used to say, that in the first few weeks of a child's existence was generally laid the foundation of its constitution, and often of its character through life. "Attend to it yourself," was always her advice to mothers; "keep it moderately warm, and scrupulously clean. Feed it from your own bosom, and do not overload its tender stomach with heavy and unsuitable food. Never be tempted to procure it sleep by means of heating cordials or poisonous drugs. Attend to all its little wants, and keep it thoroughly comfortable, and then it will sleep as much as is necessary or beneficial. Do not grudge good nursing for a few months; the liveliest children are soonest out of hand. Do not drag it about, and attempt to make it walk before it has strength and knowledge to guide itself. Let its limbs be free and easy, and it will be sure to walk all in good time." I once asked her how early she thought a child could be made to mind, because I had heard some women say it was of no consequence how a child was humored the first few months, while it knew no better. She replied, "If a child can be *humored*, it can be *managed;* and whatever silly people may say about its knowing no better, its crying when any thing is done for it, or when it wants to get hold of any thing, is just the trial whether the child or the parent shall be master. You will soon find, when you wash and dress your child, if you leave off for its crying, next day it will cry the louder; but if you go quietly on, the child will soon be quiet too. If you put the child to pain, there would be a reason for its crying; but washing and dressing, if properly done, do not hurt it, but are very refreshing to it. What can it cry for, except it be in order to get its own way? This, then, is the easiest time for teaching it that it cannot have its own way, but must be content with something better; and you can hardly imagine how valuable this lesson, thoroughly learned in infancy, will be to the child in future life."

Another of this lady's rules was this—"If children are to

be made obedient and tractable, both parents must be of one mind. If one denies an indulgence and the other grants it; or if one corrects and the other pities and soothes, and says, 'Poor thing! it did not mean any harm,' the children are not likely to regard either parent. It is the father's part to insist upon it that the children obey their mother both in his presence and in his absence, and the mother's part to teach them to love and respect their father. By this means both may hope to maintain their just authority, and to preserve order and harmony in their family." I set down some more of her sayings. "Remember your children are born with depraved inclinations, which soon show themselves in a spirit of selfishness. This you must very early resist, not only by making your children obey yourselves, but by teaching them to be kind one to another, and to find pleasure in giving up a thing they like for the gratification of another. This is the way to make them beloved by others, and happy in themselves. Whatever you do, set a good example before your children. Never say a word or do an action that you would not like them to imitate. Be not hasty or passionate in correcting them. When you find it necessary to correct, let the child see that it is according to the sin of the action committed,—not according to the inconvenience it may occasion you; and make your children sensible, by your calm, serious and affectionate manner, that you correct them from a sense of duty, and a desire for their real advantage.

"Never deceive children in the smallest matter or the greatest. Never promise that which you cannot perform, or which you do not intend to perform. Never get them to act as you wish, by telling them a thing is different from what it really is, or by any foolish threats of 'an old man,' 'a black man,' 'a chimney-sweeper,' 'a ghost,' &c. It is foolish to make them fear what has no being, and wicked to make them fear or hate what does exist, but would never injure them. People talk of 'white lies' to children; there are *no* white lies; but some of the blackest are those which, by deceiving children, teach them to practise lying and deceit themselves. 'A trick helps once, but hinders ever after.' If you tell a child that bitter physic is sweet, you may get him to take it that once; but do you think he will ever believe you again? or, what is of more consequence still, do you think you can ever convince him that there is any harm in telling a falsehood when he can gain his purpose by so doing?

"Have no favorites, but treat all your children alike, according as their circumstances require, and their conduct deserves. If children are treated alike when all things are equal, it enables the parents to make a difference with advantage when circumstances require. A naughty child is not jealous at seeing its brothers and sisters enjoy pleasures or notice which he feels he has justly forfeited; but he is stimulated to better conduct in future, which may deserve the same kindness, and which he knows he shall receive if he deserves it. None of the children are jealous of the particular attention paid to a sick child; but by observing that the parents consider such a distinction necessary, tender feelings are awakened in their minds on behalf of the sufferer, and a desire to do or avoid any thing in their power by which its comfort may be promoted.

"Parents who always treat their children with justice, fairness, and affection, will find little difficulty in inducing the many to forego their noisy sport for the sake of the one, or to give up any thing they possess for his gratification. These things are comparatively easy in families where an habitual good understanding is maintained between all parties; and these kind dispositions, thus early cultivated, generally mark the intercourse of the brothers and sisters through life.

"The Rev. C. Cecil, speaking of the influence of the parental character, observes, from his own experience—Where parental influence does not convert, it hampers; it hangs on the wheels of evil. I had a pious mother, who dropped things in my way; I could never rid myself of them. But in the exercise of this influence there are two leading dangers to be avoided. Excess of SEVERITY is one danger. My mother, on the contrary, would talk to me, and weep as she talked. I flung out of the house with an oath, but wept too when I got into the street. Sympathy is the powerful engine of a mother. I was desperate; I would go on board a privateer. But there are soft moments to such desperadoes. God does not at once abandon them to themselves. There are times when the man says, 'I should be glad to return, but I should not like to meet that face,' if he has been treated with severity. Yet excess of LAXITY is another danger. The case of Eli affords a serious warning on this subject. Instead of his mild expostulation on the flagrant wickedness of his sons, "Nay, my sons, it is no good report that I hear," he ought to have exercised his authority as a parent and a magistrate, in restraining and punishing their crimes.'"

"Be frugal in the use of rewards and punishments. It is the part of wisdom to effect all possible good at the least possible expense. Rewards and punishments are like money, valuable according to the value set upon it, and the advantages it will procure. If sending to bed an hour earlier than the rest of the children is found sufficient to impress on the mind of the offender a sense of the evil of his conduct, and the folly of repeating it, it would be a pity to waste a more severe punishment, which should be reserved for some great and special occasion. In some families, a kiss, or a quarter of an hour's conversation or reading, or being employed in some little commission for the parents, forms a more powerful reward, or the withholding them a more effectual punishment, than the lavishing of costly gifts, or exercising severe flogging, or starvation, or imprisonment would do in others. But this is managed by firmness: a very small punishment, which is sure to be inflicted, will intimidate more than a much greater punishment, where there is a hope of getting off.

"Children should be early taught to employ their time in doing something useful. There is no surer way to make a child respect himself and have a regard to his character, than to let him feel that he is of some use to his parents; and nothing so effectually keeps children out of mischief as the habit of having something to do.

"When children are to be seen gambling, or tormenting a

mouse, a worm, or a cockchafer, it just makes good what the little hymn says,—

> 'For Satan finds some mischief still
> For idle hands to do.'

"If these children had been taught to take pleasure in making baskets or nets, in gardening or carpentering, as their turn might be, it is most likely they would never have thought of cruel, mischievous sports. The mind or the hands unemployed resemble an empty dwelling with a board, *This house to let;* and some tempter or other is sure to get access to it.

"Children should not only be well employed in a general way, but they should early be taught some regular employment by which there is a prospect of their getting a livelihood. Old Mr. Dod, the puritan minister, used to say, 'Give them a Bible and a calling, and God be with them.'

"Children should be early trained to an orderly attendance at the house of God. It is not for us to say at how early a period, religious impressions of a saving kind may be made on the minds of children. Some children have given decided evidence of them very young indeed; but whether or not a child of three years old may be benefited by what he hears, it is a disgrace that a child of three years old should keep some one at home to mind him. A mother who manages her infant well, may very safely take it in her arms the first six or eight months. It will then perhaps become so lively as to disturb the solemnity of worship; but if it is brought under control, and accustomed to habits of propriety at home, at eighteen or twenty months old it may be made sensible that at such a time and place it must be quiet. In families where no servant is kept, or only one, and where religious privileges are prized, it will be no small acquisition to be enabled to take children early to the house of God; and to the children themselves the early formation of this habit may prove of unspeakable advantage. What a lovely example does little Samuel present! the child who was weaned and brought to wait upon the Lord, and who was as eminent for steadfast piety as he was for early devotedness; and what a pleasing proof that his fond and pious parents had been exemplary and successful in the exercise of early discipline! A well-behaved child in the house of God is a credit to its parents, and proves that it has been well instructed and well disciplined at home.

"It is of great importance early to impress on the minds of children sentiments of respect and reverence for the ministers of the gospel. Children are very observant even of tones and manners. Happy are those children whose earliest associations are connected with the minister as the most esteemed friend of the family; one who was always welcomed with affectionate cordiality; always spoken of with respect and gratitude; his advice sought; his approbation valued; his instructions treasured up and enforced; and the success of his labors made a constant matter of prayer. Many such families have I known, and I have observed that the young people in those families have been distinguished by a modest sedateness of manners, and a reverence for sacred things in general; which, though not in themselves amounting to a saving change, nor by any means to be substituted for it, are yet very lovely and desirable, and which are often the companions or the precursors of an ear and a heart opened to receive the saving impressions of divine truth.

"I have also known families—yes, and schools,—professedly religious, where the dinner-table conversation of the heads of the family on a Sabbath day was generally occupied in censuring some expression of the minister, or ridiculing something in his tone or manner. And the effects have been lamentable. Some young minds, on which impressions had been made by the sermons so ridiculed, were thus encouraged to postpone the convictions they had begun to admit, and to shut their hearts against the instructions they were thus taught to despise. Some have even advanced from contempt of an individual minister, to indifference, contempt, and scepticism on all religious subjects. This is not a fiction or a fancy, but a *fact*; a fact, it is to be feared, by no means uncommon; and one which, perhaps, in some measure accounts for a frequent wonder in the religious world, namely, how it is that the children of religious parents, and those brought up in religious schools, so often become indifferent or opposed to religion. A great and beneficial hold is laid on the feelings of a child who has been taught to reverence his minister.

"Parents who know the value of their own souls, will hardly neglect the religious instruction of their children. Perhaps they may feel their own ignorance and inability to teach; yet let them be encouraged to try. It is very remarkable that the means of instruction most expressly charged on parents in the word of God, is that which is within the reach of the poorest and most illiterate. It requires no great learning to talk in a familiar way with our children. Who is there that sits down to a meal, and rises up in silence? Who takes a walk with his children, and says nothing as they go along? Now, scripture expressly enjoins, that this free and affectionate intercourse between parents and children, should be made subservient to the purposes of early religious instruction. The only pre-requisite for employing this best and most efficient means, is a heart thoroughly alive to the importance of the subject. 'And these words which I command thee this day *shall be in thine heart*, and thou shalt teach them diligently unto thy children, and shalt talk of them when thou sittest in thine house, and when thou walkest by the way, and when thou liest down, and when thou risest up. And thou shalt bind them for a sign upon thine hand, and they shall be as frontlets between thine eyes, and thou shalt write them upon the posts of thine house, and upon thy gates.' That is, all the habits and observances of the family should be calculated to keep alive a constant remembrance of religion, and to present it in a lovely and attractive form to all around. A child brought up in a consistent family, when it goes out into the world, will look anxiously for a Bible, and feel the want of it a deficiency for which nothing can compensate. He will wait for the summons to family prayer, and if no such call be heard, he will feel that a most important part of the business of the day has been neglected, and a most delightful part of its daily enjoyments withheld.

"Parents who are sensible of their own deficiencies, and yet desirous that their children should be well instructed, will surely avail themselves of the valuable advantages of Sunday school instruction. Indeed, every young person, in whatever station of life he may be placed, ought to be either a Sunday scholar, or a Sunday school teacher. It is a pity that either pride, indifference, or love of pleasure, on the part of the young, or false indulgence on that of parents, should withhold the attendance of so many children and young persons, who ought to be employed in getting good or doing good. Parents should enforce the attendance of their younger children as learners, and encourage and stimulate their diligence, devotedness and perseverance as teachers, when arrived to sufficient maturity.

"One word more on the subject of children. Parents ought not to make the care of a family an excuse for negligence in the great affairs of personal religion. It is hardly possible to manage a young family so as to occasion *no* privations and sacrifices of attendance on the public means of grace; but by early discipline with the children, and a good understanding among those who have the care of them, the labor may be so lightened and so divided, as that no one person need be confined from public worship a whole Sabbath, except in case of illness. On the other hand, there are some mothers who need a caution against indulging themselves in frequent attendance on week-day services, to the neglect of a young family. It was well said by a worthy minister, on finding a family of children in dirt and confusion at a late hour in the morning, while the mother was up stairs at her devotions, 'What! is there no fear of God in this house?' In other families, the children have been exposed to bodily danger, or to the greater danger of being corrupted by evil example and impious companions, while the mother was seeking her own pleasures in the house of prayer, or perhaps engaged in religious gossip in a neighbor's house, but neglecting the obvious duties of life. This kind of neglect is perhaps less frequent than the other extreme; yet both should be guarded against. The care of children will not atone for the neglect of the soul; but the truly consistent Christian will give to every duty its proper place and proportion, and, by early rising and good contrivance, will secure time for religious duties, without neglecting her duty to the bodies and souls of her children: 'These ought ye to have done, and not to leave the other undone.'"

The indirect influence of a mother upon the formation of her children's character is very great.

"Mr. Cecil's mother was a woman of real piety. Her family, for generations back, were pious characters. It was a special mercy to Mr. C. that his mother was a partaker of the same grace with her ancestors. She labored early to mpress his mind, both by precept and example; she bought him Janeway's 'Token for Children,' which greatly affected him, and made him retire into a corner to pray; but his serious beginnings wore off, and he at length made such progress in sin, that he gloried in his shame.

"Lying one night in bed, he was contemplating the case of his mother. 'I see,' said he to himself, 'two unquestionable facts: first, my mother is greatly afflicted in body and mind, and yet I see that she cheerfully bears up under all, by the support she derives from constantly retiring to her closet and her Bible; secondly, that she has a secret spring of comfort of which I know nothing, while I, who seek pleasure by every means, seldom or never find it. If, however, there is any such secret in religion, why may not I attain it as well as my mother? I will immediately seek it of God.' He instantly rose in his bed, and began to pray. But he was soon damped in his attempt, by recollecting that much of his mother's comfort seemed to arise from her faith in Christ. 'Now,' thought he, 'this Christ have I ridiculed. He stands much in my way, and can form no part of my prayers.' In utter confusion of mind, therefore, he lay down again. Next day, however, he continued to pray to 'the Supreme Being.' He began to consult books, and to attend preachers: his difficulties were gradually removed, and his objections answered, and his course of life began to amend. He now listened to the pious admonitions of his mother, which he had before affected to receive with pride and scorn; yet they had fixed themselves in his heart, like a barbed arrow; and though the effects were, at the time, concealed from her observation, yet tears would fall from his eyes as he passed along the streets, from the impressions she had left on his mind. Now he would discourse with her, and hear her without outrage; which led her to hope that a gracious principle was forming in his heart, and more especially as he then attended the preaching of the word. Thus he made some progress; but felt no small difficulty in separating from his favorite connections. Light, however, broke into his mind, till he gradually discovered that Jesus Christ, so far from 'standing in his way,' was 'the *only* way, the truth, and the life, to *all* that come unto God by him.'

"'My first convictions on the subject of religion were confirmed from observing, that really religious persons had some solid happiness among them, which I had felt that the vanities of the world could not give. I shall never forget standing by the bed of my sick mother. 'Are not you afraid to die?' I asked her.—'No.' 'No! Why, does the uncertainty of another state give you no concern?'—'No; because God has said to me, "Fear not: when thou passest through the waters, I will be with thee; and through the rivers, they shall not overflow thee." The remembrance of this scene has oftentimes since drawn an ardent prayer from me, that I might die the death of the righteous.' The seeds sown in tears by his inestimable mother, though long buried, now burst into life, and shot forth with vigor; and he became a preacher of that truth he once labored to destroy.

"'Where parental influence does not convert, it hampers

—it hangs on the wheels of evil. I had a pious mother, who dropped things in my way—I could never rid myself of them. I was a professed infidel; but then I liked to be an infidel in company, rather than when alone—I was wretched when by myself. These principles and maxims spoiled my pleasure. With my companions I would sometimes stifle them; like embers, we kept one another warm.—Besides, I was a sort of hero; I had beguiled several of my associates into my own opinions, and I had to maintain a character before them: but *I could not divest myself* of my better principles. I went with one of my companions to see the Minor: he could laugh heartily, but I could not: the ridicule on regeneration was high sport to him—to me it was none; it could not move my features. *He* knew no difference between regeneration and transubstantiation—*I* did. I knew there was such a thing. I was afraid and ashamed to laugh at it. Parental influence thus cleaves to a man—it harasses him—it throws itself constantly in his way.'"

Mrs. Huntington gives the following account of her mode of educating her children :—" I begin to have my children in the room at prayers, within the month after their birth; and they always continue to be present, unless they are sick, or are excluded the privilege as a punishment for having been very naughty. It is difficult, when they are quite young, to keep them perfectly still. But the habit of thinking they are too young to be present at family devotion, is a bad one. And, besides, if they do not come in, some one is obliged to remain out with them, and is thus deprived of a precious privilege, and an important means of grace. After they get to be two years, or more, old, and are able to understand the meaning of your conduct, if they play, or in any other way make a disturbance, they may be taken out, and compelled to remain by themselves till the service is over; which will generally be felt by them to be so great a punishment, that they will not soon commit a similar offence. I would not do this, however, on every slight deviation from perfect order, as children cannot be expected to conduct themselves like men.

"As to government, I have always made it a rule never to give a child what it is passionately earnest to have, however proper the object may be in itself; because, otherwise, an association would immediately be formed in the mind between importunity and success. Were a child always told, when he cries for a thing, 'You shall have it when you show a proper temper,' it would soon teach him to be reasonable. I think it the destruction of government to be capricious; to refuse, one day, what, in circumstances not seen by the child to be different, is granted on another; to let fretting and teasing carry a point at one time, when, at another, they would bring punishment. Children very soon see whether we are consistent; and little deviations from an established rule afford great encouragement for the next time. These little deviations do great mischief, and are often slidden into very imperceptibly by the parent, though the child is quick-sighted enough to observe them.

"One thing, my dear friend, I think of the greatest importance, and that is, that children be made always to mind, and consider the parent's word as their law. Giving up once, after a command has passed, may lay the foundation, and lead to the establishment, of a principle of insubordination as troublesome as unconquerable. For this reason, absolute commands should be as few as possible. I also think it dangerous to play with children in the way of command, saying, 'Do this or that,' when you do not mean that the thing must be done. It weakens parental authority. I never like to tell very small children to kiss strangers, as they often feel a degree of backwardness very difficult to overcome; and if they refuse, it is necessary to pass it over without compelling obedience, which should not be, or to have a combat with them before the company, which hardens them to reproof. It is better to say, if a stranger offers to kiss them and they refuse, and it is thought best to say any thing, 'Your kisses are of no great consequence; they may be dispensed with, I dare say.' This leads the child to think he is not of so much importance as he might otherwise be led to suppose.

"It is also very necessary to good government that punishment should be proportioned to offences. If we make no distinction between intentional and complicated offences, and careless inadvertencies, the child, by the frequent recurrence of these latter faults, and the sharp rebukes they bring upon him, will become so accustomed to severe reproof, that he will not mind it. Tenderness of heart is the most powerful human engine of parental government; and when this is lost, it seems to me all is lost, unless the grace of God interposes. The inevitable consequence of frequent reproof is, a heart blunted in its sensibilities, and unmoved by the parent's displeasure. Of course, all temptations should, as much as possible, be put out of the way of children. Many little things should not be observed, which, if you were conscious the child knew you had observed, ought to be reproved. A harsh and angry tone should never be used, unless a gentle one has previously failed. And I believe, where the authority of the parent is early established by the mild and gentle means to some of which I have alluded, severe measures need be resorted to very seldom."

CHAP. XXX.

FAMILY PRAYER.

When any of the young people were married who had been brought up in the Sunday school, or were in any way connected with the good family, our minister made a point of urging on them to begin by setting up family prayer. He always advised them to begin at first; "for," said he, "if it be omitted the first day, it is more likely to be deferred the second, and perhaps deferred till conscience shall have left off to feel the omission; or till the difficulties of making a beginning seem almost insurmountable."

I wish I could recollect the whole of a beautiful sermon,* which he once read to us on this subject, but I will set down a few of his sayings, addressed to different persons, and meeting the difficulties and objections which those who had lived in neglect were too ready to urge against beginning.

" Prayer is a key which unlocks the blessings of the day, and locks up the dangers of the night." " It is the part of wisdom, as well as of duty, to seek the blessing of the Lord on all our undertakings, for, ' Except the Lord build the house, they labor in vain that build it. Except the Lord keep the city, the watchman waketh but in vain.' " " What can you do without the blessing of God ? And if you neglect to ask it, you can hardly expect to have it."

" There are five special errands which should bring every family daily to the throne of grace, and which cannot so well be carried either in public or in secret prayer :—

" 1. *To own our dependence on God.* It is he who sets the solitary in families; and on his free goodness in Jesus Christ we depend for all things that pertain to life and godliness. On him we depend for all our supports and comforts here below, and for all our hopes of heaven hereafter; and to him we are accountable for our improvement of the various relations in which he has placed us, and the various talents he has intrusted to our hands. These things should be daily acknowledged, that the remembrance may be kept alive and acted upon in the family.

" 2. *We have family sins to confess.* The best of families have to confess daily sins of infirmity; failing to do to each other as much good as we might have done; leading one another into sin and folly; much vain and unprofitable conversation; perhaps some irritability of spirit or unkindness of speech, instead of provoking one another to love, and to good works. In many things we all offend God and one another; and a penitent confession in prayer, together

* Sermon on Family Religion, by Matthew Henry.

with believing application to the blood of sprinkling, will be the most effectual way of reconciliation with God, and with one another. The best families, and those in which piety and love most prevail, in many things come short, and do enough every day to bring them on their knees at night.

"3. *We have family thanksgivings to offer.* It is of the Lord's mercies we are not consumed. When the family comes together safe in the morning from their respective retirements, and meets safe at night after their various employments, what can be so natural as that they should kneel together and bless the Lord, who daily loadeth them with benefits, even the God of their salvation? Has the family been preserved from sickness? or has health been restored where it had been interrupted? Does God bless our substance, and prosper the work of our hands; give us bread to eat, and raiment to put on; make us happy in our family relations, and rain down about our tents the manna of the gospel? Surely, where these mercies are enjoyed, the voice of rejoicing and thanksgiving should be heard in the tabernacles of the righteous.

"4. *We have family mercies to seek.* Daily bread is received by families together, and we are taught to pray for it together: 'Give *us* this day *our* daily bread.' We want daily directions as to the path of duty; we want wisdom for the management of family affairs; success to crown our endeavors; or grace to prepare us for disappointment: all these blessings should be sought of God in prayer. Then, too, we want the blessing of God to crown the instructions, which, as a family, we have been receiving in the sanctuary, and to crown the instructions and counsels given by parents to children. It is true, we cannot give our children grace, and in prayer we humbly acknowledge that we cannot; but then in prayer also we commit them to him who can give them grace, and who has declared that for all these things he will be sought unto by the house of Israel to do it for them. Besides, children hearing their parents fervently implore the grace of God for them, is a likely means to awaken them to a sense of the value of the grace of God, and to move them to pray for it themselves. A young lady, who had been piously brought up, but up to the time of her marriage had not imbibed any thing of the spirit of her pious parents; who had daily heard their fervent prayers, but had never joined in them with feeling interest,—when she entered the house of her husband, and found that family prayer was not observed, became wretched and desolate for the want of it. She was led to see the value of the privileges she had hitherto slighted, and the infinite importance of a personal interest in the salvation, of which she had so often heard with indifference. Her convictions were deep and lasting. She became, from that time, a decided Christian, and deeply anxious for the spiritual welfare of her husband and her household. In this respect her prayers were heard, and her endeavors succeeded. Her husband joined her in the way to Zion, and their children and household were taught and commanded after them to keep the ways of the Lord. What a rich reward to her pious parents, who had for so many years gone forth sowing precious seed, and weeping in the fear that it was devoured by the fowls of the air, or rotting beneath the clods!

> 'Though seed lie buried long in dust,
> It shan't deceive our hope:
> The precious grain can ne'er be lost,
> For grace insures the crop.'

"5. *We have intercessions to make for others.* Perhaps some of the family are at a distance, for the purposes of health, business, or education. These should be recommended in prayer to the grace of God. Perhaps relations dear to all the family are in circumstances of sickness, danger, or distress. God should be sought unto on their behalf for succor and deliverance. The benefit of prayer can extend far. He who hears prayer, can extend the hand of his power and mercy to the utmost corners of the earth, and to them that are afar off upon the seas. Beside this, we should pray for the land of our nativity, and make supplication for the king and all in authority. Our children should go forth into life with the testimony lodged in their bosom of the loyalty and patriotism of their parents. Then every Christian family should pray for the peace of Jerusalem. They shall prosper that love Zion; and the real saint looks forward with the greatest pleasure to seeing his children's children, when it is coupled with peace upon Israel. Then there is the world that lieth in wickedness; and while we think of the mercies our families enjoy, we must be stimulated to pray for the families in bondage and slavery, in ignorance and idolatry; and the remembrance of them in our family prayers will stimulate us and our families to do what we can for their relief, and engage the divine blessing, by which alone our efforts can be rendered successful.

"The habit of family prayer is of great value as a check to sin, and a pledge for consistency of conduct. 'Praying will make a man leave off sinning, or sinning will make him leave off praying.' He who daily meets his family in prayer, will be induced to check the rising temper, and to suppress the angry expression, that would be inconsistent with his prayer for meekness, gentleness, and self-possession. He will be ashamed to say or do any thing that his prayers would reproach.

"Family prayer tends greatly to secure family order, harmony, and subordination. It often places a happy restraint on the giddy and headstrong passions of youth. Family prayer often fixes something in the minds of children, which, in after life, perhaps when the parents are far distant, or dead, springs up as a shield against temptation, or an encouragement to return, after long wandering, to a refuge, to which the wanderer remembers his parents used to resort.

"Some would object that they have not time for family prayer. They have forgotten the true sayings, 'Prayer and provender hinder no journey;' 'There is nothing got by sinning, or lost by praying;' 'Work for earth is done best when work for heaven is done first.' The busiest have most need to pray for composure of mind in the midst of a bustle, and for strength of body and mind to discharge their various duties. 'There is a season for every thing, and a time for every purpose under the sun;' and surely the most important purpose of all need not be shut out of this wise regulation. By order, economy, and diligence, time might be redeemed, in every family, for the necessary duty of family prayer; and the habits of order, diligence, and regularity, thus acquired and cultivated, would soon be found more than to make up for the time given to devotion.

" Some plead their want of ability. They would not make this an excuse if they could not have a mouthful of food till they had prayed for it: ' where there is a will, there is a way;' and where there is a sincere desire to pray, though the words be few and simple, even should they be confused and broken, the exercise will be neither unacceptable nor unprofitable. ' A heart without words is better than words without a heart.'

" Want of capacity is too often another word for want of inclination. Those who begin in humble distrust of their own ability, will find their ability increase by exercise. Besides, there are many excellent forms of prayer for those who need them, and in the use of which many truly pious persons have found their devotional feelings kindled, and their spirits greatly refreshed.

" Some have so long neglected the duty of family prayer, that they are ashamed to begin. Here is a saying for them too: ' Better late than never;' ' It is a shame to neglect a duty, but never a shame to return to it.' When family prayer is omitted, the sweetest bond of family union is wanted. There is a continual want of something to stay the mind under the daily hurries, irritations and disappointments of life. If these wants and inconveniences begin to be felt, *now* is the proper time for setting about to meet them. Let shame and indolence, and every other opposing influence, be set aside; let the duty of family worship be *this day* set up in the house under feelings of deep contrition for the guilt of past neglect, with earnest supplications for pardon through the blood of Christ, and for the gracious influences of the

Holy Spirit to enable you to persevere in the path of duty; and then (as it was said to the Jews, to encourage them to build the temple, a work which they had long neglected) take notice whether from this day forward God do not remarkably bless you in all you have and do."

CHAP. XXXI.

OBSERVANCE OF THE SABBATH.

There is one thing to which every family should pay particular attention, and that is the observance of the sabbath. I tremble to think in how many ways it is broken, even in decent, respectable families. I shall mention a few, in which our good friends succeeded in persuading persons that they might do better if they would try in good earnest; and I believe, in several instances, their endeavors were made the means of bringing persons, who had lived in indifference and neglect, to esteem the Sabbath a delight, holy of the Lord and honorable.

Among those who seem to have some sense of religion, it is too common a thing for the mother of a family to take it for granted, that her duties at home necessarily confine her from public worship. Such persons have been heard to say, they were very sorry for it, but it was not their lot to get out for months together. Where there are young children, who cannot be taken to the house of God, or when there is illness in the family, some one, of course, must remain at home to attend to them; but it ought not always to fall upon the mother. The husband should willingly take his turn; and neighbors should, in this respect, be neighborly, and so extend each other's privileges, without abridging their own. Two or three children may be looked after by one person, and by this management each mother will have her turn in the house of prayer.

Some people make a great mistake in thinking that as they must stay at home, they might as well have a bit of dinner to cook, or something else to do. No. In a well-ordered family, it will be so managed that the person who stays at home may have an opportunity of reading the Bible, and employing the time in a manner suitable to the day. To remain at home with a sick person, or a young child, may be an act of necessity and mercy; but to employ the time not occupied in attending on them in cooking, or drudgery of any kind, is certainly, to all intents and purposes, Sabbath-breaking.

But there are many families whose Sabbath-breaking goes to a much greater extent still. Without descending to the slothful and profligate, hundreds of families may be found in all parts of the country to answer the following description:—

The man's weekly wages are received late on Saturday night, perhaps on Sunday morning. Early in the morning, the husband is seen digging and planting his garden, for the cultivation of which Sunday mornings are reserved as the regular and appointed opportunity. Meanwhile the wife is busy ironing the linen and cleaning the house. The boys are nutting, cowslipping, or birds'-nesting, and the girls lying in bed, or beginning the preparations for their evening finery. After breakfast, the children are sent to shop; and while those who know the value of the sacred day are going to the Sunday school, either as learners or as teachers, or to public worship, they are continually pained by meeting these neglected children in every direction, loaded with meat, flour, butter, eggs, candles, &c., the regular marketing of the week, or perhaps with a pair of new shoes, a hat, or a jacket, the purchase of several weeks' saving.

During the time of public worship, all hands are engaged in preparing the dinner: a good dinner on the Sunday must be secured, if they have not one all the week beside. After dinner, the boys clean the shoes of the family, the girls retire to curl their hair, and plait their frills and caps, the father takes his pipe and jug of beer, perhaps borrows the newspaper, perhaps drops asleep. By the time that this is over, the wife has washed up the dinner things, and made the house tidy, and then the best coat and best gown are put on "in acknowledgment of the day." On a fine summer evening, the family take a stroll in the fields; perhaps call at the skittle-ground or tea-gardens. The little remains of weekly earnings are spent in drink; the man joins a worthless set of fellows, disputing about politics, and infusing a spirit of discontent, or perhaps ridiculing religion, and sneering at the Bible; the wife joins other women in vain and idle gossip; the boys learn to gamble on the skittle-ground, and the girls listen to foolish, frivolous, and corrupting discourse, which paves the way to their ruin. The family return home, and retire to rest without a thought of acknowledging God, and more wearied with the grovelling pursuits and labors—miscalled pleasures—of the day, than if they had been engaged in their regular calling on the days of labor.

Some of the good people of our village made great efforts to promote the observance of the Sabbath. They persuaded the masters to pay their men either on Friday evening or at noon on Saturday. This was one great step gained. Those who chose had full opportunity of going to market on Saturday; and none had the excuse of saying that they were obliged to go to shop on Sunday. The more thrifty wives soon found that their penny would go further in the open market than in the Sunday shop. Indeed, from laying together several facts and incidents, the good women were led to the conclusion, that those who do not scruple to break the laws of God and their country, by keeping open shop on the Sabbath, are not very likely to scruple at cheating, or taking advantage of their customers, when they can do it without detection.

Then our friends would endeavor to convince the people of the great advantage of the Sabbath, even as a humane and useful provision for the rest of the weary. They argued with the men, that it would be much more for their real advantage to work an hour or two longer every day in the week, and keep the Sabbath as a day of rest; and they proved to the women how easy it would be, by good management, to get their domestic business accomplished in good time on Saturday, and on the Sunday morning to have the pleasure of sitting down quietly in a clean house.

But the *rest* of the Sabbath, and its sacred improvement, are two very distinct things. It will not be supposed that any real friend to the best interests of his fellow-creatures could be satisfied with accomplishing the lesser, unless it were made subservient to the greater. Step by step our zealous friends induced the parents to attend public worship, and to send their children to Sunday schools. Thus inquiry was awakened, and a thirst after sacred knowledge was excited. It was found that the Sabbath evenings could be spent in reading the Bible, and good books furnished to the children, more pleasantly and profitably than in their former strolling and dissipation. It was found also that the money which used to be spent in Sabbath-breaking added materially to the comforts of the week; and that the family became much more united and happy in spending their leisure hours among themselves, than when they used to pass them in society where scandal or politics formed the prevailing theme. Thus, in very many families, a great and advantageous reformation was effected by means of the kind and well-directed efforts of these judicious friends. Nor was this all. In several happy instances, persons were not only brought to attend on the means of grace, but the gospel became to them "the power of God unto salvation." I could refer to several families, to which the following description is now as applicable as the former description had been in days gone by.

Through the whole of the week, the Sabbath is borne in mind, and the employment that used to burden its morning hours, is divided between the other six days. Instead of working in his garden the whole Sabbath morning, the good man does this half an hour or an hour daily, either at his meal-times, or when his regular day's work is over. His wife, desirous of enjoying the Sabbath, soon began to find that it is inconvenient to wash late in the week; and then it struck her that there was no sort of advantage in doing it; that the linen might just as well be ironed and put away on Wednesday or Thursday, as be driven to Saturday or Sunday. Besides, it is even comfortable and respectable to know that one has a change of things for the family in the drawer or chest, instead of having to put on every rag the moment it is ironed, scarcely waiting to mend it as required, or even properly to air it. One good thing involves another; and what, with the saving of Sunday expenses, and the better management exercised during the week, it has been found easy by degrees to increase the family stock of substantial and useful clothing; and the whole aspect of the house bears marks of comfort and respectability seldom seen in the dwelling of the Sabbath-breaker.

But still, manage how you will, Saturday *is* a busy day. The only way to get all in order in comfortable time, is to employ every minute to the best advantage, and let every member of the family have an allotted share in accomplishing the business. Yes; in a family accustomed to " remember that to-morrow is the rest of the holy Sabbath of the Lord their God," the mother may be seen hastening to market for the weekly supply of bread, meat, and grocery; not loitering on the way to gossip with one neighbor and another, but quietly passing on, like one who has something to do, and who knows the value of time. Meanwhile, one girl is directed to sweep and dust the bed-rooms, another has to clean the fire-irons and candlesticks; one boy is digging potatoes and getting in firing to serve through the Sabbath, and another is helping the mother to bring home her errands. All know that the mother will soon come home, and that their allotted tasks must be performed by the appointed time.

Then the Sunday dinner is prepared. Sometimes it is dressed and left cold; but most plain folks, who work hard all the week, like a bit of hot dinner on the Sunday. In this case, the good woman, who is determined to employ the whole of the Sabbath in a proper way, soon becomes an adept in devising and preparing such dishes as occasion no trouble on the Sabbath. A stew, nearly done on the Saturday, wants little more than re-warming. It is set over the fire when the family go out in the morning, and is ready for dinner when they return ; or a meat pudding, made on the Saturday, and tied up securely, wants only to be put in the pot on Sunday morning, with a fire made up so as to keep it boiling ; or boiled meat, of almost any kind, may be so managed as to require no further attention after it is once set on.

Having arranged all these little matters, and set every thing ready for use on the Sunday, the house is cleaned, the stockings mended, the best clothes laid out, the shoes cleaned, the children thoroughly washed and combed, and the frugal meal prepared against the husband and father returns from work. Then an hour is happily spent in more immediate preparation for the sacred services of the coming day;— but who shall say that all the humble, simple detail of domestic duties, discharged in their appointed time, are not most important subservient preparations? Yes; the punctuality and order of the family have much to do with a tranquil, holy frame, for entering on more sacred engagements; and, surely, this is a beautiful feature of the religion of Jesus Christ, that, while it imparts strength for the greatest and most arduous duties of the Christian life, it sanctifies and ennobles what might seem the most mean and trifling.

Let the soul be brought under its influence, and then there is dignity and importance even in the good management of the kitchen fire-place. Be " diligent in business," that you may be " fervent in spirit, serving the Lord." Think nothing beneath the attention of a Christian, which may, in any degree, conduce to his waiting on the Lord without distraction; but " whatsoever ye do, in word or in deed, do all in the name of the Lord Jesus."

To return to the Saturday evening of the happy, because pious, family. The children once more look over, or repeat to each other, their several lessons for the Sunday school. The texts and instructions of the last Sabbath are recalled and talked over, the Bible is read, the cheerful hymn of praise is sung, and the lifting up of the hands is as the evening sacrifice. The sacred morn is not profaned by either sloth or toil. The family rise refreshed and grateful, duly appreciating and welcoming the sweet day of rest on which they have entered; regarding it, not as a day of restraints to be endured, but of privileges to be enjoyed, and every necessary secular engagement, as a duty to be performed, not an indulgence to be allowed. This is the great turning point of a well or ill-spent Sabbath; whether or not the heart is in it. If holy things be the choice and delight, the individual or the family will be fertile in expedients to improve and multiply opportunities to enjoy them; but, if the Sabbath be a weariness, there will be no lack of pleas and excuses for violating it.

A holy cheerfulness and seeming enjoyment play on every countenance, and mark every movement of the happy family on the sacred day. In what little of a worldly kind must necessarily be done, each is prompt in taking a share, that all may be performed without bustle and confusion. In family union, they implore a blessing on the more public engagements of the sacred day. The Sunday school, public worship, and private reading, meditation, and conversation, divide the sacred hours; and the day closes with some such joyful sentiments as these: "How amiable are thy tabernacles, O Lord of hosts! A day in thy courts is better than a thousand! We had rather be door-keepers in the house of our God, than dwell in the tents of wickedness. One thing have we desired of the Lord; that will we seek after, that we may dwell in the house of the Lord all the days of our life—to behold the beauty of the Lord, and to inquire in his temple.

> " 'Tis religion that can give
> Sweetest pleasure while we live;
> 'Tis religion must supply
> Solid comfort when we die:
> After death its joys will be
> Lasting as eternity.
> Be the living God our Friend,
> Then our bliss shall never end."

CHAP. XXXII.

ADVICE TO YOUNG TRADESMEN.

It is often the case, that when a young man first sets up in business, he wants advice. I here insert a little for the benefit of such.

"In order to succeed in business, it is absolutely necessary that you should maintain the character and appearance of an honest man. The easiest and most effectual way of doing this, is to be really so. If principles of strict integrity reign in the heart, there will be no little tricks and meannesses to conceal and glaze over, in words or actions. It is the most honorable and valuable character that can be established by a young tradesman; and a certificate that will carry him through life.—' He is thoroughly upright and transparent in all his dealings; he is incapable of an action that could raise a blush on his countenance, if all the world beheld it.'

"Let your standard of honesty and integrity not merely be to keep clear of those things that would expose you to disgrace and punishment; but do nothing to your neighbor or your customer, that you would not think upright if he did the like to you. The golden rule of our Lord Jesus Christ, if universally acted upon, would set aside quarrels and lawsuits. There may be a few cases, in which persons do not know what is legally right, and may find it necessary to consult a lawyer; but ninety-nine cases out of a hundred begin in a failure of attending to this rule, and are carried on in determined opposition to it.

"Detest the petty acts of fraud by short weights and measures, by delivering goods inferior to sample, or by making incorrect entries in your book. 'Divers weights and divers measures are an abomination unto the Lord.'

"Punctuality is a great friend both to integrity and peace. Therefore, deliver and receive all things by exact number, weight, or measure; and take regular accounts of all things sent out or received in.

"For every thing you buy or sell, let or hire, make an exact bargain at first, and neither suffer nor practise the common evasion, 'Never mind the price; we sha'nt disagree about trifles.' This is a common source of disagreement, and often an intentional cloak for fraud.

"Let your books be always kept in such a state as would be no disgrace to yourself, or injury or trouble to others, if sudden death should throw them into the hands of your executors, or unexpected calamity should put them in the power of your creditors.

"Be diligent to know the state of your own affairs. Do not deceive yourself by getting in a good stock, and thinking your shop is well filled, and you have good debts on your books, and ready money for your use, while you have not paid your wholesale dealer. Have your accounts so that you can tell at one view what you owe, what you possess, and what is due to you, and then reckon your own property at less than half the balance that stands in your favor.

"Never forfeit a good conscience, or a good name, for the sake of gain. The gain will be found but momentary, the injury lasting as life. Honesty is always the best policy. Wise men take things in the long run; and they know very well, that to get ten pounds a-year, for life, is better than to get twenty or thirty by one crafty action. To the very poorest a good character is better than ten pounds a-year, and will be found worth more than that in the long run. Let the poor, struggling, honest man look back, and he will find reason to say, 'I got such a one's work, and such a one's good will, and such a one's assistance, by bearing an unblemished character. Where should I have been without a good name for honesty?' While the crafty, unprincipled man is often obliged to think, though he does not choose to say, 'Such an advantage I lost, because I was looked upon with suspicion; such an appointment would have been mine, but they did not like to trust me; I might at this moment have been a richer man, if I had strictly kept to the paths of integrity.' Craft generally outwits itself; as the wise man says, ' The wisdom of the prudent is to understand his way ; but the folly of fools is deceit.' How true are the sayings, ' Tricks and treachery are the practice of fools, who have not sense enough to be honest ;' and, ' that which is unjustly gained, will prove like a barbed arrow, wounding the conscience as it enters, and, still more, the character, when it is torn back with violence.'

" If you wish to maintain a clear conscience and a good name, avoid the very common crime of defrauding government. In all your dealings, whatever duties are levied, or taxes required, let them be punctually rendered, according to the scripture precept, ' Render to all their dues ; tribute to whom tribute is due; custom to whom custom.' Many people, who imagine themselves very honest, think, ' it is no crime to cheat the king.' But there are, at least, three principles on which the dishonesty of such conduct is very evident :—Government must be supported; and every one who shares the protection of government, is bound to contribute his share towards its support. Then, if a certain sum is to be raised amongst a certain number of persons, and if one or more evade paying their share, the deficiency must be made up among the remainder. So, the person who says there is no harm in cheating the king, is, in fact, guilty of cheating the whole community. Then, again, the tradesman who evades any duty, is especially guilty of injustice to other tradesmen in the same line of business. If they pay the duty which he evades, he is enabled to undersell them ; or, if he maintains their price, he gains a much larger profit, and so an end is put to all fair competition. In addition to this, it may be observed, that those who begin by smuggling, or in any way defrauding government, generally go on to acts of private fraud. Their conscience is hardened ; they are in the daily practice of deeds at which they would once have revolted ; they become mean and ungenerous in all their habits ; integrity and respectability are forever sacrificed.

"Avoid as much as possible either taking or giving credit. Nothing establishes the character of a young tradesman more than applying his first returns of ready money to paying debts before they become due, and taking the discount. Many a young tradesman has been ruined by suffering his customers to run up bills with him, which they were unable to pay, and he, in consequence, has been unable to meet the demands of his wholesale dealers. Never seek to promote your own interest by injuring a brother tradesman. It is a common saying, 'Two of a trade can never agree;' but this ought not to be the case, especially among those who profess to be under the influence of religion: 'Live, and let live,' 'The world is wide enough for us both,' are much better sayings. Those who maintain uprightness, candor, and good feeling, may live in the same town, and carry on their respective operations in perfect harmony, and find, in the end, that their mutual interests have been promoted by such a course. But any spiteful attempt to injure a brother tradesman will generally meet the reward that Solomon speaks of, 'He that rolls a stone, it shall return upon him.'

"In a certain small town there were two tradesmen in the same line of business. A nobleman in the neighborhood wished to give equal countenance to every honest tradesman, and directed that the custom of his house should be divided between the two. Both these men were of a sly and spiteful disposition, and each endeavored to undermine the other. Whenever an order was given, or a bill was paid, the one who received it took the opportunity of hinting something to the disadvantage of his neighbor. After endeavoring for several years to cure them of this meanness and malignity, the nobleman became so much disgusted that he took away his custom from both, encouraged a third to set up in the town, and both the former were ruined.

"Be faithful and punctual to your employers. Never crib the articles intrusted to you to make or repair, nor run them to needless expense, for the sake of lengthening your bill. Never draw persons in to put a job into your hands, by inti-

ADVICE TO YOUNG TRADESMEN. 171

mating that the expense will be smaller than you know will really be the case. Such tricks will not serve more than once or twice.

"Never promise customers to get their work done by a certain time, which you know it is impossible to accomplish. Many tradesmen, unwilling to turn away a job, will promise one and another that their work shall be sure to be done by the time desired, at the same time well knowing that almost every one of them must be disappointed. The wives of some tradesmen will boast of their ingenuity in inventing falsehoods to appease an angry customer whom their husband has disappointed. It need scarcely be added, that such tradesmen soon lose their best customers, as well as forfeit their integrity and respectability. An eminently pious tradesman said, 'For many, many years, I have never omitted this supplication in my morning prayer, 'Let integrity and uprightness preserve me, for I wait on Thee.' His prayer was heard and answered; amidst every trial he was preserved in peace of mind; and maintained a character for integrity that the bitterest enemies of religion dared not impeach.

"Integrity is the young tradesman's first requisite, and industry the second. He must keep his shop, if he wishes his shop to keep him. Rise early in the morning. 'The early bird catches the worm.'

> 'Early to bed, and early to rise,
> Is the way to be healthy, wealthy, and wise.'

'Sloth makes all things difficult; but industry makes all things easy.' 'Let your shop be open, and your hammer be heard, the first in the street.' There is no time when the hands and spirits are so nimble, and when all is so free from interruption, as early in the morning; therefore, 'Take time by the forelock, for he is bald behind.' 'One to-day is worth two to-morrows.' 'Defer not till to-morrow what should be done to-day, else you will have a day's work the more to do, and a day less to do it in.' But rather, if you have something that must be done to-morrow, strive if possible to do it to-day, and 'drive your business, rather than let your business drive you.' 'He that rises late, may trot hard all day, and shall scarce overtake his business by night; while Laziness travels so slowly that Poverty soon overtakes him.' It is a common saying that, 'Diligence is the mother of good luck.' We do not talk about good luck, for we know there is no such thing, but that all is under the direction of a wise and righteous Providence; but we know also the Book that says, 'The hand of the diligent maketh rich.' 'Love not sleep, lest thou come to poverty; open thine eyes, and thou shalt be satisfied with bread.' The blessing of God is commonly seen to rest on honest industry. Therefore,

'Plough deep while sluggards sleep,
And you shall have corn to sell and to keep.'

"Let the following sacred proverbs be deeply engraven on your memory: 'The way of the slothful man is as a hedge of thorns, but the way of the righteous shall be made plain.' 'Slothfulness casteth into a deep sleep, and an idle soul shall suffer hunger.' 'The sluggard will not plough, by reason of the cold; therefore he shall beg in harvest, and have nothing.' 'The desire of the slothful killeth him, for his hands refuse to labor.' 'The slothful man saith, "There is a lion without, I shall be slain in the street."' 'I went by the field of the slothful, and by the vineyard of the man void of understanding, and, lo! it was all grown over with thorns, and nettles had covered the face thereof, and the stone wall thereof was broken down. Then I saw, and considered it well. I looked upon it, and received instruction. Yet a little sleep, a little slumber, a little folding of the hands to sleep: so shall thy poverty come as one that travelleth, and thy want as an armed man.'

"The very appearance of diligence is advantageous. The young tradesman should always be found at home, and in some way employed. Busy, meddling neighbors have their eyes always open. You had better weigh and measure your old stock, than let them see you doing nothing. Indeed, it is no bad plan to spend your leisure moments in weighing out pounds or ounces of such things as take no injury, and it is a great saving of time in the bustle of market-day. The very principle and habit of finding a handy little job to fill up every vacant minute is of great value.

"The young tradesman's three best instructers are Necessity, Habit, and Time: from these every thing may be learned, common sense alone excepted, the peculiar and rarest gift of Providence. At his starting in life, Necessity teaches him that if he hopes to live, he must labor; Habit turns the labor into an indulgence, and Time gives to every man an hour for every thing, unless he chooses to throw it away.

"Beware of pride; it has been the bane of many a promising young tradesman: 'pride often breakfasts with plenty, dines with poverty, and sups with infamy.' If you wish your business to befriend you, never be too proud to own your friend. Wear an apron, if such be the custom of your business, and consider it rather a badge of distinction than a mark of disgrace. It will gain you respect and credit with the wise and good. Let there be no part of your business, however inferior, which you do not thoroughly understand, and to which you cannot turn your hand, if occasion require.

"If you have men or boys employed under you, be among them early and late; 'the master's eye does more than both his hands.' Much waste and fraud would never have been practised, if servants could not have ensured themselves with 'Master won't be up for this hour or two,' or, 'Master is safe enough at the public-house.' Not to oversee workmen, is to leave them your purse open; trusting too much to others, is the ruin of many.

> 'He who by the plough would thrive,
> Himself must either hold or drive.'

'If you would have your business talked of, send; if you would have it done, go and do it yourself;' 'if you would be sure of a faithful servant, serve yourself.' These are the sayings of a philosopher, who gained his knowledge, not from books, but men.

"If you would wish to prosper, do not despise small jobs or little customers. You are not to expect, as soon as you set up, that people will leave their old tradesmen, and deal with you; and yet they may sometimes send to you for a small article, or to do some little thing in haste. Receive their orders civilly and thankfully, and take as much pains to do them well, as if they were ten times as great. You will get your proportion of profit; and these little things may lead to greater—perhaps, in time, to the whole custom of the parties who came at first to your shop on some little two-penny errand, for mere convenience. But the carpenter, shoemaker, or tailor, who rudely scorns a little mending job, from those who do not employ him on new work, stands a fair chance of driving away all his customers, both little and great, new and old.

"You may sometimes meet with those who do not treat you with as much courtesy as you think you have a right to expect. It might be very *natural* for you to resent these little indignities, but it will be much more for your peace and advantage if you pass them by: the noble lion is not soon roused to resentment, but the insignificant cur is always ready to snarl and bark. There is much true dignity, as well as sound wisdom, in passing by little affronts. But in order to this, the pride of corrupt nature must be mortified; '*that* would break a proud man's heart, which would hardly break a humble man's slumber.'

"The celebrated Benjamin Franklin, many of whose maxims are here recorded, was early instructed in this useful lesson, 'Learn to stoop.' Having called on the Rev. Cotton Mather, that gentleman, when he took his leave, proposed to show him a shorter way out of the house. It was through a narrow passage, crossed by a beam over head: as they were still talking, Mr. Mather hastily said to his young friend, 'Stoop! stoop!' He did not understand the warning, until he struck his head against the beam. On this, Mr. Mather observed to him, 'You are young, and have the world before you; stoop as you go through it, and you will miss many hard thumps.' 'This advice,' said Franklin, many years afterwards, 'thus beat into my head, has frequently been of use to me; and I often think of it, when I see pride mortified, and misfortunes brought upon people, by carrying their heads too high.' 'Pride goeth before destruction, and a haughty spirit before a fall,' and 'before honor is humility.'

"Beware of false dependences and sudden elevations; go steadily on, laboring and earning, buying and selling, and 'be content to spend a penny less than thy clear gains.' Many have been ruined by calculating on an expected legacy, or an extraordinary run of business. As to legacies, never think about them till you have actually got them. If you do, you may be insensibly led into expenses, which your present circumstances do not justify, and which future circumstances never may; and instead of being benefited by occasional gain, you may be exposed to embarrassments through life. In like manner, if a peculiar season, or some public change of peace or war, should give you a brisk and prosperous run of trade, remember it will not last always. Be not hasty in enlarging your expenses, or making a more showy appearance on the strength of it. Let extra gains go quietly towards increasing your capital, and then they may prove a real and permanent advantage; but if spent on appearance or present gratification, they will only excite in yourself a taste for indulgences and gratifications, that you cannot continue to enjoy, and in your neighbors an estimate of your circumstances which truth and time will not support.

"Always act by a plan. It is said, 'A good contriver is better than an early riser.' Now, early rising is a piece of good contrivance, that no person deserving the character will ever omit. Those who waste their morning hours in bed, are generally notorious for indolence and ill-management throughout the day. Indeed, their life is a scene of lazy bustle and laborious confusion. However, though every good contriver is an early riser, it does not follow that every early riser is a good contriver. The great matter is, to have an allotted and profitable employment for every hour of the day, and something always at hand to fill up the odd minutes. Much time may be wasted in considering what to set about next; and much time frittered in pursuits not worthy our attention. 'As every shred of gold is precious, so is every moment of time. Time is the stuff that life is made of,' and he who wastes his moments is a kind of self-murderer. He does not live so long as he might do. Remember, 'time is money;' if you loiter away an hour, you might just as well, perhaps better, throw away the money you might have earned in that hour. If you spend an hour or half a day in diversion, you must reckon that it costs you, not merely the money you pay, but the money you neglect to earn; and you ought also to take into account the offence given to neglected customers, and the loss of character sustained.

"Do not be regardless of appearances, or of the remarks that are made of you: every man may command respect, and it is his duty to do so. If he conducts himself well, bad people may hate or envy, but they cannot despise him; and all good people feel a pleasure in manifesting respect towards one whose character is respectable. A wise man will neither seek nor despise a good name. He does right, because it is right; and in so doing, he finds the advantage of being reputed to do so, in the confidence and respect he gains; but he who professes to despise what men may say, is likely to be very careless whether he does right or wrong. It is an advantage to a young tradesman, and will be found to set him higher in the esteem, both of his creditors and his customers, to have it known that he spends his evenings at home with his family, and his Sabbaths at the house of God, than if his voice were heard in the tavern, or at the billiard table, or skittle ground.

"Wherever a man goes, his good or his ill character will be sure to fly before him, or at least to tread on his heels; and it will rather generally be grounded on small habits than on great acts.

"Idleness leads to extravagance: for that reason they are often coupled together in the book of Proverbs: thus, 'he that is slothful is brother to him that is a great waster;' 'the drunkard and the glutton shall come to poverty, and drowsiness shall clothe a man with rags.'

"Shun a public-house; it is the grave of a tradesman's respectability and prosperity, and a snare to his soul. Avoid making bargains or paying wages in a public-house; the very appearance is not creditable, and the habit is highly injurious. Form no connection with a club that holds its meetings at a public-house. Savings banks and life insurances will answer your purpose better, and neither cost you a farthing in drink, nor run the hazard of exciting in you a love of liquor. There are two houses which a thrifty young tradesman will never enter—the public-house or liquor-shop, and the pawnbroker's. Every pound borrowed at the pawnbroker's amounts, in the course of a year, to at least three pounds, and sometimes (according to circumstances) to as much as sixteen pounds. This may seem incredible, but it is a fact.

"Every pound spent at the public-house should be reckoned as two pounds, at the end of three years, and sixteen pounds, at the end of twenty-four years. Many a tradesman who complains that he cannot get on for want of capital, forgets how much capital he has wasted by littles. 'He that despises small things, shall fall by little and little.' Do not say it is *only* a penny, *only* a shilling, but remember that 'a pin a day is a groat a year, and a groat a day is six pounds a year.' Besides, if a groat a day be spent the first year, sixpence a day will hardly suffice for the second year; and so a man may go on spending, till what would keep his family in bread, meat, and grocery, shall scarcely suffice for his own selfish and sensual expenses: many a good estate has been swallowed from a wine glass. Well has the wise man said, 'He that loveth pleasure shall be a poor man; he that loveth wine and oil shall not be rich.'

"The young tradesman who wishes to thrive, must avoid all needless expenses, both in his shop, his person, and his household concerns. There is nothing got by ostentatious display in the fitting up of your shop; every sensible customer says, 'I must pay for part of this finery.' The brightness of your shop windows is much more likely to attract profitable notice than the size of the panes; and the neat and tasty selection and arrangement of your goods, than the mahogany counters on which they are served.

"Every tradesman should maintain a clean, neat, and respectable appearance; but if he becomes foppish and extravagant in his dress, he will be suspected of either imposing on his customers, or of running the way to his own ruin; and except frugality preside over all his personal and household expenses, whatever be his gains, his ruin is certain.

"In order to secure economy in the management of household expenses, as well as many other important advantages, it will be his wisdom to choose an industrious, prudent and discreet wife, rather than a showy one. For in vain will he earn and spare, if she be wasteful and extravagant. He who has an extravagant wife, as the saying is, 'may keep his nose to the grindstone all his life, and not leave a groat behind him at last;' 'a fat kitchen makes a lean will.'

"Check the first inclination in yourself or your wife to lay out money on mere gratifications: 'Those who buy superfluities are likely soon to sell necessaries;' 'silks and satins put out the kitchen fire.' Do not be induced to buy things merely because they are offered cheap : 'a cheap bargain is a pick-pocket.' When you feel inclined to buy any thing, it will not take long to ask yourself the following questions, and may be the means of saving you from ruin.

"Can I afford it?

"Is it fit and becoming to my station in life?

"Can I not do very well without it?

"Might not the money be turned to a better purpose?

"Many families, for the sake of a fine showy appearance, endure the want of real comforts; their miserable, confined, ill-furnished bed-chambers and kitchen, but ill agree with their drawing-rooms and sofas, their ribbons and feathers: but, as the saying is, 'pride is as loud a beggar as want, and

ADVICE TO YOUNG TRADESMEN.

a great deal more saucy;' 'when you have bought one fine thing, you must buy ten more, that your appearance may be all of a piece.' It is easier, therefore, to suppress the first desire, than to satisfy all that follow it.

"Beware of the folly of hankering after things, either in dress or furniture, merely because your neighbor has them; perhaps his means are above yours; if they are, you would only make yourself as ridiculous as the frog in the fable, who killed himself in trying to swell as large as the ox. If your neighbor's means are not larger than your own, there is no reason why you should make a fool of yourself merely because he chooses to do so. Those who strive to make an appearance above their circumstances, are often reduced to seek assistance of those who are content with living a little below theirs. And so 'a ploughman on his legs, is higher than a gentleman on his knees.'

"If you have a little money in hand, and are tempted to take a little for extra diet, and a little for fine clothes, and a little for grand entertainments, remember that 'many a little makes a mickle,' 'a small leak will soon sink a great ship,' and 'if you are always taking out of the meal tub, and never putting in, you will soon come to the bottom.' If you act thus, and come to poverty, don't be laying the blame on bad times and heavy taxes: 'you are taxed twice as much by your idleness, three times as much by your pride, and four times as much by your folly; and from these taxes the commissioners cannot ease or deliver you by making an abatement.'

"'My neighbor,' says one, 'had a terrible itching for auctions:' 'never mind,' he used to say, 'I'll have *that*, it will not ruin me; knock me down that other thing, it is dirt cheap; I don't much want these things, but there is nothing that will not come in use once in seven years.' He was sadly out here; he filled his house with useless lumber, and made good the saying, 'Feather by feather, the goose was plucked.'

"One great evil of extravagance is, that it leads to running in debt; he who, having ready money, cannot resist the temptation to spend it on superfluities, when he has no ready money, is more likely to run in debt than to deny himself; and then what follows? You will be ashamed to see your creditor, ashamed to speak to him, and driven to make poor, pitiful, sneaking excuses, till you come by degrees to lose all principle, and sink into base, downright lying, as it has been well said, 'Lying rides on debt's back.' 'The second vice is lying, the first is running in debt;' and again, 'It is hard for an empty bag to stand upright.'

"Poverty, brought on by extravagance, often deprives a man of all spirit and virtue. Very different this from honest poverty; a poor man, his wife, and family, may labor hard and fare hard, perhaps go to bed supperless, but when he rises, he feels that he owes no man any thing, and goes forth cheerfully to earn the daily bread in its day, happy to think that he is not burdened with the expenses of yesterday; and if he begins with one honest penny in his pocket, he feels himself a little prince, compared with that man, who, for past gratifications, is suffering nightly disturbances and daily apprehensions. The way to be rich and respectable is to 'let industry make a purse, and frugality find strings to it; let the strings only be drawn as frugality dictates, and there will always be found a useful penny at the bottom.'

"The prosperous young tradesman is generally one whom his customers find at home; if a customer calls again and again, without seeing the master, it is likely he will seek elsewhere. Many a good order has been lost, for want of the master being in the way, to make hay while the sun shines; 'as a bird that wanders from her nest, so is a man that wanders from his place.' All his plans are likely to be defeated, and the whole to issue in a failure.

"Whatever is amiss in your circumstances, do not indulge a restless, discontented spirit, and try to lay the blame any where but on yourself; it is bad enough if you have brought yourself to inconvenience, but if you can come to the conviction that this is the case, by all means cherish the conviction rather than stifle it, for after all it affords the best hope of mending matters. Surely you have more power to correct your own follies than the follies of other people. Industry and patience can remedy almost any common grievance; but discontent and despair only increase them. 'The foolishness of man perverteth his way, and his heart fretteth against the Lord.' Instead of indulging this repining spirit, submit yourself; humble yourself under the mighty hand of God; acknowledge that you have deserved all you suffer, and much more. Resolve to act differently for the future, and beg of God to give you strength and grace to keep your resolutions. Let the fear of God rule in your heart; this will make you think well and act well, and when you most need it and least expect it, God may raise you up a friend, or open to you a way of deliverance.

"Do not meddle with politics. I never knew a young tradesman either do good or get good, who was fond of political debates or Sunday newspapers: 'fear the Lord and the king, and meddle not with them that are given to change.' 'Let God govern the world, and the king the nation, and mind your own business.'

"If you wish to prosper, you must be persevering as well as industrious. Be not discouraged if you do not at first enjoy as much success as you could desire, but try again and again, still humbly depending on the blessing of God, and sooner or later you will in some measure succeed, perhaps far beyond your present expectation. One great man was encouraged to perseverance by observing a spider, which, in attempting to reach the beam on which to fix its web, failed twelve times, but succeeded the thirteenth. Another person, when forced to take shelter from the pursuit of his enemies, concealed himself in a ruined building, and remained there several hours. While meditating on his hopeless condition, he saw a little ant carrying up a high wall a grain of corn much larger than itself. He numbered the efforts made by this diligent little creature to accomplish its object; sixty-nine times the grain fell to the ground, but the seventieth time the ant successfully reached the top of the wall. The lesson thus imparted was never forgotten.

"It is greatly to the honor of a young tradesman, instead of consuming all the gains of his industry, to lay by a portion for old age or sickness.

> 'For age and want, save while you may;
> No summer's sun lasts a whole day.'

Lay up while young, and you will find it when you are old. A prudent care and forecast may be cherished without yielding to a mercenary or distrustful spirit.

"But with all your industry, perseverance, and good management, guard against worldly-mindedness. 'And seekest thou great things for thyself? seek them not.' 'Labor not to be rich; cease from thine own wisdom. Wilt thou set thine heart upon that which is not? for riches certainly make themselves wings; they fly away as an eagle towards heaven.' Money is only valuable for the good it will procure; in itself, it is very mean, and unsatisfying, and uncertain; and riches unsanctified are a curse. 'They that will be rich, fall into temptation and a snare, and into many foolish and hurtful lusts, which drown men in perdition and destruction.' While laboring diligently, never forget the solemn question, 'What will it profit a man, if he gain the whole world, and lose his own soul? or what shall a man give in exchange for his soul?' In your pursuit of wealth, never be drawn to neglect *the one thing needful*, or to alienate time, especially sacred time, from the concerns of your soul. 'Prayer and provender hinder no journey.' Real success will never attend that cause on which the blessing of God is not sought; but the blessing of God is seen to rest, in an especial manner, on that house in which the worship of God is maintained, his Sabbath sacredly observed, and his sanctuary frequented; while those who have been induced, for the sake of worldly gain, to slacken their attendance on religious duties, have generally fallen, both in property and enjoyment, instead of rising.

"Never forget your entire dependence on Providence. Though the advice here given is consistent with sound reason and sacred wisdom, 'Do not depend too much on your own industry, frugality, and prudence, though excellent things, for they may be blasted without the blessing of Heaven; and, therefore, seek that blessing humbly, and be not uncharitable to those who at present seem to want it, but comfort and help them.'

" 'Except the Lord build the house, they labor in vain that build it; except the Lord keep the city, the watchman waketh but in vain. It is vain for you to rise up early, to sit up late, to eat the bread of carefulness.' Constantly remember the Lord thy God, for it is he who giveth thee power to get wealth, or who in wisdom withholds it. He it is who appoints thy straits or thy sufficiency. In either, his blessing alone can make truly rich and happy. The only security for a blessing, on either prosperity or adversity, is in being found among those 'for whom all things work together for good, even them that love God, and are the called according to his purpose.'

"Now the question is—whether all this good advice will be taken heed to, or whether it will be suffered to run off, like clear water from a duck's back. We can give counsel, but we cannot give conduct. 'One man can lead a horse to the water, but twenty cannot make him drink;' but remember, that 'they who will not be counselled cannot be helped,' and 'if you will not hear reason, she is likely to rap your knuckles.' 'Therefore, hear counsel, and receive instruction, that thou mayest be wise in thy latter end. Keep sound wisdom and discretion, so shall they be life to thy soul, and grace to thy neck; for the wise shall inherit glory, but shame shall be the promotion of fools.' "

The following is part of a letter from Rev. James Hervey to his brother, while he was an apprentice:—

"As soon as you are bound, you are at your master's disposal, and not at your own: he has then a right to your hands, your strength, and ALL that you can do. He becomes a sort of parent to you; and though not a natural, yet a legal father. You are also obliged, not only by the laws of your country, and the tenor of your indentures, but by the fifth commandment of God, to pay him all due submission and honor. To do this is a most material part of your duty as a Christian, as well as your undeniable debt as an apprentice. It is required of you by God, in Holy Scripture, and you must not once imagine that you do what is pleasing to him unless you conscientiously perform it. Now, that you may know what it is that your master will expect from you, and what it is that the Lord has enjoined you with regard to him, remember it consists, first, in reverence of his person; secondly, in obedience to his commands; and, thirdly, in faithfulness in his business.

"First, in reverence of his person. You must esteem him very highly for his superiority's sake and the resemblance he bears to God. For God, who made you, and has an uncontrollable power over you, has communicated some of that power to your master; so that you are to look upon him as the representative, in some sort, of the divine majesty, and invested with some of his authority. Accordingly, St. Paul says, 1 Tim. vi. 1, 'You must count him worthy of all honor;' all, that is, internal and external, that of the actions and words, as well as that of the heart. It is not enough to maintain a worthy estimation inwardly, but you must let it appear on all occasions outwardly, by behaving yourself very obligingly to him before his face, and by speaking very respectfully of him behind his back. Suppose you should discern failings and infirmities in him, you must by no means divulge them, or make yourself merry with them, much less must you dare to set light by any of his orders. Whatever you have reason to think will grieve or displease him, or will be prejudicial or offensive to him, that you must cautiously forbear.

"Secondly, obedience to his commands. See how full the apostle speaks to this purpose, Col. iii. 22. 'Servants, obey in all things your masters according to the flesh.' Observe, likewise, from this passage, not only the necessity, but also the compass and latitude of your obedience, how large and extensive it is. It reaches not barely to a few, but to all and every instance. If you should receive orders that are ever so much against the grain of your own inclination, you must force yourself to comply with them; receive them as you used to do nauseous physic; though they may be unpleasant at first, they will do you good, and be comfortable to you afterwards; your own pleasure must always stoop, and give way to your master's. If he sets you a task that is mean and ignoble, and such as (according to the expression of the world) is beneath a gentleman's son, do not scruple it, dear brother, but despatch it cheerfully. Remember who hath said, 'Servants, obey your masters in all things.' And, oh! remember that, however well born and bred we are, yet He that was higher than the highest of us all, even the most excellent and illustrious person that ever lived, condescended to the lowest and (such as our fine folks would account) most shameful offices. The Lord Jesus Christ, though 'the brightness of his Father's glory,' disdained not to wash his disciples' feet. Neither be dejected because you are treated in an unworthy manner, or set to do some mean and low office for your master, or his family; but rejoice rather in that you are made like unto your Redeemer, and in the happy prospect you will have of becoming great in heaven, by being little on earth. I am aware this piece of advice is not so unexceptionable as the rest; it may possibly be adjudged the mark of too yielding and sneaking a spirit; but never forget that the things which are most highly esteemed by God, are held in least repute by men. I know, and am sure, that if any apprentice would make such a compliance for the sake of preserving peace, and out of conscience to the command of God, and with an eye to the example of Christ, there is a day coming when he will not repent of it; when it will not be deemed a blot in his character, but be 'an ornament of grace to his head, and more comely than chains about his neck.'* Well, you see your obedience must be universal; you must come when he calls you, and go

---

* Prov. i. 9.

where he bids you; do all that he commands you, and let alone all that he forbids you. This must, moreover, be done, not grudgingly, or of necessity, but readily and gladly : for hear what the scripture saith, ' Whatsoever ye do, do it heartily ;'* and again, ' with good will doing service ;'† so that we must not creep, but be quick and expeditious in our business, however disagreeable. You must not go about it with grumbling words and muttering in your mouth, but with so satisfied an air as may show that you are pleased with whatever pleases your master.

"Thirdly, in faithfulness in his business. This is the last branch of your duty to your master ; and since Moses has obtained an honorable testimony on this account, be you also 'faithful in all his house.'‡ You may find this, as indeed all the qualifications of a good servant, described by St. Paul, Tit. ii. 10. ' Not purloining,' says he, ' but showing all fidelity.' You are charged not to purloin, that is, not to keep back from your master, nor to put into your own pocket, nor convert to your own use, any of that money which, in the way of trade, passes through your hands. You were taught from your childhood to keep your hands from picking and stealing, and I hope you abhor such abominable practices from the bottom of your heart. You must not sell at a cheaper, and buy at a dearer rate, in order to have some valuable consideration made you privily in your own person. These differ from robbing on the highway, only in being less open and notorious ; but they are flagrant acts of dishonesty, and will cry to Heaven for vengeance. Such tricks and villanies do the same thing by craft and treachery as housebreakers do by force and violence. Therefore, dear brother, renounce, detest, and fly from them, as much as from fire, arrows, and death. Besides, you are not only to abstain from such clandestine knavery, but also to show all good fidelity. What is meant by this you may understand by reading how Joseph conducted himself in Potiphar's service. Your master, it is likely, will commit the

---

* Col. iii. 23. † Eph. vi. 7. ‡ Heb. iii. 5.

management of some of his affairs to you; and you must endeavor, by a discreet behavior and a pious life, to bring the blessing of the Lord upon all that you take in hand. You must lay out your time, and your labor, and give all diligence to answer the trust reposed in you. You must not delay the business which is urgent, nor do your work by halves, nor transfer that to others which it is expected you should do yourself. 'The slothful man,' says Solomon, 'is brother to him that is a great waster;' therefore you must avoid idleness and carelessness. In a word, you must do nothing knowingly and wilfully that is likely to impoverish your master, but seek by all lawful and laudable means to increase his substance. All this you must observe, not only when he stands by you, and inspects you, but when his back is turned, and you are removed from his view; otherwise your service is nothing but eye-service, such as will prove odious to man, and is already condemned by God. For if you appear to be industrious, and in earnest, before your master, and loiter and trifle when out of his sight, you will be chargeable with hypocrisy, a sin extremely hateful to Christ, and grievously pernicious to the soul. But I am afraid I tire you; this one sentence, therefore, and I have done. You must carry yourself, throughout the whole course of your apprenticeship, so respectfully, so obediently, so faithfully, that at the end of it you may truly say with Jacob, 'With all my power I have served.'"

CHAP. XXXIII.

HELPING ONE ANOTHER.

It is a remark, which I have often heard addressed both to fellow-servants, and to the members of a family in general, "Know your own places, but be always willing to help one another:" these two rules will do much to promote family order and harmony. "What is every body's business, is nobody's care." It is both the occasion and the excuse of neglect. Duty is often altogether neglected of which it may be said, "Most likely Jane has done it," or "I dare say Richard will be home in time to do it," or "I thought Betty had done it." For that reason it is desirable that every duty, however small, should be regularly assigned to Jane, or Richard, or Betty. But, then, it is equally desirable, that a general feeling of good-will should be cherished among them; that each, having performed his or her own part, should be ready to render assistance to any one who may happen to be a little behind with theirs, and all should cheerfully join in making things comfortable when any extra work occurs, either through illness or visitors.

I know a large family, whose house is the seat of order and harmony; and this is how they manage. They keep no servant, but the industrious and judicious mother has brought up her children to a thorough knowledge of the management of domestic affairs in general. Each, also, has a particular department assigned, according to the particular turn discovered; and the least agreeable services are taken by each in turn. One daughter takes care of the pantry, and another of the bed-rooms; a third is chiefly employed in making up the clothes of the family; one superintends the laundry; and another the nursery and sick room. One son takes care of the garden, another manages the horse and other animals, and a third attends to the brewery and wine-making. But, though each knows and keeps his own department, each takes pleasure in lending a helping hand to the other: thus all is managed without bustle, confusion, or altercation.

I have also heard a story of a humorous old gentleman, who, hearing a dispute between two of the servants, inquired what was the matter. The house-maid replied, that, being very tired, she had asked the coachman to fetch her a pail of water from the well, which was at some little distance from the house: this he ill-naturedly and surlily refused. "Nay," said the master, "I could not have thought, John, that you could be so ungallant as to refuse to assist a female." John sulkily muttered, "that it was not his place to fetch water—he was not hired to do it." "True, true," replied the master; "I beg your pardon for supposing that you would do any thing that you were not hired to do. Go directly, put the horses to, and bring the carriage to the door." In a few minutes, the carriage was announced, when the master directed the house-maid to get in with her pail, and ordered John to drive her to the well as many times as she required. "Whenever young people feel a grudging disposition, and unwillingness to render any little service that they are not expressly hired to perform, let them remember the old gentleman's humorous reproof, and remember, above all things, the precepts of the holy Book, which, if acted on, would prove the cure of all selfishness and ill-will: 'Look not every man on his own things, but every man also on the things of others. Bear ye one another's burdens, and so fulfil the law of Christ.'

CHAP. XXXIV.

CHANGING PLACES.

"THINK twice before you act once," said a man to a journeyman, who talked of leaving his master for the sake of higher wages. "You may, perhaps, get higher wages for a few weeks, just while the run lasts, but how will it be all the year round? Besides, think how ungenerous it would be, in the busy time, to leave a master who has kept you employed when trade was dull.

"When I was in business," said this man, "I had many men in my employ, and was always desirous of keeping them in constant work, at such wages as would enable them to live. I never turned off hands at a time when work was dull, but found them employment in what I hoped afterwards to bring into use. I seldom had occasion to take on extra hands at a busy time, and I made it a rule *never* to take on a man who had once deliberately left my employ. If any one signified his intention of leaving, I generally advised him to sleep upon his resolution, and to remember that, if he once left, he would have no chance of being taken on again. By steadily maintaining this plan, I and my men came to understand each other; they were satisfied that moderate gains, all the year round, were, on the whole, preferable to an occasional flush and frequent destitution; they lost the restless desire of changing, and I had the pleasure of leaving in the employ of my sons, scores of men who had worked many years for their father—men who had maintained their families in decency, and who had most of them laid by a snug trifle for a rainy day."

CHAP. XXXV.

SUPERSTITION.

"Don't put those hams in salt to-day, whatever you do," said self-conceited Mary to the cook, who was preparing the ingredients for that purpose. "Why not?" asked the cook. "Because it is Friday," answered the silly girl, "and no good luck ever comes to any thing begun on a Friday."

"And are you really weak enough to believe that can have any thing to do with the matter?" asked her mistress, who happened to be passing the pantry door at the moment.

"Every body knows that's true, ma'am; at least all country people do. There is not a farmer's wife round, that would put hams in salt, or begin making cheeses, on a Friday. It is certainly true that they never prosper."

"And, pray, do you know the reason why Mrs. Thomson's bacon was spoiled last autumn, which she was so very careful to put in salt on a Saturday?"

"No, ma'am, I do not know."

"Then I will tell you. It was because the weather was

warm, and the meat was not salted early enough to preserve it. If it had been salted on the Friday, it is very likely it would have proved good bacon; but it was sacrificed to the silly prejudice of not putting it in salt on Friday.

"Much in the same manner Mrs. Taylor suffered her baby to scratch and disfigure its face, because she had a notion that it is unlucky to cut the nails of a child under a year old; and Nanny Scott, the old washer-woman, is sure that another death will happen this year in the family, because, when her sister-in-law was taken out to be buried, somebody shut the door before the corpse was under ground, and so shut death into the house. Another neighbor expects a similar event, because a single raven flew over the house, and the cricket chirped on the hearth, and she saw a winding-sheet in the candle.

"My dear women," continued the lady, "how can you be so silly as to embitter your lives by such foolish superstition? It is very likely that death will enter the house within the year, for no doors nor bolts can keep it out, and it is very likely that you may be its victim. You have more reason to think so than any of your silly omens can give you."

"Dear, ma'am, what reason?" asked one of the women in terror.

"Because the Bible tells us that it is appointed to *all men* once to die, and warns us to be *always* ready, because we know not the day nor the hour when we shall be called."

"But, ma'am, don't you believe in any thing that is a token of death, or of good or ill luck?"

"In nothing whatever. There is no such thing as luck, either good or bad; for luck means chance; but every thing, great and small, is under the wise and gracious direction of God; nothing can happen without his permission, and He permits nothing but what, in his wonderful plans, He designs to work about for good. We are kept in ignorance of the particular events that are to befall us, in order to keep up in us a constant sense of our dependence on God, and a constant obedience to the directions of his word, by which alone we can be prepared for the dispensations of his providence."

"Should you not think me very silly," continued she, "if I were to say, Some dirty rags were put into the mill, and by good luck they came out clean paper? You would say luck had nothing to do with it. It was the intention of the master to make those rags into paper, and every part of the mill was contrived for that very purpose; for that he sets the different machines to work, and employs the various substances which he knows will bring about and effect the change he intends.

"Now, though I don't know much about paper-making, I know you employ different materials and different methods, according to the different kinds of papers you want to produce. But suppose I were to say, 'A raven flew over the mill, and therefore I know the pulp in this tub will come out brown paper. The cat mewed for some meat, or purred over her kitten, and that is a sure sign that the pulp in this other vat will become white paper.' Well, the paper turns out white or brown, just as I had said; but should you not think me very silly indeed, if I could for a moment suppose that the raven or the cat had any thing to do with making it so?"

"Very true, ma'am; it could have nothing to do with it: we know better than to think it could: but then we know all that is done to make the rags into paper, and to make the paper white or brown, as the master pleases."

"Yes, my friend, and we know, too, that every event, both great and small, is under the direction and control of God, and all are employed in effecting his plans. Then, as to our having a knowledge of any particular event beforehand, God, in his infinite wisdom, has seen fit to withhold such knowledge. It would only unfit us for our duty; and it is both vain and wicked to endeavor to obtain it, or for any one to pretend that they possess it. The Bible tells us quite enough of futurity to teach us to prepare for it, as far as it rests with us to prepare; and as to the particular strength and assistance we shall need when any particular trial comes upon us, it is much safer and better for us to know that a God of infinite mercy is exactly acquainted with our circumstances and need, has all resources at his disposal, and will bestow upon his people, in answer to prayer, *what* and *when* is really best for them, according to his riches in glory by Christ Jesus. We do so with our little children; we give them food or medicine as we see necessary, and tell them to come to us when they are in want or in pain; but we never think of telling them exactly what and when we intend to give them next, though we take care to provide such things as are necessary.

"Had it been according to the will of God, and for our real good, that we should know every thing beforehand, we may depend upon it, the information would have been given us in God's holy word, or gathered from general instruction and observation, as we find all kinds of knowledge are obtained that are worth possessing. It certainly would not have been left to creaking doors, and croaking ravens, and ill-made tallow candles."

A lady once lent us an excellent little story about Tawny Rachel, showing the wickedness of those people who pretend to tell about the future, and the folly of putting any faith in dreams, omens, and conjurers. I was mightily pleased with the whole story, and shall here copy a few of the concluding remarks.

"Listen to me, your true friend, when I assure you that God never reveals to weak and wicked women, the designs of his providence, which no human wisdom is able to foresee. To consult these false oracles, is not only foolish but sinful; it is foolish, because they are themselves as ignorant as those whom they pretend to teach; and it is sinful, because it is prying into that futurity which God, in mercy, as well as in wisdom, hides from man. God indeed orders all things, but when you have a mind to do a foolish thing, do not fancy you are *fated* to do it; this is tempting providence, not trusting God. It is indeed charging Him with folly; prudence is his gift, and you obey him better when you make use of prudence, under the direction of prayer, than when you madly rush into ruin, and think you are only submitting to your fate. Never fancy you are compelled to undo yourself, or to rush upon your own destruction, in compliance with any supposed fatality. Never believe that God conceals his will from a sober Christian, who obeys his laws, and reveals it to a vagabond, who runs up and down breaking the laws both of God and man. King Saul never consulted the witch till he left off serving God; the Bible will direct us best; conjurers are impostors; and there are no days unlucky but those which we make so by our vanity, folly and sin."

CHAP. XXXVI.

THE HOUSEKEEPER'S CHAPTER OF SUNDRIES.

Cleanliness.—" Have your house clean, your dress clean, your body clean, and your mind clean."

> "Let thy mind's sweetness have its operation
> Upon thy person, clothes, and habitation."

And truly the connection is much nearer than would appear at first sight; purity, commencing in the heart as the fountain, extends itself to every little rill of conduct and appearance.

"Cleanliness," says the proverb, "is next to godliness;" we will not dispute about the exact degree of relationship. Cleanliness ought never to be set up as a substitute for godliness, but it certainly is, or ought to be, a constant attendant upon godliness.

All physicians agree that cleanliness does much to preserve and to restore the health of the body; by frequent washings, the skin is kept clear from disease, and the circulations go on freely; by frequent change of bed-linen, the sleep is more refreshing, and general health and cheerfulness are promoted. Children, in particular, have their temper, as well as their health, affected by the cleanly or the negligent habits of those who nurse them; and it is not improbable that many a fretful, irritable temper, through life, may be traced in the beginning to this very circumstance.

Clean skin, clean walls, and clean furniture, will do more to keep off infectious disease than all the scents and perfumes in the druggist's shop.

A healthy air, like pure water, should be quite free from every kind of taste and smell.

To enter a close and dirty apartment is no less injurious than it is disgusting; but thorough cleanliness is at once inviting to the eye and refreshing to the spirits.

Families who are thoroughly cleanly in their habits, generally enjoy more peace and contentment than those of an opposite description; and the unexpected entrance of a visitor produces no feeling of shame or irritation. Then, again, cleanly people are generally forecasting and prudent in other respects; their furniture and clothes are carefully preserved, and so last longer. Time seems turned to a better account; a cleanly person is never indolent. Neither is half the time occupied in cleaning, by persons who are habitually cleanly; hence they have more time to devote to every other proper purpose, and, in particular, more time to attend to the duties and enjoyments of religion. It is a very common excuse for neglecting public worship,—" We have no decent clothes to appear in :" this is not the plea of the cleanly; however poor, they can always command a decent appearance, and are generally distinguished for their orderly attendance on public worship. Thus we make good the assertion, that cleanliness is the handmaid both of peace and godliness.

Keeping things to their proper uses.—The three well-known rules of domestic economy ought to be affixed in some conspicuous part of every kitchen and cottage, at least until they are transcribed into the memories and habits of the inhabitants:—

> Do every thing in its proper time;
> Put every thing in its proper place;
> Keep every thing to its proper use.

It is a perpetual source of vexation in families, and a disgrace both to mistresses and servants, when household articles are either mislaid or injured, in consequence of having been used for improper purposes:—a good table-knife hacked with cutting wood, instead of a saw or a chopper; the prongs of forks bent or broken, by having been made to do the work of a corkscrew; a dresser or table made to serve for a chopping board, and a chair for a pair of steps; a table-cloth cut by having been used as a knife-cloth, and a good cloak or blanket scorched by being made to serve as an ironing-blanket. Many such sights may be seen in slatternly families; and they generally indicate that the owners will one day be destitute of things for their use.

"Only for once,"—"It does not much signify,"—"It is not worth while to fetch it,"—with the whole train of similar foolish apologies and excuses, should always be heard with suspicion and disgust; and where young people find themselves at all inclined to set up such excuses, they should immediately stand self-convicted of the beginning of mischief, and should at once resolve to do the thing properly, and to acquire a habit of so doing.

Kindness to animals.—In most families, one or more domestic animals are kept: as they are removed from their natural state, in which they could have supplied their own wants, and that for the use or gratification of man, they have a claim to be properly supplied and kindly treated. "A merciful man regards the life of his beast, but the tender mercies of the wicked are cruel."

Every domestic animal should be distinctly understood to be the charge of an individual; else there is great danger of its being forgotten or neglected, under the idea that another person has supplied it. The person who undertakes this charge, should have a regular time allotted for fulfilling it, and a regular place assigned, in which supplies are to be put as they accumulate; the fragments of the cookery, and of the table, for the poor dog and cat, and even the crumbs for the chickens or sparrows. Let nothing be wasted that can contribute to the happiness of any living thing; there is something delightful in a benevolence resembling that of the bountiful Creator, who provides for the meanest creatures of his power, and takes pleasure in their happiness.

Children should early be taught to be kind to dumb animals; encouraged to supply them with food and water; taught to know what food is suitable for them; and never, on any account, be allowed to torment them in sport.

Cleanliness is as conducive to the health and comfort of animals, as it is to the human species. Even those that bear the character of the dirtiest animals, thrive astonishingly better if kept thoroughly clean; and their being kept so is essential to the health and comfort of those who live near them.

Borrowing.—" If you would borrow a thing a second time, use it well, and return it speedily the first." Avoid a habit of borrowing: remember, "the borrower is servant to the lender." The proverb runs, "He that goes a-borrowing, goes a-sorrowing;" and so, indeed, does he who lends to some people. They are only concerned for their own immediate convenience, and have no due regard to their neighbor's property. They will even forget that the article does not belong to them, or imagine that it was returned long ago, and will feel offended when the owner applies for it. This is very frequently the case with respect to books, the benefit of which a benevolent man would wish to extend to his friends; but is often, by repeated losses, discouraged and deterred in his kind intentions.

In household affairs, people should take care to have their own articles kept in good repair and fit for use, that they may not often be compelled to trouble their neighbors. If any article is borrowed, special care should be impressed on the minds of all concerned, to remember that it *is* borrowed, to preserve it from injury, and to return it to the owner as soon as done with.

It is wise to have a separate place, in which to put borrowed articles, especially borrowed books; lest, being put among others, the circumstance of their being borrowed should be forgotten, the lender injured, and the borrower disgraced.

Vessels used in cookery.—Every housekeeper should be aware that some kinds of vessels, used for kitchen purposes, render the food dressed in them unwholesome; but frequent accidents have occurred through the ignorance or thoughtlessness of cooks.

Copper is generally used for tea-kettles and saucepans, on account of its appearance and durability; and, for the former purpose, there is no objection; but then it should be understood that any *greasy*, *salt*, or *acid* substances, permitted to remain in them, produce a green scum, called *verdigris*, which is highly poisonous. To avoid this danger, observe,

1. To keep every copper saucepan well tinned: at the same time, do not depend on this. However well tinned, copper will affect the food, if it be suffered to remain in the vessel.

2. Do not suffer any thing to remain in the vessel a moment after the process of boiling has ceased. It is when the liquid begins to chill, or even to coddle slowly, that the mischief begins to arise.

3. As soon as the food is poured out, let the saucepan be filled with cold water, and so remain until it is convenient to clean it. In cleaning it, be very attentive to see that every part of the vessel is thoroughly cleaned, and then immediately dried by the fire before putting away.

Some cooks are rash enough to boil a half-penny with greens or pickles, to make them a very bright green; but it renders the articles so dressed highly pernicious. In boiling greens, peas, broccoli, cauliflowers, &c., every good end may be answered by attention to the following particulars:—

Have a large saucepan of common tin, which will boil very quickly. Rain or river-water, if very fresh and clean, is preferable to pump-water. Let the water boil just at the moment it is wanted. If it has boiled several minutes before the vegetables are put in, or if it has boiled and stood on the hob, and has to be boiled up again, the vegetables will be discolored. The moment the water boils, put in the vegetables, with a table-spoonful of common salt, or a tea-spoonful of salt of wormwood; put the lid on instantly, and make them boil up very fast. When they do so, *but not before,* remove the lid, and put it on no more. Keep them fast boiling. When done, they will sink. Take them out, and drain the water from them, and their color will be found as bright a green as if the most injurious expedients had been used to secure it. *Lead* is still more pernicious than copper. Many people are not aware that the glazing of white or colored earthenware is a preparation of lead, which is easily acted on by acids of every kind, and by salt and sugar in a liquid state. Hence the common white jars are improper for either pickles or preserved fruit. For the same reason, glazed red pans are improper for salting meat. Unglazed stone ware is the best for pickle jars. Glass also is very proper, either for pickles or preserved fruit; and, for salting meat, there is a kind of stoneware, smoothed inside and out, but not glazed with any substance that salt will act upon.

Charcoal is sometimes used in cooking, or for airing rooms. It is generally burnt in a stove, or chimney furnace. This is very pernicious, unless there is a free current of air, as the fumes of the burning charcoal occasion violent head-aches and faintness, and will sometimes instantaneously deprive a person of consciousness and of the power of breathing; and if a person be not instantly removed into the fresh air, life will probably be destroyed.

Charcoal, however, may be safely and beneficially used for the purpose of preserving meat from putrefaction. A few small bits of charcoal laid over meat or game, that is required to be kept a considerable time, will preserve it from taint, or boiled with meat that has a little gone by, will effectually remove both the unpleasant flavor and injurious property.

Boiling potatoes.—This valuable root is now an article of daily consumption in almost every family, from the highest to the lowest, and yet many even professed cooks have never acquired the art of dressing it properly. Nothing is more unwholesome than an ill-boiled potato, especially to the delicate stomachs of children and invalids.

The people in Ireland and Lancashire pay great attention to the manner of boiling potatoes, and have brought it to great perfection, as will be found by trying the following method :—

The potatoes should be as much as possible of a size, the large and small ones boiled separately. Let them be washed clean, just before boiling, but neither scraped nor peeled; the saucepan in which they are boiled should be large enough to leave an inch or two above the top of the potatoes. Set them on in cold water, not quite enough to cover them, as they produce a considerable quantity of fluid themselves. When they boil, throw in a little cold water to check the boiling, and a spoonful of salt, or a tea-cupfull of brine in which meat has been salted. If the potatoes are large, it will be necessary thus to check them with cold water two or three times as they come to boil; otherwise the outsides will break, while the inside is not half done. When boiled enough, pour off the water, and again set the vessel over the fire for a short time, that all the moisture may be carried off by steam, and the potatoes remain perfectly dry: they will then be mealy and wholesome.

Potatoes should never be boiled with meat, or in liquor which is to make soup or broth; as the watery juice which boils out of them is very injurious, and renders the liquor unwholesome in which they have been boiled.

Coal-balls.—Fuel is a very expensive article in all families, and yet it is essential to health and comfort to have a sufficiency of it. Many persons may be glad of a hint by which a little may be made to go a great way.

Take one part of mud, and two parts of small coal; mix them well together, and make them up into round balls about the size of a turnip. They burn best on the hearth, without any grate. First light a few cinders, and when they begin to burn, pile the coal-balls upon them, making every layer narrower and narrower, till they rise to a point at the back of the chimney. Then plaster over the outside with the mixture the balls are made of; with the poker, make a hole in the front, and another at top, by way of vent. They will then burn well, throw out a strong heat, and last many hours.

Sunday dinners that keep nobody at home.—Many people like to have a hot dinner on Sunday, perhaps the only day in the week when all the family sit down together; and yet they do not wish to detain any person from public worship to dress it, nor yet to employ a baker to do it; by which, though forty or fifty families may be accommodated by one or two people, that one or two are injuriously detained from public worship, and employed in a manner unsuitable to the day. The guilt must rest somewhere, whether with the baker, who does it for the sake of gain, or the families who employ him, for the sake of self-indulgence. By good management it may be provided against. Several dishes may be so prepared the day previous, as to require nothing more than boiling up on the Sunday morning, and then banking up the fire, so that it will keep the vessel boiling while the family are gone to public worship. A little experience will soon give the habit of regulating a fire, so that it shall be neither too fierce nor too dull; and the dinner will be found as well cooked as if some one had been standing by the whole morning to watch it.

A pudding of beef-steaks or other meat, in a light crust, made with either suet, dripping, or lard, may be put in the basin, and tied up on Saturday; one egg will bind the crust and prevent its breaking.

A boiled leg or neck of mutton will take about the time to do, that people are usually absent at public worship.

Mutton-broth will take about the same time; the barley or rice, onions and turnips, may be put in as soon as it boils, which should be before it is left.

A suet-pudding is all the better for long boiling; so is a currant-pudding; and both are improved by being made the day before. They are much lighter made with water than with milk. This is also preferable in hot weather, as more likely to keep.

These hints will not be despised either by Christian mistresses or Christian domestics, on whom it is incumbent that the houses in which they preside or serve, should be models of good management to observers, and of comfort to the inmates. It is no small part of Christian duty to make all connected with us as comfortable as our means and circumstances will admit. "If a Christian," said Mr. Newton, "is but a shoe-black, he ought to be the best in the parish."

CHAP. XXXVII.

REVERENCE TO THE AGED.

A GENTLEMAN was once passing through a village, and happened to see a poor feeble old woman let her stick fall, and stand a moment in perplexity, not knowing whether she dared stoop to pick it up, or attempt to reach her home without it. Just by the spot where the accident happened, a group of boys were playing at marbles; some of them took no notice, others rudely mocked the poor old woman's distress; but one kind-hearted lad threw down his marbles, ran to her assistance, and helped her into her house. She thanked him, and said, "God Almighty's blessing be upon you, for your kindness to a poor old woman!" The gentleman saw and heard the whole, and made inquiry after the lad, in whom he felt deeply interested. He found that he was already in the Sunday-school, and, in all probability, had there learnt the scriptures, that inculcate reverence to the aged. From that time he had him instructed in writing and accounts at an evening school; when old enough, assisted in apprenticing him, and in course of time had the satisfaction of seeing him a respectable and flourishing tradesman.

I recollect his mentioning the circumstance to his wife as soon as he came home; and he then said he thought that boy discovered the rudiments of a good character, and that he should be greatly disappointed if he did not turn out one whom it would be a credit and satisfaction to have put forward in life: after years fully proved that his opinion was correct. This, and some other circumstances, led the gentleman to make many remarks on the treatment the aged should receive, which deeply impressed my mind, and which I have endeavored to preserve.

"The hoary head is a crown of glory, if it be found in the way of righteousness." "Thou shalt rise up before the hoary head, and honor the face of the old man, and fear before the Lord thy God." Such are the express precepts of scripture. So reasonable in itself, and so clearly commanded by God, is reverence from the young to the aged, it may be fairly said, that the young person who fails in so obvious a duty is a stranger to the fear of God, and destitute of those dispositions which alone can render youth amiable, manhood virtuous, and old age honorable.

Honor the aged, because God has put an especial honor upon old age; and to treat old people with respect, to study their comfort and credit, and tenderly to soothe their infirmites, is an act of obedience to God.

Honor the aged, because they have generally a claim on your gratitude. Perhaps some feeble, decrepit old person, whom the thoughtless youth may be inclined to ridicule and despise, has, in days that are past, nurtured his infancy, or rescued his heedless steps from danger, or administered a medicine that was the means of saving his life, or in some way or other been instrumental in giving him a good education, or introducing him to some advantage in society, which he now enjoys.

Honor the aged, because the time was when they were as blooming and lively and active as yourselves; and if you live to old age, you will probably be as feeble and decrepit as they; and then, how can you expect sympathy, kindness, and respect, if in your youth you have not shown them to others?

Honor the aged, because outward infirmities do not necessarily enfeeble the mind, and much valuable instruction may often be derived from persons laboring under the weakness and sufferings of age. "Days should speak, and multitude of years should teach wisdom." "Ask now thy father, and he will show thee; thine elders, and they shall teach thee." Young people might find it greatly to their advantage to listen to the experience of the aged, and to treasure up and improve their observations; to ask, and to attend to their counsels, rather than to follow the dictates of their own ignorance and self-conceit. But it is only a respectful, soothing deportment on the part of the young, that can invite the aged to bring forth the rich stores of their experience. Wise is the youth who never suffers such an opportunity to pass unimproved.

Honor the aged, because a disposition in youth to give due honor to age, is one of the fairest indications of general excellence of character; and a particular blessing is often seen to rest upon those who have treated the aged with conscientious respect. On the other hand, the youth who can despise and ridicule the aged, gives sad evidence of a generally vicious and depraved disposition. He often becomes a tyrant in his family, a quarrelsome neighbor, a despiser of religion, perhaps a murderer! And many instances are on record (besides that of the children of Bethel, who mocked the prophet Elisha) in which the divine displeasure has evidently rested on those who refused the honor due to old age.

I have somewhere met with the following narrative by an eye-witness.

"My duty calls me every morning to pass through a certain busy town; and as I take my walk, I cannot help making observations upon what I see as I go by, and sometimes as I call at the shops and houses of the inhabitants. I have been especially struck with the different treatment which old age meets with, in the various families where I have had an opportunity for taking notice. There is one family, in which I observe a very old woman, who has been the slave of her children and grandchildren for many a year, for which she now receives nothing but neglect. I have seen her wait most diligently on her three unruly sons; and if it was a wet day, she would stand and entreat of the one who was going out, to put on a great coat, or take an umbrella, lest, '*dear fellow*,' as she said, he should take cold; and I have seen that son snatch it from her hand, throw it aside, and, calling her an old fool, set off without, in defiance of her: yet she would meet his return with a smile, forgetting and forgiving all; his warm tea would be ready, and his slippers and dry clothes by the fire, and no remarks made on his ill conduct to her. To the children of her three sons she was a complete drudge. I think I see her now stooping to lead them and teach them to walk, till her poor old back was almost broken; but she never did enough to give satisfaction: the three wives of her sons thought fit to despise her. She is now a paralytic, and sits in the chimney corner to bear the insults of the youngest child: a kind word is never given her; and all think it no use to pity her, for she is always grumbling. I never see her, without hoping that God will in mercy soon give her a joyful release, lest her children should fill up the measure of retribution which they are preparing for their own old age.

"I have observed another scene. The dwelling is hardly to be called a cottage, for that gives one the idea of a neat pretty abode, with white-washed walls covered with roses: this is a little, old, dirty house, consisting of two rooms; the people pretend to sell green-grocery; and I see the grandmother fetching dead sprouts and parched greens to set out on a block before the door. Poor old creature! her face is one mass of wrinkles; her steps are tottering, and her hands tremble; her daughter is a widow, a hard-working charwoman; want of cleanliness is her chief fault, and her greatest excellence filial affection to her poor old mother.

As I pass their door, the aged creature is sometimes entering with her bundle of greens. I have often seen the daughter come out to meet her, saying, in a kind tone, 'Mother, why do you carry so many? Come sit down, and let me give you something to eat and drink, for I am sure you must be faint.' There is a large family of children; and one day I heard the eldest boy give his grandmother an impertinent answer, for which he received from the mother a hearty box on the ear: 'That is to teach you not to answer your grandmother in that manner, sir,' said she; 'go and beg her pardon this moment.' Away went the young culprit, and did as he was told. There are perhaps better systems of family discipline than this: the woman is dirty and slatternly, and I fear she has very little thought of religion; but her behavior to her aged parent is a pattern to many.

"There is one old woman, who has five sons and one daughter: the sons are all married and prosperous for their station in life, but they forget their mother. She is a high-spirited old woman, and does not like to ask them for help: for many a day she worked hard for them, and succeeded in making them what they are, clever workmen. Her daughter, who is a notable girl, obtained a good service, and had such wages as enabled her to dress very respectably: she lived also at a plentiful table. Her fellow-servants were a cheerful, pleasant set, and the situation had many advantages; but several times, when she went home to see her mother, she found her overdone with work, infirm, and wanting attention. 'I cannot live here,' said the good girl, 'and see my mother in this state. How can I enjoy my health, and sing, and be happy, while her age is fainting under hard work? Can I enjoy a meal while she wants? No.'—So home she came, and mother's bed was taken down and washed, and her room scoured very clean, and her easy chair placed at the window; and there sits mother now, like a lady: no work will Fanny suffer her to do, but works hard herself: and when she carries up her nice, nourishing basin of beef-tea, or her cup of coffee when she wakes, the showers of blessings from a mother's lips, make Fanny happier and richer than a princess. O what a store of comfort is she laying up *for herself!*

"I know one poor servant girl, who is a credit to her class: her mother lives with a married daughter, who does all she can for her; but many a comfort would she want, were it not supplied from the wages of Jenny—a bit of fish, when she can purchase it at a cheap rate, a little ripe fruit, or any other nicety which is within her power to obtain, a pair of easy warm shoes, and, at Christmas, a few yards of new flannel, to keep off the rheumatism—these things my own eyes have seen bestowed, and many a crown and half sovereign with them, by a hard-working servant girl, on an aged mother! And may God send his best of blessings into the cup of that dutiful child!

"I passed the house of one who had ever been accounted dutiful to her mother: she married, and had herself become the parent of three children, when called to that mother's death-bed, during the period of whose sickness her tender care was required; but she was so taken up with her three children, that she could not spare an hour for her dying parent; no, these little new-comers so engrossed her affections, that the old tried friend, who had so carefully reared her, who had been ever ready with advice and help for her, when in difficulty, was now forgotten: if food required preparing for the sick mother, she was sure to be making up a smart cap for the baby. She never would contrive matters so as to devote an hour to her mother, and yet not neglect her children—no, the love, the gratitude of the daughter was lost. Let her take care, lest her three idols pass unheedingly by her dying bed: they are three beautiful children; but I never see her fondle them without thinking of the poor old mother's last, lonely hours.

"There is one old lady—she is quite a lady in manners and fortune—whose fine house I pass; but her estate, and her set of servants, cannot help her under her infirmity of mind, which is *the fear of death;* she is a holy, good woman, and none who know her, save herself, doubt of her eternal safety. She has a daughter who is a great comfort to her; and the constant effort of this good girl is to smooth the mother's passage to the tomb. She knows her gloomy fears, and is ever pointing out some new, and beautiful, and cheering view of the heavenly Canaan. She will draw the mother's attention to the beauties of nature, and lead her trembling steps in the green pastures, and beside the still waters; and then, while she is enjoying all, will remind her,

> "If such the sweetness of the stream,
> What must the Fountain be?"

She often reads to her, how 'the arrow sharpened with love let easily into the heart,' was Christiana's token, when she was called to go over the river; and how Despondency's last words were, 'Farewell, Night! Welcome, Day!' and how his daughter Much-afraid went through the river singing; and 'how glorious it was to see how the open region was filled with horses and chariots, with trumpeters and pipers, with singers and players on stringed instruments, to welcome the pilgrims as they went up, and followed one another in at the beautiful gate of the city.'

"Reader, how is it between you and your parents? Perhaps they are gone—they no longer need your kindness. But if they still live, and your heart tells you that you have not showed them all the tenderness and respect which you might have done, oh, begin this moment to endeavor to soothe their few remaining, painful days: think of the satisfaction it will yield you, when they are no more. The pleasures of earth are going from them: you and your children are in health, cheerfully looking on to prosperity and many happy days of joy; but your aged parents' eyes are closing to all things under the sun; life and its joys are become tasteless: they may adopt the words of Barzillai to King David, when he said, 'Come over with me, and I will feed thee in Jerusalem. And Barzillai said unto the king, How long have I to live, that I should go up with the king unto Jerusalem? I am this day fourscore years old; and can I discern between good and evil? Can thy servant taste what I eat, or what I drink? Can I hear any more the voice of singing men and singing women? Wherefore, then, should thy servant be yet a burden unto my lord the king? Let thy servant, I pray thee, turn back again, that I may die in mine own city, and be buried by the grave of my father and of my mother.' And is this the case of your parents, and do you not deeply feel for them? Can you see those trembling hands, and forget that they cherished your infancy; or watch those tottering steps, and forget how often in their strength they have hasted to comfort you? Look back, when absent from home and among strangers, how the sudden sight of your mother or your father has caused your young bosom to swell with joy, and brought kindly tears to your eyes: you have flown to them, and felt at home. Did ever stranger watch your sick bed as they have done? Did ever stranger, gay and pleasant as he might be, show the daily, the constant, the deep, the self-denying interest for you that they have done? When trouble has overtaken you, the world has passed heedlessly on, busy and cheerful—what did it care whether you did well or ill? But there was one, whose countenance fell when you were in sorrow; one who thought of you, and wept for you, and prayed for you, yes, and acted for you, when and where he could—it was your father. There was one whose deep sighs and many tears told how her heart bled for you—it was your mother. Can you forget all this, and suffer their gray hairs to go down to the grave with sorrow? Oh, turn, before it is too late. Let their weak hands and their feeble knees plead for your tenderness now, as your weak hands and feeble knees once pleaded with them. They were ready to forgive your faults, to hide your defects; oh, let the same love look over and pass by the peevishness, the defects of their old age: recollect how much that was disagreeable they put up with in you, and that not grudgingly, but out of a heart overflowing with love. Pay them back liberally the debt of gratitude you owe; and as ye would that your children should do unto you, do ye even so unto your parents."

CHAP. XXXVIII.

JESTING, FOOLISH SPORTS, AND FOOL-HARDINESS.

It is a considerable attainment always to preserve seriousness without gloom, and cheerfulness without levity. I never knew a more cheerful family than that of Mr. White's. Parents, and children, and servants, all had a happy expression of countenance: all tried to make each other happy: all, I believe, had a conscience void of offence both towards God and man; and, as they felt really happy, they always appeared really cheerful; but levity and folly they could not endure; light, foolish jests were never heard, either in their parlor or kitchen. I have heard there many remarks on the subject, the truth of which I have seen exemplified in many other families, though not in theirs; and have observed, that families where a spirit of jesting is indulged, though they are sometimes very merry, are at other times very gloomy, and generally very contentious. Their conduct and temper reminds one of the saying of Solomon, "The laughter of fools is like the crackling of thorns under a pot,"—a great blaze and soon over; and often "in the midst of laughter the heart is in heaviness."

How strikingly the apostle cautions us against "foolish talking and jesting, which are not convenient." Indeed they are not; and it may be questioned which is greatest, the folly of jesting, or the mischief arising from it. A jester is a most contemptible or a most dangerous person; no one either respects or trusts him. He who delights in puns, scruples not to make himself the ape or the buffoon of a company.

He who indulges a more pungent and malignant kind of evil-speaking, spares neither the feelings nor the character of others ;

> " Who, for the poor renown of being smart,
> Would stick a dagger in a brother's heart."

Another poet has it,

> " Laugh at the reputations she has torn,
> And holds them dangling at arm's length in scorn.'

The contemptible light in which jesters are held by all men of sound wisdom, is evident in many cautionary maxims left on record, such as, " Commit no business, no secret of importance, to a jester."—" Let not a fool play with you in the house, lest he play with you in the market."—" The joking of wits, like the play of puppies, often ends in snarling." —" He that makes himself the common jester of the company, has but just wit enough to be a fool."

The jester has seldom any reverence for sacred things; the sacred name of God, or some sentiment or precept of his holy word, is often perverted, to give point to the strokes of his profane levity. " It may be wit to turn things sacred to ridicule, but it is wisdom to let them alone."—" Sin is too bad, and holiness too good, to make sport of; the one demands repentance, and the other reverence."—" They are fools who mock either at sin or holiness."

It is a great pity that even religious people sometimes indulge themselves in repeating the puns or mistakes of others on the words of scripture, which are thus associated in the mind with improper and ludicrous ideas; and the sacred influence of the passage is entirely lost. Some ministers have declared themselves precluded from preaching on one or more very solemn and weighty passages of scripture, from being unable to divest them of some ludicrous association imprinted on the mind, perhaps in the days of youthful vanity and folly, or perhaps, which is still more to be lamented, presented more recently by some one who ought to have had enough sacred wisdom to restrain this frivolous wit.

Not less foolish or injurious are those practical jests which the young and thoughtless often practise on each other for mere sport. Many persons, as long as they live, never recover the effects of some sudden surprise or fright, thus wantonly inflicted; some now living, and once possessed of the finest faculties, fitting them to be the ornaments of society and great benefactors to mankind, have been thus reduced to a mere state of idiocy, and present an affecting wreck of former capabilities thus wantonly shattered and destroyed. Truly, he is a "madman who casteth about firebrands, arrows and death; so is the man who deceiveth his neighbor, and saith, Am I not in sport?"

Even in cases where neither death nor derangement result from such foolish jesting, it is often attended with consequences which, though less serious, occasion real suffering and inconvenience through life. A child was terrified to silence by a wicked servant assuring her that if ever she mentioned some misconduct which she had witnessed, the birds would fly down and peck her—(the hangings of the bed in which the child slept were copper-plate printing, in which trees, fruits and birds were introduced.) Young as the child was, she knew enough to be sure that this was impossible; yet an undefined terror possessed her mind, which seriously affected her health and endangered her life. She could never afterwards have a quiet night's rest in that bed, nor could she see a bird, either living or dead, without an agony of terror. Even in mature life, (though by no means of a timid disposition,) she suffers more at having to pass near half-a-dozen harmless barn-door fowls, than if they were really fierce and destructive creatures of another species. More than once, in peculiar circumstances, her health and even life have been endangered by this ungrounded and yet unconquerable apprehension.

Surely this ought to be a caution to those intrusted with the care of children, never to fill their minds with imaginary terrors; and to young people, in their moments of sport, never to venture on a play or a joke, which may wound the feelings of a companion, and perhaps endanger his reason or his life.

This is a good place to caution young people against such sports as would endanger themselves, or such feats of strength as, if accomplished, can scarcely fail to injure the constitution. There is no true courage in fool-hardiness; and no person can trifle with his own safety and health without sin. Our health and strength are talents bestowed on us by God, which we are to employ for the purposes intended, and for which we must be accountable; but it is no part of a man's duty, nor at all to his credit, to display the strength of a horse, for mere idle boasting of what he can do. Let a man, who possesses great bodily strength and courage, carry them meekly and quietly on ordinary occasions; and when a real emergency arises, let him rush forward, regardless of labor and fearless of danger, to save the life of a fellow-creature. This is a cause worth his exertion, and will secure, as it deserves, the admiration, respect, and gratitude of others. But he who hazards his health, limbs, or life, for the mere idle boast of what he can do, is as deservedly despised, even by those whom he amuses; and, were it not for the awful futurity awaiting him, others would be apt to form an estimate similar to his own of the worthlessness of that life which he so wantonly endangers.

One of our kings gave a fit rebuke to fool-hardiness. When a man, who had climbed to the top of Salisbury cathedral, presented a memorial to the king, hoping to be rewarded for his feat, the king immediately replied that he would grant him a patent for performing it,—strictly forbidding all his other subjects to attempt the like, on pain of death.

A sailor had often run by the mouth of a cannon at the moment of its firing. Many of his comrades had admired the feat, and laid wagers on his performing it; but others, more sober, entreated him to desist from so presumptuous an attempt, and even endeavored to pull him back; but he persisted, and in an instant was blown to atoms,—an affecting picture of those who, in spite of all the warnings of the word of God, and the remonstrances of pious friends, madly rush on in the ways of sin, and sport on the very edge of the pit of destruction. This is fool-hardiness indeed; for a puny worm of the earth to rush forward and contend with his Maker, and dare the Almighty to do his worst,—to dance over the embers of sin and corruption, which one breath of Jehovah can kindle into everlasting burnings. "Who ever hardened himself against God and prospered?" "Oh that they were wise, that they would consider this!"—"He that, being often reproved, hardeneth his neck, shall be suddenly destroyed, and that without remedy."—"Now, consider this, ye that forget God, lest he tear you in pieces, and there be none to deliver."

CHAP. XXXIX.

CHRISTIAN PATRIOTISM.

A Christian ought never to be a noisy, disputing politician, but he ought to be a patriot. Every man who shares the blessings and protection of a civilized country, ought to have its interests at heart: he is bound to pray for the peace and prosperity of the land he lives in; he is bound to cultivate and exemplify that righteousness which exalts a nation, and to discountenance and weep over that sin which is a reproach to any people, and which, sooner or later, brings down the judgments of a righteous God. When the Lord was about to pour forth his dreadful judgments on the wicked Jews, the few truly pious and patriotic were thus distinguished: "And the Lord said unto him, Go through the midst of the city, through the midst of Jerusalem, and set a mark upon the foreheads of the men that sigh and that cry for all the abominations that be done in the midst thereof."

A friend often said that he reckoned my father a true patriot: father was surprised at this, and said he thought it belonged only to great and learned men: "No," said his friend, "that is quite a mistake; even a poor and unlearned man may be the support and honor of his country, while he guides his affairs with integrity and discretion; while, by his patient industry, he renders the natural produce of the land available to the supply of the community in general, as well as his own; while he rules well his own household, and trains up a family of good subjects to the state; and while he prays for kings and all that are in authority, that they may rule over men in the fear of the Lord, and that all the subjects of the land may lead quiet and peaceable lives, in all godliness and honesty; —such a man is a true patriot, and has as loyal and patriotic an interest in ' his own hearth-stone,' ' his own vine and fig-tree,' as a noble lord has in his splendid mansion and extensive estates. 'Better is the poor that walketh in his integrity than he that is perverse in his ways, though he be rich.' Sometimes it is seen that 'though the rich man is wise in his own conceit, the poor that hath understanding searcheth him out.' Solomon tells us that ' there was a little city, and few men within it, and there came a great king against the city and beseiged it, and built great bulwarks against it: now, there was found in it a poor wise man, and he, by his wisdom, delivered the city. Then, said I, Wisdom is better than strength;' and 'by a man of knowledge and understanding the state shall be prolonged.'

"Remember, then, every one may be a true friend to his country—not by blustering about politics, and shouting at elections, but by acting well himself, and setting a good example to all around him. The best reform will be, when every one sets about, in earnest, to reform himself. 'When every one sweeps before his own door, we shall soon have a clean street;' and when every man is what he ought to be, we shall have a whole nation fearing God and working righteousness; meanwhile, let every one look to himself, and do his part towards it."

CHAP. XL.

GOOD AND ILL REPORTS.

A GOOD man's character is very dear to him—it ought to be so—he is commanded to follow those "things that are of good report." This is a point in which bad men are always ready to injure him; as they hate their brother, because his works are good and theirs are evil; his goodness reproves their badness, and therefore they cannot bear to have it appear that he is as good as he is. They will not scruple to invent, or pervert and circulate, stories to his prejudice; they will misrepresent facts and malign his motives. This is very trying to the spirit of a man who desires so to live that he may adorn the doctrine of God, his Saviour, in all things; but "to do well, and be ill-spoken of, is characteristic of the Christian."

When men are troubled in this way, it is better, in nine cases out of ten, to take no notice at all, but let malice run itself out of breath. A great philosopher, on being told that some had spoken ill of him, replied, "It matters not; I will endeavor so to live that nobody shall believe them." Malicious aspersions cast upon the character of a good man, will, in time, wear off, and his righteousness will appear as the light, and his judgment as the noon-day: indeed, the very attacks of malice may prove a benefit to the Christian. Those who lay to his charge things that he knew not, may bring to his notice imperfections which he had not observed, and lead him to correct them. It has been prettily represented, that the Christian goes through the world as with a rich silk garment, that glistens in the sun; but the spite and malice of men follow him, and cast dirt upon his garment, and then call upon others to observe how it is bespattered: he goes on his way, perhaps grieved at the injury he has sustained—perhaps unconscious of it—but, by-and-by, the dirt rolls off, one piece after another, and proves to have been nothing more than fuller's earth; it cleanses the garment of some spots it had contracted, and leaves no trace of the dirt that had been maliciously cast upon it.

It is a just observation, that as those who for every slight illness take powerful medicine, do rather injure than repair their health, so they, who for every trifle vindicate their character, do rather weaken it.

The best defence, against both oppression and malice, is a harmless life and a peaceful spirit. While we suffer in the way of well-doing, we need not plead our own cause, but commit it to Him who judgeth righteously—who will execute judgment for the oppressed, and bring to light every secret work of darkness.

We should, however, make it our concern to act prudently as well as harmlessly, and not provoke opposition by a rash and meddlesome spirit. Every man ought to be ashamed of suffering as a babbler, a mischief-maker, or a busy-body in other men's matters; but if he is assailed with unmerited opposition and unfounded malignity, then he suffers as a Christian; and let him glorify God in this behalf, and commit the keeping of his soul unto God in well-doing, as unto a merciful and faithful Creator.

CHAP. XLI.

COMPANIONS AND SECRETS.

We should labor to impress on young people, especially at their first going out into life, the importance of prudence and caution in the choice of companions. It is a generally-received maxim that "you may know a man by the company he keeps;" and if two are seen familiarly to associate together, it is concluded, that the worst will corrupt the best, rather than the best reform the worst,—for such is the natural tendency of corrupt human nature; therefore, take heed of being infected by the breath of a profane or a polluted heart. What good can you expect from bad company? If you are truly good, they will taunt or despise you; if you are unsettled, they will surely corrupt you.

We are not, however, to refuse all worldly dealings with ungodly men; for then, as the apostle says, we must needs go out of the world. But the Christian's intercourse with such men should resemble that of "the physician in an infected apartment, or of a lawyer conversing with his client in a shower of rain;" neither will hesitate to discharge their duties; but, having done so, both will be glad to hasten on. The Christian is not required to be either surly, uncharitable, or fanatical; on the contrary, he is commanded to be courteous to all men. In worldly matters, he should act with worldly men as a citizen of the world, but always under the influence of Christian principles; so that worldly men who deal with him shall be made to feel that they may trust him to the uttermost, but they dare not take liberties with him. As to his *chosen society*, he should say with the Psalmist, " I am a companion of all them that fear thee, and of them that keep thy precepts." " I have not sat with vain persons, neither will I go in with dissemblers. I have hated the congregation of evil doers, and will not sit with the wicked. O Lord, gather not my soul with sinners, nor my life with bloody men!"

In all the conduct of consistent Christians, that wisdom of the prudent which is profitable to direct, will be manifested. Divine wisdom in the heart lays the best foundation for human prudence and profitable conversation.

In reference to social intercourse, the following maxims are worthy to be observed: "Beware of strangers, and behave with caution in mixed companies."

"Censure not persons nor principles before strangers, or in mixed company."

"Never listen or peep at doors or windows; never ask a man what he carries covered; never peep behind a curtain, nor look into other men's books or papers."

'Believe not all you hear, nor repeat all you believe."

"Suspect a tale-bearer, and a great talker—in the multitude of words there wanteth not sin, and he is not worthy of being trusted with thy secrets who is fond of entertaining thee with another man's."

"Tell not thy secrets to thy servant, lest he become thy master."

"Say little of persons whom thou canst neither commend without envy, nor censure without danger."

"Those who are eager to know a secret, are sure to be fond of telling it; therefore, trust not any who press for thy confidence."

"Rather persuade thyself than thy friend to keep thy counsel; for how should another keep that secret which concerns him not, when thou canst not keep it thyself, whom it does concern?"

"Impart not to thy friend such things as cannot benefit him to know, but may prejudice thee, if discovered. 'A fool uttereth all his mind, but a wise man keepeth it in till afterwards.'"

"Trust not him that flatters with his lips. Flatterers have generally some interest of their own to serve, as the eagle is said to lift up the tortoise, in order to get something by his fall."

"Know thyself, and then no flattery can deceive thee."

"Love thy friend, with all his faults; thou art not perfect thyself, therefore expect no perfection in others."

"Respect both thyself and thy friend."

"Too much familiarity breeds contempt."

"Be not too eager in counselling others. Ill success sometimes attends good counsel; then the blame is laid to the adviser's charge, though the success attending good advice is seldom thanked for."

Seek the company of those who are capable of instructing you, especially in the things which relate to your soul or your calling, and improve every opportunity of converse with them to treasure up some piece of useful knowledge, some maxim or motive for prudence or spiritual improvement. It is a pity to look back on hours, or even minutes, spent in the society of wise and good men, without having derived some real profit from it. In all our intercourse with society, it should be our constant aim either to do good or to get good; but false modesty too often prevents the one, and self-conceit the other.

The sacred book of Proverbs abounds with precepts and cautions in the choice of companions, which the young should treasure up in their memories and hearts. "My son, if sinners entice thee, consent thou not." "Go from the presence of a foolish man, when thou perceivest not in him the lips of knowledge." "He that followeth vain persons is void of understanding." "Enter not into the path of the wicked, and go not in the way of evil men; avoid it, pass not by it, turn from it, and pass away." "Make no friendship with an angry man, and with a furious man thou shalt not go, lest thou learn of his ways, and get a snare to thy soul." "He that walketh with wise men shall be wise, but a companion of fools shall be destroyed."

CHAP. XLII.

THE GOVERNMENT OF THE TONGUE.

This comes in very near connection with the last subject. Many maxims apply to both. It is a very common mistake of wicked men to say, "Our lips are our own; who is lord over us?" Even good people often fail in circumspection here, and speak as if they thought words were of very little consequence. But our Lord has taught us, that "for every idle word that men speak, they must give an account thereof in the day of judgment;" and the apostle James speaks of the government of the tongue as one of the highest and most difficult points of Christian attainment, and an indispensable mark of the sincerity of our Christian profession. "If any man offend not in word, the same is a perfect man, and able also to bridle the whole body." "If any man seem to be religious, and bridleth not his tongue, but deceiveth his own heart, that man's religion is vain."

There is great danger of sinning with the tongue, because the depravity of our own hearts inclines us to it. "The heart is deceitful above all things, and desperately wicked;" and "out of the abundance of the heart the mouth speaks."

There is danger of sinning, because it is so very easy to do so. Some sins require time, preparation, exertion; and while all this is going on, a better thought may come in, and check the mischief; but the instant an improper thought or feeling enters the mind, what can be so easy as for the doors of the mouth to fly open, and give it utterance? Hence the too frequent apology, "I am sorry I said it—I meant no harm—it was but a hasty word—I spoke without a thought." *Not quite*, we may say, for speaking is but thinking aloud; but the fact is, we should think twice before we speak once.

We are in danger also from the frequency of speech; that which we do but seldom, we are more apt to weigh well, and take pains to do properly; but we are obliged to speak many times every day of our lives, and it is a great wonder if we do not often speak amiss. To avoid this, it is wise not to speak without real occasion; for in the multitude of words there wanteth not sin. "God has given us two ears and but one tongue, as if to intimate that we should be twice as ready to hearken as to speak." "Let every man be swift to hear, slow to speak." "Life and death are in the power of the tongue, and they that love it shall eat the fruit thereof." "Seest thou a man hasty in his words? There is more hope of a fool than of him." "Even a fool, when he holdeth his peace, is counted wise; and he that shutteth his lips is esteemed a man of understanding." The following are excellent maxims of wisdom in this particular:—"There are times when we may and ought to say nothing, and there are times when we may and ought to say something; but there will never be a time when we should say all things." "We must never say any thing but the truth, nor must we say the truth at all times." "One often repents of saying too much, but seldom of saying too little." "Better say nothing than nothing to the purpose." "Great talkers discharge too thick to take good aim." "To one you find full of questions, it is better to make no answer at all." "Praise no man too liberally before his face, nor censure any man severely behind his back." "Say nothing to any one in a fury, for that is like putting to sea in a storm." "In times of joy and grief, set a special guard upon the tongue, for then you are most in danger of speaking imprudently." "Words spoken in meekness and wisdom, not from an angry spirit, are most searching to him to whom they are addressed, and most comfortable to him that speaks them."

"Answer not a fool according to his folly, lest thou also be like unto him: answer a fool according to his folly, lest he be wise in his own conceit." This paradox has been well explained.

"The *fool*" is one who does not make a proper use of his reason. When he speaks in the folly of *passion*, answer him not with like folly, but give 'a soft answer, which turneth away wrath.'

"Answer not the folly of mere *talkativeness* with similar folly. Perpetual prating about nothing may often be put down by a dead silence. Answer not the folly of *unreasonableness, false argument,* or *prejudice,* by like folly; but 'prove all things, and hold fast that which is good.'

"Answer not the folly of *profaneness* by folly like his own, but by marked silence, or well-timed reproof. (The Rev. John Howe, walking in the park, met two gentlemen, who, in eager discourse, repeatedly uttered the awful word 'damn,' to each other. Mr. Howe took off his hat, and, with much solemnity, said, 'Gentlemen, I pray God to save you both.' 'A word spoken in season, how good is it!')

"Answer not the folly of *malignity* with like folly. 'There is that which speaketh like the piercings of a sword;

but the tongue of the wise is as a healing medicine. In the mouth of the foolish there is a rod of pride; but the lips of the wise shall preserve them.'

"Answer not the folly of *peevishness* according to its folly, but pity, forbear, and forgive; and

> ' The tear that is wiped with a little address,
> May be followed, perhaps, with a smile.'

"Answer not the folly of *captiousness* with similar folly. Be not displeased when you are contradicted; above all, do not wait for an opportunity of contradicting in your turn, to pay off the supposed affront.

"Answer not the folly of *flattery* according to itself, but turn to it a deaf ear, and a disgusted heart; for he that flattereth his neighbor, spreadeth a net for his feet. Flattery cherishes pride, self-love, and self-ignorance.

"But 'answer a fool according to his folly, lest he be wise in his own conceit;' that is, answer him so as to refute him on his own false principles, lest his being left without an answer, should lead him to suppose that his folly is unanswerable, and so confirm him in his mistake. Answer him, if he fancies himself right when he is clearly in the wrong, if possible to prevent him from deluding others."

I remember hearing a sermon read, in which the laws of speech were thus laid down, by which our conversation should be governed.

"The law of *prudence*.—This condemns idleness and folly; for no one has a right to talk nonsense. It condemns, also, all that is impertinent and unsuited to the place, the company, and the season. 'A wise man's heart discerneth both time and judgment.' 'A word fitly spoken, O how good is it! It is like apples of gold in pictures of silver.' All 'foolish talking and jesting' are forbidden by the apostle, while he enjoins, 'Let your speech be always with grace, seasoned with salt, that ye may know how to answer every man.'

"The law of *purity*.—This forbids all ribaldry, and not

only every thing that is grossly offensive, but all indecent allusions and insinuations, however artfully veiled: 'but fornication and all uncleanness, let it not be once named among you, as becometh saints.'

"The law of *veracity*.—This condemns every thing spoken with a view to deceive, or spoken so as to occasion deception, which may be done by a *confusion* of circumstances; by an *omission* of circumstances; by an *addition* of circumstances. 'Wherefore, putting away lying, speak every man truth with his neighbor; for we are members one of another.'

"The law of *kindness*.—This condemns all calumny and tale-bearing, the circulation of whatever may be injurious to the reputation of another. This requires that, if you *must* speak another's faults, you do it without aggravation; and that you do it, not with pleasure, but with pain; and that, if you censure, you do it as a judge would pass sentence on his son. 'Let all bitterness, and wrath, and anger, and clamor, and evil speaking, be put away from you, with all malice.'

"The law of *utility*.—This requires that we should not scandalize another by any thing in our speech; but contribute to his benefit by rendering our discourse instructive, or reproving, or consolatory. 'Let no corrupt communication proceed out of your mouth, but that which is good, to the use of edifying, that it may minister grace to the hearers.'

"The law of *piety*.—This requires that we should never take God's name in vain, never speak lightly of his word or worship, never charge him foolishly, never murmur under any of his dispensations. It requires that we extol his perfections and recommend his service."*

The following remark is worth preserving and noticing. "A cause which has a strong tendency to destroy religious seriousness, and which almost always prevents its formation and growth in young minds, is levity in conversation upon subjects connected with religion."† "Who is a wise man, and endued with knowledge among you? Let him show out

---

* Rev. W. Jay.   † Paley.

of a good conversation his works with meekness and wisdom."

There is, perhaps, no fault more common than gossiping; I mean telling and hearing the little news and idle chit-chat of the neighborhood. Few masters and mistresses like to have many comers and goers in their kitchen; and none would be willing to have all their concerns talked over with the domestics of their neighbors. Every considerate head of a family will be willing to indulge his domestics with liberty to visit their friends, at proper times; and of this you will do right to avail yourself; but when you are sent on an errand, or other necessary concern, call to mind the injunction given by the prophet Elisha to his servant, which you may find by turning to the second of Kings, chap. iv. ver. 29, and act accordingly; or, if civility requires you to give or return a salutation, be sure you do not stop and waste your time in foolish tittle-tattle. This is no unnecessary caution. Often have I beheld a whole group of domestics standing together for half an hour or more, gossiping about what one's master says, and another's mistress does; who is just gone from this house, and who is expected at that; and fifty other things as little worth knowing or relating; while, perhaps, three or four helpless infants have been all the while exposed to the bleak winds, or set down upon the cold stones; and many a one has been condemned to drag crippled limbs, or suffer excruciating pains throughout their whole lives, who might date the commencement of their sorrows to such unpardonable negligence. Ever stand at the utmost distance from all such practices; and if any one is so imprudent as to ask you questions relative to the concerns of the family with which you live, check at once their foolish curiosity by replying, " that it is no part of your business to inquire into such matters, nor would it be right to divulge them, even if known to you." You will say, perhaps, " What! am I never to talk?" Yes, I am sure you will, whether I give you leave or not; nor do I wish to prohibit it. Man is a social creature; and the gift of speech, when properly exercised, is not only one of the distinguishing, but one of the noblest blessings, bestowed upon him by the great Author of his existence. Use it with thankfulness, but use it also with discretion. Converse with your friends and acquaintance freely and cheerfully; but take care that your conversation is inoffensive, that it does not interfere with your duty, that it is never slanderous or censorious. Remember who has said, that " for every idle word that men shall speak, they must give an account in the day of judgment." Matt. xii. 36.

CHAP. XLIII.

READING.

" READING is an invaluable art. It is a key which can unlock all the treasures of wisdom and knowledge. It furnishes a pleasing employment and solace for the hour of solitude, and fits us for appearing in society with advantage. It enables a man to avail himself of the knowledge and experience of others, with whom, but for reading, he would have had no medium of communication. It brings him into familiar acquaintance with whatever may concern his present or future well-being through time and eternity.

" But, like every other machine of vast power, there is a proportionate danger of its becoming the instrument of destruction. Books have been made subservient to the purposes of vice as well as of virtue—the vehicles of every thing that is polluting and profane; and the young cannot be too cautious in making their selection.

" A taste for reading is, in itself, desirable and commendable. It has been the means of keeping many a young man from imbibing a taste for the public-house, the ball-room, or the gaming-table. Every young man will do well to connect himself with some society, by means of which he may be furnished with a judicious selection of profitable books. There are many subjects affording mines of pleasing and interesting information, which invite the research of the student, and which are now happily treated of in so simple and common-sense a manner as to render them intelligible to persons of an ordinary education. Biography, history, travels, geography, mechanics, natural and experimental philosophy, and general science, will afford a pleasing variety to every unperverted taste.

"But guard against the love of light, trifling reading. At best, it wastes the time and enfeebles the mind, disqualifies it for the relish of more solid subjects, and, by giving a false and delusive coloring to the scenes of human life, excites unreasonable expectations, unfits for common duties, and produces discontent with the sober realities of life.

"The youth, or the head of a family, who is alive to the great interests of eternity, will devote a considerable portion of his leisure to the perusal of such books as have a direct tendency to promote his moral and spiritual improvement. Very far from considering religious books dull and insipid, he will esteem them most interesting and savory; and, without excluding or despising works of general information, he will consider those connected with his spiritual interests as the most indispensable. Above all, the holy scriptures will be the book of his daily perusal. Whatever other book is consulted or dispensed with, this cannot be done without. It will be the man of his counsel, the light of his faith, the consolation of his spirit."

The above remarks were made by a gentleman at the formation of a reading society, or lending library, among the young men of the village. He originated the plan, and was for many years the president of the society. There was a little opposition at first: what good thing ever was set afoot that did not meet with some opposition? One or two of the farmers were sadly afraid of making the people too learned, and that there would be none left who would be content to labor. The master of a circulating library opposed it, because he feared that the new books recommended would cut out his foolish novels and romances; and the inn-keepers objected to it, when they found that the meetings of the society were to be held in the school-room, and not in a public-house. However, the plan succeeded, and outlived all their opposition: together with Sunday-schools, in which this gentleman and his whole family were actively engaged, I think this reading society was highly beneficial in promoting the civilization and respectability of individuals, and the comfort of families. Indeed, I recollect several instances of young people in humble life so improving these means of instruction, that they have been instrumental in fitting them to fill very respectable stations in society; so they have found the truth of the old saying, that "learning is better than house and land."

The following remarks I have met with elsewhere.

"There are many books," said Mr. Newton, "which I cannot sit down to read; they are indeed good and sound, but, like half-pence, there goes a great quantity to a little amount. There are *silver* books, and a very few *golden* books; but I have one book worth more than all, called the Bible; and that is a book of *bank notes.*"

To a man who knows the value of the word of God, it is nearer than his friends, dearer than his life, sweeter than his liberty, and pleasanter than his daily comforts.

Every man who prays loves the scriptures; for we speak to God in prayer, and He speaks to us in his word. Such a person reads the threatenings of God, and considers them as a call to him to repent. He reads the promises, and they call upon him to believe. He reads the commands, and feels himself sweetly called upon to obey; and often he bursts into exclamations like those of the Psalmist, " How sweet are thy words to my taste! yea, sweeter than honey to my mouth; moreover, by them is thy servant warned, and in keeping of them there is great reward." " Thy statutes are my songs in the house of my pilgrimage."

All arguments against the word of God are fallacies; all

conceits against the word are delusions; all derision against the word is folly; all opposition against the word is madness.

The Bible is open to all; but each should receive it as if addressed to himself alone: let it speak to each in the words of Nathan to David, " Thou art the man "

This one book is worth all the books in the world beside. He who reads this book with attention, humility, prayer, and self-application, can never be ignorant of that which it chiefly concerns him to know. " Therein are contained the words of eternal life. It has God for its Author, salvation for its object, and truth, without mixture of error, for its matter."

> " Holy Bible! book divine!
> Precious treasure! thou art mine!
> Mine, to tell me whence I came;
> Mine, to teach me what I am;
> Mine, to chide me when I rove;
> Mine, to show a Saviour's love;
> Mine thou art, to guide my feet;
> Mine, to judge, condemn, acquit;
> Mine, to comfort in distress,
> If the Holy Spirit bless;
> Mine, to show, by living faith,
> Man can triumph over death;
> Mine, to tell of joys to come,
> And the rebel sinner's doom.
> O, thou holy book divine,
> Precious treasure! thou art mine!"

CHAP. XLIV.

COMMON SENSE.

COMMON SENSE is a most valuable quality. " The wisdom of the prudent is to understand his way;" to see promptly what is the best thing to be done in the circumstances in which he is placed; and what is the best way of setting about it. Of some people it may be justly said, they have every sense but common sense; they can tell you about the stars, and write fine poetry, and make fine speeches, and draw fine pictures, and play fine music; but, as to handling a spade, or a hammer, or a stocking-needle, they are as helpless as a babe or an idiot. They have scarcely an idea of the food they eat, or the clothes they wear; to know how, where, and by what means, they are procured, and what they are made of; but they depend altogether upon the skill, care and industry of other people. And if they (like Robinson Crusoe) should be cast on an uninhabited island, though surrounded with the means of subsistence, they would perish for want of a notion how to bring them into use. They go through the world without opening their eyes to any of the common objects around them.

One of these learned simpletons having had a hole cut in his study-door to admit a favorite cat, when the said cat brought him a kitten, deemed it necessary to send for a carpenter to cut a smaller hole, through which the kitten might pass; never once imagining that a cat and a kitten could pass through the same hole.

Another, walking round a favorite meadow, about a mile in circumference, when he had gone three parts of the way, looked at his watch, and finding it was near dinner-time, thought he had not time to go quite round, but must hasten back as quickly as possible; thus making his walk a mile and a half instead of a mile! A poor day-laborer would have known better than to commit such a blunder. But "fine sense and exalted sense are not half so useful as common sense."

As every man knows that he cannot live long on earth, but will live in another and an unknown world forever, it would be the part of common sense to be more concerned and more active in securing the interests of that long futurity, than those of this short and fleeting time; but this is one sad proof of human depravity, that the generality of persons are "careful and troubled about many things" that concern their present interest, ease, and gratification, and disregard "the one thing needful,"—the interests of their souls, and their preparation for eternity. "O that they were wise; that they understood this; that they would consider their latter end!" "What is a man profited if he shall gain the whole world and lose his own soul, or be cast away?"

CHAP. XLV.

POLITENESS.

Some people are very fond of affecting a rude coarseness of manners, and despise politeness among friends, as though it were inconsistent with freedom and sincerity. How important that politeness should be cultivated in every family; not the foolish, unmeaning ceremony of the world, but a gentle, obliging demeanor towards all around us. "Politeness is not affection, but it is one of the outworks of it; like a wall or a hedge round a garden, which preserves it from being entrenched upon or trampled down." True politeness is *benevolence in trifles*. Some people are naturally polite, and others naturally churlish, or rather selfish; for selfishness is the great enemy to politeness, as well as to generosity; and many persons, even in polished life, who make loud professions of benevolence and attachment to their friends, are yet too selfish to deny themselves some trifling gratification, though at the expense and inconvenience of a whole party. On the other hand, some, even among the rustic classes of society, discover much native politeness.

One mark of true politeness is, that it never seeks to obtrude itself on the notice of those whom it accommodates; but rather conceals than displays the personal sacrifice at which it promotes their pleasure. It is noiseless in conferring a kindness, and is never known to recall the attention of others to it; but seems to forget, or rather actually forgets, acts of kindness, which are no strange things, but perfectly habitual to it.

Another branch of genuine politeness is, not to bring forward a subject of conversation which is not understood by the party in general, by which they cannot be really benefited, or in which they cannot harmoniously unite.

Another feature is, that true politeness, without compromising any thing that duty or fidelity requires to be brought forward, observes proper times and seasons for saying and doing things. Every thing is beautiful in its season; nothing is beautiful out of it; "As vinegar to nitre, so is he that singeth songs to him that is of an heavy heart." So is he that rudely reminds the fallen of past greatness; that treats a superior with insolence; an inferior with contempt; an equal with unkindness; that ostentatiously overburdens gratitude, by heaping upon it favors that it is unable to repay; or that pains the generous and delicate mind by compelling it to decline giving that which it is unable to bestow.

Politeness may even be regarded as a Christian virtue; our Lord and his apostles both practised and inculcated it; we are repeatedly admonished to be kind, patient, gentle to all men, pitiful and courteous. Among other instances that might be given, the Epistle of Paul to Philemon discovers, in every sentence, the very essence of politeness; and the whole character of the Saviour presents a living and perfect model.

"My dear Redeemer and my Lord,
I read my duty in thy word;
But in thy life the law appears
Drawn out in living characters.
Be thou my Pattern—make me bear
More of thy gracious image here."

"It is of no small importance that those especially whose office it is to recommend religion to others, should cultivate a kind, gentle and winning deportment. "We were gentle towards you," said the eminently successful apostle of the gentiles, "as a nurse cherisheth her children." A very simple incident will serve to illustrate this sentiment. Many years ago, the son of a highly respectable family was placed in business with his grandfather, where it was his duty to answer the applications of persons calling on business. On one occasion, a stiff, prim, powdered divine came up, and in a haughty tone addressed the youth: "Is your master at home?" Not long afterwards, a cheerful, benevolent-looking gentleman called, and, on being answered by the same youth, good-humoredly said to him, "Now, can you manage to ride my horse up and down a few minutes while I go in and speak to Mr. ——?" With cheerful alacrity the youth complied with the request; and, contrasting the kind and condescending manners of this visitor with the repulsive haughtiness of the former, from that moment imbibed a strong prejudice (if such it might be called) in favor of the religious instructions imparted by the latter gentleman, and against those of the former. The attractive visitor was the Rev. Richard Cecil, who was remarkably successful in winning the attention of young persons to the great truths that belong to their everlasting peace; and herein, probably, was part of the secret of his success. Gentleness and kindness of manners in the teacher will not indeed carry the gospel in power to the heart; but they may do much in removing the covering of prejudice from the ears. It is something to gain the gospel a favorable hearing; for faith cometh by hearing: and the manners and deportment of both ministers and private Christians should be such as to echo every invitation of the gospel, saying, "Come with us, and we will do you good."

The following is an example of humanity inculcated by a queen, which will interest the reader.

Queen Caroline, consort of George II., being informed that her eldest daughter (afterwards the Princess of Orange) was accustomed, at going to rest, to employ one of the ladies of the court in reading aloud to her till she dropped asleep, and that on one occasion the princess suffered the lady, who was indisposed, to continue the fatiguing duty until she fell down in a swoon, determined to inculcate on her daughter a lesson of humanity. The next night, when in bed, the queen sent for the princess, and commanded her to read aloud. After some time, her royal highness began to be tired of standing, and paused, in hope of receiving an order to be seated. " Proceed," said her majesty. In a short time, a second pause seemed to plead for rest. " Read on," said the queen again. The princess again stopped, and again received an order to proceed; till, at last, faint and breathless, she was forced to complain. " Then," said this excellent parent, " if you thus feel the pain of this exercise for one evening only, what must your attendants feel, who do it every night? Hence learn, my daughter, never to indulge your own ease, while you suffer your attendants to endure unnecessary fatigue."

On a journey, one frequently has an opportunity of observing and contrasting the different manners of coachmen, guards, waiters, and other persons employed for the accommodation of travellers; and the truth of the sentiment often presents itself to the mind, " Nothing is cheaper than civility—nothing is more odious than scorn."

A venerable divine, little accustomed to regard, still less to display, the well-earned academical honors he possessed, had been visiting at the house of a friend, who felt fully disposed to give honor to whom honor is due, and who, having undertaken to cord and direct the packages the doctor had to take with him, wrote on each, " The Rev. —— D. D., passenger." In the course of his journey, the doctor was induced, by the false representations of either a book-keeper or coachman, to take his place by a coach which they assured him would convey him to the town he desired. Having secured the fare, the parties made little scruple of setting down their passenger several miles distant from the place of his destination. In vain he remonstrated, appealing to the assurances which induced him to take his place, and stating the importance of his reaching the town specified. To injustice the coachman added gross insolence—

concluding, from the plain dress and simple manner of his passenger, that he was some humble mechanic, whom he might insult with impunity; and, accompanying his rudeness with profanity, advised him to cease his complaints, and called him " a grumbling old blacksmith." But in an instant his tone was changed, when the porter, unloading the luggage, called out, " Whose is this trunk ? The Rev. ―― D. D." " That trunk is mine," returned the insulted passenger,—and immediately the crest-fallen coachman came up, bowing and cringing, entreating the Rev. doctor's pardon, assuring him he had no idea who he was, and offering to meet his disappointment, as far as possible, by providing him entertainment free of expense at the inn, and a conveyance to the place of his destination early the following morning. His submission was accepted, with a good-natured hint for the future to treat all persons, whatever their appearance, rank, and profession in life might be, with that civility and courtesy which are due to all; and especially, in all his intercourse, to bear in mind the sacred injunction, " Swear not at all. The Lord will not hold him guiltless that taketh his name in vain."

As a contrast to the conduct of this coachman, there is pleasure in recording the following simple fact. On mounting a coach, a passenger asked the coachman whether he might depend on reaching a certain place he wished, in time to take the next coach, for a place which it was important for him to reach that night. " Yes, sir," replied the coachman, " you may depend on it. If all be well, my coach will reach there twenty minutes or half an hour before that coach starts." As they proceeded on their journey, the coachman addressed his passenger : " I think, sir, you have been at W., assisting at the missionary meetings there ?" " Yes," replied the passenger; "did you attend them?" " I attended all that my occupation would allow; I had the pleasure of hearing you once, and a very happy time we had of it." This opened a pleasing conversation, which occupied the time till they arrived at the desired place, punctual as the moment to the engagement of the coachman, who, it may be observed, being a religious man, regarded his word, treated his passengers with civility, and had no inclination to loiter and drink at every inn he came to. Certainly, if religion does a man any real good, it makes him more to be depended on, and teaches him to behave with propriety to all with whom he comes in contact. On leaving the coach, the civil coachman begged his passenger to hasten into the inn and get his dinner, engaging himself to secure a place the moment the coach came in, and to transfer the luggage safely. Having done so, he respectfully took his leave, saying, " If you should travel this road again, sir, I shall be happy if it falls to my lot to drive you ; and wherever you go, I hope the blessing and protection of God will attend you, and crown all your efforts in the Redeemer's cause." Such an interview will long retain a pleasing place in the memory of both parties.

A similar contrast was observed between two female servants, at different inns. At one inn, the servants came forward, inviting the passengers to alight and take refreshment. Some declined, others complied. One outside passenger ordered a glass of beer, of which he offered part to a poor woman, who seemed to stand in need of refreshment, but who had declined taking any, apparently from inability to bear the expense. She thanked her fellow-traveller for his kindness, but said she could not drink without eating a morsel of food. He ordered the servant to bring her a little bread, or bread and butter. With no very good will she went, and, as she returned, rudely called out to another servant, " What am I to charge a woman on the coach for bread to eat with beer that a gentleman has given her ? " then, throwing it up in such an awkward, ungracious manner, that, out of three morsels on the plate, two were dashed into the gutter, demanded of the poor woman sixpence for the scanty and churlish accommodation.

In another town, the servants in like manner surrounded the coach door to inquire after the wants of the passengers.

An elderly lady declined getting out, saying she felt very unwell, but requested the maid-servant of the inn to bring her a glass of water. Here was an opportunity for a churlish spirit to have spurned at the unprofitable commission; but this young woman, with cheerful alacrity and good humor, hastened to comply with the request, and presented the simple draught in a glass as clear as crystal, on a polished waiter, and with as much kindness of manner as if it had been the most costly beverage. On the lady offering her money, she briskly replied, "O no, thank you, ma'am; you are heartily welcome; I could not think of taking any thing for a cup of cold water; indeed I had rather not; you know there is a reward for giving that." Kind-hearted girl! may her heart have admitted the vital principle " for Christ's sake," and then verily this simple act of kindness shall not lose its reward!

CHAP. XLVI.

HELP AND PITY.

Some people seem to make it their employment to go about, from house to house, to find out the calamities of their neighbors, only to have the pleasure of carrying the news to the next house they go to. I once heard one of these gossips. She had nearly talked herself out of breath, with " Shocking news, I hear! poor Mr. Green is dead, and has left a large family without a shilling to help them ; and Mrs. Perry has fallen down stairs, and broken her leg; I saw the doctor ride by, as I came along; and Farmer Smith's house has been burnt down ; and Mrs. Wyman's eldest daughter has lost her place, at a minute's warning. Dear, dear, what troubles there are in the world; it really makes one's heart ache to hear of them."

" And pray," asked a good man, who stood near, and who

was quite as ready himself to lend a helping hand as to give a word of advice, "what have you done to help all these people in their distress?"

"O, sir, it is not in my power to help them."

"Indeed, I think you might find out some way of being useful to them; if you only spent, in rendering help, the very time that you squander in idle gossip, about their misfortunes, which, I can't help thinking, seems to afford you a sort of pleasure. I will tell you a story: A traveller passing over a miserable road, the wheel of his carriage stuck in a deep rut. He labored with all his might to extricate it, but in vain; presently some one passing by said to him, 'You are in an awkward situation, sir; pray how did the accident happen?' Another came up, 'Dear, dear, what is the matter? Well, what a good thing your neck was not broken; but this road ought to be indicted: there are continually accidents of one kind or another.' A third addressed him, 'I'm really sorry to see you so much heated and fatigued, sir: I fear, too, your horse and carriage are injured. I am very sorry.'—'Come then,' replied the unfortunate traveller, 'if you really are sorry, be so good as to put a shoulder to the wheel; a grain of help is worth a bushel of pity.'"

The idle and impertinent curiosity of some people, in the time of a neighbor's distress, is ill concealed under professions of sympathy and pity, while, like the priest and the Levite in the parable, they only come to the place and look, and then pass by on the other side of the way. If sympathy and pity are really felt, let them lead to conduct like that of the good Samaritan; for our Lord says to each of us, "Go thou, and do likewise."

CHAP. XLVII.

MAXIMS AGAINST SIN.

THE maxims on sin, and on several other subjects that follow, I have gleaned as opportunity offered, partly from books, partly from the conversation of friends. I wish they may be remembered by my children, and prove profitable to them in the hour of temptation.

" It is the mischievous property of sin, that it not only puts the soul into hell, but puts hell into the soul."

" That should be our chief trouble, which is the cause of all the trouble in the world."

" Nothing worth having is got by sin. Nothing worth keeping is lost by holiness."

" 'Tis bad trading with sin and Satan, since we ourselves must pay for all at last."

" By suffering we may avoid sinning; but we cannot by sinning avoid suffering."

" Fools make a mock at sin," but "it will be bitterness in the end."

" He that makes light of small sins, is in the ready way to fall into great ones."

" If we would not fall into things unlawful, we must not venture to the utmost bound of things lawful. To tread upon the edge of a precipice is dangerous, if not destructive."

" 'Tis folly for a person to do that now, which he must shortly undo by repentance, or be himself undone forever."

" Carefully avoid those vices which most resemble virtue. They are a thousand times the most ensnaring." *Covetousness*, which looks very much like *Prudent Care*, is *Idolatry!*

" Never do evil that good may come thereby. That would be serving the devil that God may serve thee."

In order to avoid sin :—

1. Run not in the way of temptation.
2. Maintain a constant watch and fear of sin.
3. Beware of pride and presumption.

4. Avoid and abhor slothfulness.

5. Remember, all strength and grace are in Christ. By faith and prayer look to Him for them.

6. Continually seek the sanctifying influences of the Holy Spirit.

CHAP. XLVIII.

CONSCIENCE.

"HEARKEN to the warnings of conscience, if you would not feel its wounds."

"Stand in awe of thine own conscience."

Prayer.
"What conscience dictates to be done,
Or warns me not to do,
This, teach me more than hell to shun,
That, more than heaven pursue."

"When no observers are present, be afraid of thyself. That which we are afraid to do before men, we should be afraid to think before God."

"Remember there is a witness every where, and a book in which every action is recorded, and from which no record is ever blotted out, except by the precious blood of Christ."

"Conscience is either a man's best friend, or his worst enemy."

The only way to have peaceful slumbers, or pleasant dreams, is by preserving a good conscience.

The state of the conscience has an amazing influence both on bodily health and mental vigor. When the conscience is pure and peaceful, the health and spirits are in a great measure preserved; and in sickness the physician finds a powerful ally within, to second all his endeavors. On the other hand, a disturbed conscience produces a burning brow, a restless, feverish state of spirits, and that which resists all the efforts of the healing art. " It is of no use," said a miserable wretch to the physician who offered him medicine ; " doctors cannot reach a diseased conscience."

It is a great mercy to have an *enlightened* conscience, that can discern between good and evil ; a *tender* conscience, that shrinks from the touch of evil; a *wakeful* conscience, that perceives the approach of evil ; a *peaceful* conscience, healed and cleansed by the blood of sprinkling ; a *clear* conscience, void of offence, both towards God and man ; a *sanctified* conscience, with which the Holy Spirit bears witness that we have in sincerity received the Lord Jesus Christ by faith, and that we are children of God, and joint-heirs with Jesus Christ.

The following story illustrates the power of conscience :— A butcher who resided in the west of England, and had for several years been in the practice of keeping a stall for the sale of meat, in one of the neighboring markets, having given way to the sin of falsehood, his heart became hardened, and he was then an easy prey to a temptation, by yielding to which, as the following particulars will show, he embittered almost the whole of his future life. It happened, on one occasion, that a lady, having purchased some meat of him, accidentally left her purse ; on discovering her loss, she returned to the butcher to inquire for it, but he firmly denied having seen it. The lady was too fully convinced that she had left it on his stall, to be easily satisfied with his denial ; but it was in vain she endeavored to bring to his recollection the circumstances relative to the transaction : every remonstrance was useless ; he still persisted that he had no knowledge of the purse or its contents. The lady, not inclining to press the subject further, submitted to the loss, (which was about four pounds,) but from that time declined having any further dealings with one who could act so dishonestly.

Some years after this, the butcher became reduced in his circumstances, and at length was under the necessity of declining his business, after which he engaged in the occupation of a pig driver. Whilst thus employed, he fell from his horse, by which he was so much injured that he was able to use but little personal exertion during the remainder of his life; and having no other means of support, he was obliged to apply to the parish for relief. In this dependent and helpless situation he survived many years, for a time noted for the sullenness of his disposition, and unaccommodating habits. But as he advanced in age, his mind became suddenly impressed with the awfulness of eternity, and a recollection of his ill-spent life became most burdensome to him, which was very evident from his general conduct, though the person with whom he lived was not aware that he was then suffering from the remorse of an awakened conscience. She had been particularly struck with the very scanty manner in which he supported himself; for, trifling as his income was, he could not be prevailed upon, by all her arguments, to spend the whole of it, nor to disclose his reasons for doing so.

At length he had by little and little saved as much as he apprehended the lost purse contained. He then related the whole affair to his hostess, acknowledged that the lady had left the purse upon his stall, that his son had concealed it with his knowledge, and that, on her application, he had denied the fact; that under a feeling of severe remorse for the wicked transaction, he could find no peace until he had restored the amount which the purse contained to its proper owner. He then gave his accumulated savings to the woman, with directions to take it to the lady, who lived about five miles from him, which she accordingly did: this happened after an interval of about fifteen years from the time the purse was lost.

From this period to his death he manifested a desire to be prepared for the final change; his general conduct was very satisfactory, and he was enabled, by faith in Christ, to look forward with a confident hope of pardon and everlasting life.

How grateful ought we to be, when awakened to a sense of our guilt! Surely it is a proof that we are not given up to the enemy of our souls: it shows that the Lord has not forsaken us. And when thus mercifully made sensible of our sins, may we be enabled by faith to behold the "Lamb of God which taketh away the sin of the world!"

It is by grace alone that we are kept from falling—may we then endeavor constantly to live in the spirit of prayer, that we may be enabled to resist temptation! How little are we able to repel the assaults of an enemy, without any preparation beforehand! May we be encouraged by the assurance that every time we are strengthened by the Holy Spirit to overcome temptation, we shall find that resistance to evil becomes more easy; but may we also remember, that every time we fall in with temptation, we are increasing the power of Satan over us, and thereby adding difficulties in our path which may eventually lead to our eternal misery! Let us therefore habitually remember our own weakness and our surrounding dangers, that we may continually say unto God, "Hold thou me up, and I shall be safe!"

CHAP. XLIX.

MAXIMS ON SELF-EXAMINATION.

"EXAMINE yourselves. What! know ye not your own selves?"

"Keep the heart with all diligence, for out of it are the issues of life."

"In the morning, consider what you have to do; and in the evening, what you have done."

"Man, know thyself; all wisdom centres here."

The following lines, by Dr. Watts, are recommended to all young people to commit to memory.

Evening Reflections.

"Let not soft slumber close your eyes
Before you've recollected thrice

> The train of actions through the day:
> Where have my feet chose out their way?
> What have I learnt, where'er I've been,
> From all I've heard, from all I've seen?
> What know I more that's worth the knowing?
> What have I done that's worth the doing?
> What have I sought that I should shun?
> What duties have I left undone?
> Or into what new follies run?—
> These self-inquiries are the road
> That leads to virtue, peace, and God."

Just as it is wise to keep clear accounts of our receipts and expenses, our debts and engagements, so it is wise constantly to examine and compare our heart and conduct with the word of God; to see what duties have devolved upon us, and whether we have discharged them, or failed in them, and what means can be adopted to promote circumspection, diligence, and fidelity in future. These reviews, if faithfully entered into, will often be humbling and painful, but they will be no less profitable. The more we know of ourselves, the less we shall be inclined to rely on our own merits, or to trust our own strength, and the more earnestly we shall desire an interest in the perfect righteousness and all-sufficient atonement of the Lord Jesus Christ, and in the influences of his Holy Spirit to purify our souls, and to quicken and sustain us in the paths of holiness.

The practice of self-examination has been recommended and observed by good and wise men in all ages. It is a pleasure to add the testimony of the present sovereign of England, King William the Fourth. He lately said, that, when a midshipman in the British navy, he was obliged to keep a log-book fairly written; and thus, he said, he acquired a habit, which he had found of the greatest benefit through life, that of recording the occurrences of the day, and submitting his actions to the scrutiny of self-examination.

CHAP. L.

SAYINGS ON REPENTANCE.

"While we live in a sinful world, and carry about with us a body of sin and death, repentance must be the work of every day."

"We brought sin enough into the world to be humbled for all our lives, though we had never actually sinned; and we sin enough every day to sorrow for it, though we had brought none into the world."

"If repentance on earth be bitter, what will be remorse in hell?"

"He that covereth his sins shall not prosper, but whoso confesseth and forsaketh them shall have mercy."

"Repentance is a plank thrown out after shipwreck—he that neglects it sinks inevitably."

"Worldly joy ends in sorrow, spiritual sorrow ends in joy."

"Let none defer repentance till another day. He that hath promised pardon on our repentance, hath not promised life till we repent."

"If we put off repentance to another day, we have the sins of another day to repent of, and a day less to repent in."

"Repentance begins in the humiliation of the heart, and ends in the reformation of the heart and of the life."

"Repentance is the tear of love, dropping from the eye of faith, when it fixes on Christ crucified. 'They shall look on Him whom they have pierced, and shall mourn.'"

"Sincere repentance is never too late, but late repentance is seldom sincere. The thief on the cross repented, and was pardoned in the last hour of his life; but we do not know that he had ever before been favored with a gospel call to repentance. If he had been frequently so called, and had refused to hearken, we have no reason to conclude that he would then have been called again. We have one such instance in scripture, that none might despair; and but one, that none might presume."

Still, however, the probability that apparent repentance, which comes at a dying hour, will be genuine, is very small. It has been justly observed, that " Sincere repentance is never too late, but late repentance is seldom sincere." The following fact will furnish an affecting illustration of this sentiment, and a solemn warning against the too common delusion of deferring the work of repentance to a dying bed :—

" The faithful and laborious clergyman of a very large and populous parish had been accustomed, for a long series of years, to preserve notes of his visits to the afflicted, with remarks on the issue of their affliction, whether life or death, and of the subsequent conduct of those who recovered. He stated, that, during forty years, he had visited no less than two thousand persons apparently drawing near to death, and who discovered such signs of penitence as would have led him to indulge a good hope of their safety if they had died at that time: they were restored to life and health, and then he eagerly looked that they should bring forth fruits meet for repentance; but alas! of the two thousand, not more than *two persons* manifested an abiding and saving change; the rest, when the terrors of eternity ceased to be in immediate prospect, forgot their religious impressions and their solemn vows, and returned with new avidity to their former worldly-mindedness and sinful pursuits, " as the dog returns to his vomit again, and as the sow that was washed to her wallowing in the mire."

CHAP. LI.

THE AWFUL STATE OF A WICKED MAN.

" A WICKED man is like one that hangs over a deep pit by a slender cord, which he holds with one hand and is cutting with the other."

A gentleman much addicted to profane swearing accompanied a pious miner to see one of the mines in Cornwall.

During his visit to the pit, he distressed his companion by many profane and abominable expressions; and as they ascended together, finding it a long way, he flippantly said, "As it is so far down to your work, how far do you suppose it is to hell?" The miner promptly replied, "I do not know how far it is to hell, sir; but I believe that, if the rope by which we are drawn up should break, you would be there in one minute!"

CHAP. LII.

SICKNESS, RECOVERY, DEATH.

In times of general sickness, God requires us to be active and kind in ministering to the temporal and spiritual wants of our neighbors, and in endeavoring to lead them to a suitable improvement of the dispensations of Providence. To those in health, we may say, "It is as great a mercy to be preserved in health as to be restored from sickness; but remember, now is the time to prepare for sickness and death. Hitherto the stroke has passed by you, but that is only to give you an opportunity to prepare for it. When God strikes your neighbor, he threatens you; when he wounds another, he warns you. Life is the time to prepare for death, and health to prepare for sickness. Delay not preparations for death till you are stretched in agony or insensibility on a dying bed. *Now* is the time to think about your soul; *then* you will have enough to do to bear the pains of the body. He that would reap comfort in sickness must sow it in health. It is in vain to defer the evil day, and put far from you the thoughts of dying; ready or unready, death will come, and there is no discharge in that warfare. Death will be most terrible to those who have not, in anticipation, died daily. None are the more likely to die for being prepared for it, nor will men's keeping it out of sight, and out of mind, keep it a single moment from their house or their persons!"

There is nothing terrible in death but what our sins have made so; and even now, death has no terrors of which faith in Christ cannot strip it. The sting of death is sin, and the strength of sin is the law; but acquittal and victory may be obtained by faith in Christ Jesus our Lord. "We should think of death, not as if we were only thinking, but as if we were also dying, and not rest satisfied with any thing short of that which would satisfy us if we knew that this moment would be our last." "Let us familiarize death by meditation, and sweeten it by preparation." "It is the great business of life to prepare for death, and to lay hold on eternal life." "Death will introduce us to the judgment-seat of Christ: if death be our friend, and the Judge our friend, then we need not fear."

That man is in a miserable state, to whom it is death to think of death, or discourse of death; and to put away the thoughts of death no more gives peace and security than the child's shutting his eyes in a storm preserves him from the danger at which he is terrified. "Death often comes without a warning, but never without a warrant, and a warrant which brooks no delays in its execution." "When a saint dies, he leaves all his bad behind, and carries all his good away; but when a sinner dies, he leaves all his good things behind him, and carries with him all his bad—a load which sinks him into the pit of everlasting perdition."

To those recovered from sickness, God seems to say, "Sin no more, lest a worse thing come upon thee." Remember, a respite is not a reprieve; and though, in your late affliction, you were nearer to death in your own apprehension than you are now, it is certain, in fact, that death was never so near you as at the present moment. Look back and reflect what it was that gave you the most pain and alarm on that bed of sickness, and avoid it, as you would avoid planting your dying pillow with thorns. A glimmering of eternity breaks in upon the sick chamber, and shows the world and sin in their true light. Accustom yourself to think of them as you then thought, and suffer not yourself to be deceived by the false glare that too often rests upon them. The world is as vain and empty, and sin as ruinous and dreadful, as they appeared when death and eternity seemed just at hand. Your answered prayers and enjoyed mercies now demand returns of gratitude and praise. The vows you made in sickness must now be fulfilled in holy obedience. "What shall I render unto the Lord for all his benefits? I will take the cup of salvation, and call upon the name of the Lord. Because He hath heard my prayer and my supplication, therefore I will call upon Him as long as I live. I will pay unto the Lord my vows, which my lips have uttered and my mouth hath spoken when I was in trouble."

I shall now set down some of those comforting sayings which I have heard a minister address to pious persons in prospect of death. "Death to a Christian," he would say, "is but putting off rags for robes—is but exchanging a dungeon for a palace." "Sin has long been your greatest grief; but that period is very near at hand when

'Sin, your worst enemy before,
Shall vex your eyes and ears no more;
Your inward foes shall all be slain,
Nor Satan break your peace again.'

Sin received its sentence of death in the death of Christ; but it does not receive its execution till the death of the Christian." "The great comfort of a believer on his death-bed is faith in Christ, hope in the promises, and interest in the covenant: by these, death is stripped of its terrors, and the glories of eternity brought full in view." "Your best friends are gone to heaven before you, or will soon follow after, and Christ is waiting to receive you, which is best of all."

That Christian* was in a happy frame who said, "My Head is in heaven—my heart is in heaven: it is but a few more steps, and I shall be there also." And another,† who, on being asked how he found himself, answered, "Well and happy, and going home, as every honest man should do

---

* The mother of Philip Henry.   † The Rev. Joseph Mead.

when his day's work is done; and I bless God I have a good home to go to."

There is nothing more grievous to a benevolent man, than to see aged persons tottering over the grave, and yet unmindful of eternity. "Oh!" he will say, "it is a dreadful sight to see old persons making more provision for life than preparation for death! What awful folly and madness, to prepare that which they cannot enjoy, and to neglect that which they cannot avoid. The steel being spent, the knife cannot cut—the sun being set, the day cannot tarry—and old age being come, life cannot long endure. It is the eleventh hour, and almost the last minute of that hour. The lamp is just flickering in the socket, and there is the whole work of a life to do, or the soul must be undone forever."

I once heard the following conversation between an old man and a Mr. Wilson:—"Well, my friend," said Mr. W., "you have had a long walk; pray how old are you?"—"Seventy-three, sir, last birth-day."—"And you are still permitted to enjoy a comfortable degree of health and vigor."—"Oh, yes, as well as ever I was in my life; *as likely to live fifty years as any body.*"—"Oh, my friend, do not deceive yourself with so very improbable an idea. It is very unlikely you should live fifty months; you have already been permitted to advance far beyond the ordinary boundaries of the life of man; and you ought to live in daily expectation of death, and in constant preparation for it. What is your hope for another world, if to-day should finish your existence in this?"—"Time enough to think about that, sir, when death is a little nearer. I hope I shan't be cut off so quickly but what I shall have time to say, 'Lord, have mercy upon me!'"—"Alas! alas! and can you venture your immortal soul on such a vain, precarious foundation? If you really think you shall need mercy, then, why do you not cry for mercy now, while the opportunity is afforded you? My soul trembles to think of your awful condition."—"Don't disturb yourself about me," said the insensible old man; "you know every tub must stand upon its own bottom; and I dare say I shall do very well at last. Good day to you, sir."

Mr. Wilson then turned to some young persons who happened to be present, and charged us to remember our Creator in the days of our youth, and not deceive ourselves with the thought that old age must needs bring piety with it.

A very few weeks after this, I saw the old man's son with a crape hat-band, and learned that his father was dead; and there was every reason to fear that he died as he had lived, without God and without hope!

"I am very poorly," said another old man to Mr. Wilson; "I have had another severe plunge since I saw you." After detailing the particulars of his affliction, he added, "I have been a great sufferer in my time. Have I not seen a great deal of affliction? Well, it is best to have it all here; it is to be hoped there will be no more of it hereafter."—" But what reasons have you, my friend, for indulging such a hope? The troubles and sorrows of this world have nothing to do with another, except so far as they produce a good or bad effect on those who are exercised by them."—"For my part, I have nothing to fear about another world; I have always led a good life; never followed any bad ways. I never cheated any body—never was spiteful—I owe nobody any thing—I am sure to do well."

> "Come, then, a still small whisper in your ear;
> He has no hope who never had a fear;
> And he that never doubted of his state,
> He may perhaps—perhaps he may—too late."

"But what have I to be afraid of?—Do you think I have been a wicked man?"

"My dear friend, I have known you for many years to be an upright, kind-hearted neighbor, one who would feel pleasure in doing good to any one. Hence you have a claim on any one who has it in his power, or thinks he has, to do you good. This very feeling of respect and gratitude urges me to press upon you a serious examination into the grounds of your hope for eternity. For my own part, I know of no other hope than what the Bible reveals; and though I have read my Bible for many years, I never yet met with a passage that intimated, that merely avoiding to cheat or injure his neighbor, would insure a man a place in heaven. Have you thought, my friend, of the relation in which you stand to God, and in what manner you have discharged your duty to him, as well as to your fellow-creatures?"

"Why, you know God Almighty is very merciful?"

"True; He is infinitely merciful. For the very best of us, with all our good deeds and kind actions to our fellow-creatures, deserve at his hands nothing but wrath and destruction. It is of his tender love and mercy that he has sent his only-begotten Son into the world to die for guilty men and women, in order that mercy might be extended to all who humbly believe and accept this great salvation. But the blessed God is never merciful at the expense of his justice. He will never set aside the demands of his holy law, nor accept our poor, worthless doings as an atonement for our sins; nor will he acquit or save any but those who believe and obey the gospel of the Lord Jesus Christ. Pardon my freedom in entreating that you will read the holy scriptures, especially the Gospels, and that you will earnestly pray for the Holy Spirit to help you to understand their true meaning;—that, if you have been in error as to your state, and building your hopes for heaven on a false foundation, you may be convinced of your error while yet there remains time and hope of amending it."

"Be so good as to examine the following passages, and seriously inquire what aspect they bear on your character and state. 'By the deeds of the law shall no man living be justified in His sight.' 'There is none righteous, no, not one:' —'for all have sinned and come short of the glory of God.' Rom. iii. 10, 20, 23. 'Except a man be born again, he cannot see the kingdom of God.' John iii. 3. 'God so loved the world, that he gave his only begotten Son, that whosoever believeth in him should not perish, but have everlasting life.' 'He that believeth on the Son hath everlasting life: and he that believeth not the Son shall not see life ; but the wrath of God abideth on him.' John iii. 16, 36. 'Neither is there salvation in any other : for there is no other name under heaven given among men whereby we must be saved.' Acts iv. 12. 'Therefore, thus saith the Lord God, Behold, I lay in Zion for a foundation a stone, a tried stone, a precious corner stone, a sure foundation : he that believeth shall not make haste (or be *ashamed,* or be *disappointed.*) Judgment also will I lay to the line, and righteousness to the plummet ; and the hail shall sweep away the refuge of lies, and the waters shall overflow the hiding-place.' Isa. xxviii. 16, 17. ' Seek ye the Lord while he may be found ; call ye upon him while he is near.' Isa. lv. 6. 'There is no God else beside me ; a just God and a Saviour: there is none beside me. Look unto me, and be ye saved, all the ends of the earth. Surely, shall one say, in the Lord have I righteousness and strength.' Isa. xlv. 21, 22, 24. 'Two men went up into the temple to pray ; the one a Pharisee, and the other a publican. The Pharisee stood and prayed thus with himself: God, I thank thee that I am not as other men are, extortioners, adulterers, unjust, or even as this publican : I fast twice in the week, I give tithes of all that I possess. And the publican, standing afar off, would not lift up so much as his eyes unto heaven, but smote upon his breast, saying, God be merciful to me a sinner. I tell you that this man went down to his house justified rather than the other : for every one that exalteth himself shall be abased ; and he that humbleth himself shall be exalted,'" Luke xviii. 10—14.

CHAP. LIII.

TRUE RICHES.

I HAVE heard of a great nobleman in the north of England, who used to boast of his great riches · on one occasion, he said to a gentleman who accompanied him in a walk, "These beautiful grounds, as far as your eye can reach, belong to me; those majestic woods on the brow of the distant hills are mine. Those extensive and valuable mines belong to me; yonder powerful steam-engine is employed by me in obtaining the produce of the mines; and those ships in conveying my wealth to other parts of the kingdom; fire, water, earth, and air, all are tributary to me."—"Well, my lord," replied the gentleman, "do you see yonder little hovel that seems but a speck in your estate? There dwells a poor woman, who can say more than all this; for she can say, 'Christ is mine.' In a very few years, your lordship's possessions will be confined within the scanty limits of six feet by two; but she will then have entered on a far nobler inheritance than your lordship now possesses—an inheritance incorruptible, undefiled, and that fadeth not away, reserved in heaven for her, who is now kept by the power of God, through faith unto salvation."

The following sayings are worth remembering:—

"He is the richest man who desires no superfluities, and wants no necessaries."

"To have a portion in the world is a mercy; to have the world for our chief portion is a misery."

"Wealth is a common gift of God's hand; but wisdom to improve it is a special grace from his heart."

"We put a price upon riches, but riches cannot put a price upon us. We must answer for them, but they cannot answer for us."

"The contented man has two heavens; one here in his own bosom, another hereafter in Abraham's bosom."

"There is no miss of the creature where there is a full enjoyment of the Creator, any more than of a candle when the sun shines at noon-day, or of a cistern when we have the fountain at command."

CHAP. LIV.

CROSSES AND AFFLICTIONS.

SUBMISSION, unreserved submission, is not only the most reasonable thing imaginable, but the most calming, consoling state of mind in this vale of tears, and produces the happiest effects on ourselves and on all around us, especially when accompanied with daily earnest prayer for those in particular whom we regard as most instrumental in occasioning or increasing our trials. Mr. Newton used to say, "A sinner has no right to complain; and a saint has no reason."

"No affliction for the present seems joyous, but grievous;" and even good people are too apt to construe their afflictions into expressions of divine displeasure against them, and to discourage themselves with the idea that they cannot be the children of God, or they should not be thus hardly dealt with. I remember hearing a conversation between Mr. Wilson and a good woman who had been exercised with a series of trials, both in worldly circumstances and family bereavements. It was something to the following effect:—

Mr. W.—"Well, my friend, the Lord has chastened you sore, but he has not given you up to death."

Woman.—"Not quite to death, sir, but almost to despair. It is a bad sign that I should need to be so hardly dealt with; I must have a deal of wickedness in my heart. Indeed, I think no one can be so wicked as I; and now I begin to think that God has cast me off forever."

Mr. W.—"It certainly is a bad sign that we need affliction, as it is a sign that we are sick when we need physic. But it is more hopeful to have medicine administered, however bitter, than to be left a prey to our spiritual diseases. 'Tis a worse sign to be always without chastisement than to be often under chastisement; and, instead of fearing that

God has cast you off, you have reason to be thankful for these merciful intimations that He designs your cure. Afflictions are God's potions, which we may sweeten by faith and prayer; but we are too apt to make them bitter, by putting into God's cup the ill ingredients of our own impatience and unbelief."

Woman.—"That's too true, sir. I wish there was more submission in my heart, and then my troubles would be more easily borne; but here I sit, day after day, thinking of what I have lost, and how I have been exercised; and every day seems to bring some new trial, and it seems as if there was no end to sorrow."

Mr. W.—"Yet do not imagine that any strange thing has happened to you. The same afflictions are accomplished in your brethren, and it is no more than what you have been forewarned of. There are daily crosses as well as daily bread; and if we are enabled to take them up, and bear them with the temper and spirit of true Christians, we have reason to hope for the gracious assistance of our Lord in bearing our burden, and in making it a real blessing to us; but as to the end of our burdens and sorrows, we are not to expect it till we lay down our burden and our life together."

Woman.—"I often think, sir, that I could have borne any trial better than my own."

Mr. W.—"Yours is a very common mistake; but these are true sayings, 'Your own clothes cannot be so well fitted to you as your own crosses.' 'It is a presumptuous child that would choose his own rod, and an unreasonable Christian that would choose his own cross.' A cross we must have; and those that are made in heaven best fit the saints' backs, while those that we make by our own folly and perverseness are the most galling and the least profitable."

Woman.—"True, sir; so I find it. The sorest of all my troubles come through the misconduct of an over-indulged child, whom I made my idol."

Mr. W.—"Ah! my friend, 'Whatever we make an idol

of will be a cross to us if we are God's children, and a curse to us if we are not.' But what a mercy it is, that though God makes our own backslidings to reprove us, and our folly to chastise us, he does not utterly take his mercy from us, nor suffer his faithfulness to fail. Your great concern now should be, to humble yourself under the mighty hand of God, to take refuge in the mercy of Him who smites you, and to see that the end of these painful dispensations is answered in you. 'Though the hand of God may seem to be against you, his heart may be towards you;' and 'Afflictions are sent, not to drive you *from* God, but to draw you *to* him.' 'By afflictions God separates the soul he loves from the sin he hates.' Grieve not too much after outward losses; God never takes from his people any earthly enjoyment, but he gives them something as good or better in its room.' 'Whatever thou hast lost in the creature thou mayest find in God; and if these sorrows bring thee to cling more closely to Him, as thy comfort in life and thy portion in death, thou mayest say, as a saint of old said, 'It is good for me that I have been afflicted.' 'Afflictions are rather promised than threatened to the people of God.' Afflictions make a large article in God's inventory of good things, and 'no good thing will he withhold from them that walk uprightly.' How much mercy and consolation are contained in that declaration, 'As many as I *love*, I rebuke and chasten!' So far, then, from taking afflictions as evidences of the divine displeasure, we should rather receive them as tokens of fatherly love; and instead of fearing that we are in the wrong road, because we find it rough and thorny, we should be encouraged by the assurance that the way to heaven is through much tribulation. Humility can draw out all the bitterness from the cup of sorrow, and faith can replace it with sweet consolation. Thus many a saint beside the apostle has found that 'as suffering abounds, consolations much more abound,' and has learned to 'glory in tribulation; knowing that tribulation works patience, and patience experience, and experience hope; and hope makes not ashamed, because the love of God is shed abroad in the heart by the power of the Holy Ghost.'"

Much more, in the same strain, the good man addressed to his afflicted friend, and marked down many precious passages of scripture for her to ponder over in solitude.

Before he left the room, he turned to me, then a gay girl, who had never tasted sorrow, and said, "Remember that your time of sorrow will come. Though you live many years, and rejoice in them all, yet remember the days of darkness, for they will be many. One great means to lessen troubles when they come, is to expect and think upon them before they come. Evils will come never the sooner for our being aware of them, but they will come the easier. 'Preparation to meet sorrow is labor well lost if it come not, and labor well bestowed if it come;' and how can we obtain preparation for meeting affliction? By having the heart established in faith on the Lord Jesus. If our sins are pardoned, the sting of affliction, as well as of death, is taken away. If the friendship of God is secured, we shall never want support, comfort, or protection. If we have a portion in heaven, we may well bear all the losses, crosses, and trials of earth. If we are the children of God, all things will work together for our good; and 'our light afflictions, which are but for a moment, will work for us a far more exceeding, and an eternal weight of glory; while we look not at the things which are seen, but at the things which are not seen; for the things which are seen are temporal, but the things which are not seen are eternal.'"

Since that time, as the good old gentleman told me, I have seen many days of trouble; and his good sayings have often come into my mind and cheered me, especially those blessed portions of scripture which encourage us in the darkest seasons to put our trust in the mercy of God through Jesus Christ: and that is among the uses of affliction; it leads us to search the blessed volume for promises on which to rest our hope. I, for one, may well say, "Unless thy law had been my delights, I should then have perished in mine affliction."

> "This was my comfort when I bore
> Variety of grief,
> It made me learn thy word the more,
> And fly to that relief."

The following lines were repeated to a minister, by a poor and pious female, when her husband appeared to be dying, leaving her with nine children :—

> "Long have I view'd, long have I thought,
> And trembling held this bitter draught;
> But now resolv'd and firm I'll be,
> Since 'tis prepar'd and mix'd by Thee!
>
> I'll trust my great Physician's skill;
> What He prescribes can ne'er be ill;
> No longer will I grieve or pine;
> Thy pleasure 'tis, it shall be mine.
>
> Thy med'cine oft produces smart;
> Thou wound'st me in the tend'rest part;
> All that I priz'd below is gone,
> Yet, Father, still, Thy will be done.
>
> Since 'tis thy sentence I should part
> With what is nearest to my heart,
> My little all I here resign,
> And, lo, my heart itself is thine.
>
> Take all, great God; I will not grieve,
> But wish I still had more to give;
> I hear thy voice; thou bid'st me quit
> This favor'd gourd—and I submit."

CHAP. LV.

THE WIDOW AND THE FATHERLESS.

It is mentioned as one prominent feature of pure religion, and undefiled before God and the Father, "to visit the fatherless and the widows in their affliction;" and those who were so ready to every good work were not backward in this particular.

I well remember, when my dear father died, that some of our kind, good friends came to see my poor mother, and one of them said to her, "This day, my friend, you become heiress to promises more numerous, full, and particular, than to any other state or condition mentioned in scripture; and from this day forward it will be your privilege to plead at the throne of grace: 'Lord, thou hast seen fit to make me a widow, and these my children fatherless; and now, remember the word unto thy servant on which thou hast caused me to hope.'"

This sentiment rested on the mind of my dear mother, and often roused her fortitude when she seemed ready to sink in overwhelming grief. And she, and those dependent on her, ever had reason to say that not one good thing failed them of all that the Lord had spoken. We had struggles, to be sure, and sometimes met with unkindness and oppression; but often friends and protectors were raised up, and sources of supply opened most unexpectedly and seasonably. We were all of us willing to work, and, under the blessing of God, our hands have been sufficient for us. Above all, the prayers of our parents were answered in our family being preserved in peace and love, and each of us, I trust, brought to love and serve the God in whom they trusted.

When we read a passage of scripture together, and any thing struck my mother as particularly suitable, she would often say, "Mark that place down, child; we may be glad to refer again to it ourselves: besides, there are many widows in Israel; and glad should I be to point out to another that which has brought comfort to my own mind."

In this manner, I got a number of passages marked down under different particulars, applicable to the case of widows and fatherless children; such as these:

1. God has taken widows and fatherless children under his special care and protection.—"The Lord relieveth the

fatherless and the widow." Ps. cxlvi. 9. "A Father of the fatherless and a Judge of the widows is God in his holy habitation." Ps. lxviii. 5. "Leave thy fatherless children; I will preserve them alive; and let thy widows trust in me." Jer. xlix. 11. "The Lord will establish the border of the widow." Prov. xv. 25. "In thee the fatherless findeth mercy." Hos. xiv. 3. "Thou art the Helper of the fatherless. Lord, thou hast heard the desire of the humble. Thou wilt prepare their heart. Thou wilt cause thine ear to hear, to judge the fatherless and the oppressed, that the man of the earth may no more oppress." Ps. x. 14, 17, 18. "Remove not the old landmarks, and enter not into the fields of the fatherless, for their Redeemer is mighty, and he shall plead their cause." Prov. xxiii. 10, 11.

Many of the laws given to God's ancient people, the Jews, express his tender concern for the widow and the fatherless. "Ye shall not afflict any widow or fatherless child. If thou afflict them in any wise, and they cry at all unto me, I will surely hear their cry, and my wrath shall wax hot, and I will kill you with the sword, and your wives shall be widows, and your children fatherless." Exod. xxii. 22—24. "The Lord doth execute the judgment of the fatherless and the widow." Deut. x. 18. "And the fatherless and the widow which are within thy gates, shall come and shall eat, and be satisfied, that the Lord thy God may bless thee in all the works of thine hand which thou doest." Deut. xiv. 29. "Thou shalt not pervert the judgment of the stranger, nor of the fatherless, nor take the widow's raiment to pledge. When thou cuttest down thine harvest in the field, and hast forgot a sheaf in the field, thou shalt not go again to fetch it. It shall be for the stranger, for the fatherless, and for the widow; that the Lord thy God may bless thee in all the work of thine hands." Deut. xxiv. 17, 19.

It is often mentioned in scripture as a good feature of character, to be kind and tender to the widow and the fatherless. Those who are so, are encouraged to pray for a blessing on their substance: "When thou hast made an end of tithing all the tithes of thine increase, the third year, which is the year of tithing, and hast given it unto the Levite, the stranger, the fatherless, and the widow, that they may eat within thy gates, and be filled, then thou shalt say before the Lord thy God, I have brought away the hallowed things out of mine house, and also have given them unto the Levite, and the stranger, to the fatherless, and to the widow, according to all thy commandments which thou hast commanded me: I have not transgressed thy commandments, neither have I forgotten them. Look down from thy holy habitation from heaven, and bless thy people Israel, and the land which thou hast given us, as thou swarest to our fathers." Deut. xxvi. 12, 13, 15.

Job, in the time of his affliction, was comforted by recollecting that, in the time of his prosperity, he "delivered the poor that cried, and the fatherless, and him that had none to help him. The blessing of him that was ready to perish came upon him, and he made the widow's heart to sing for joy." Job xxix. 12, 13, xxxi. 16, 17.

Such conduct is mentioned as an evidence of genuine piety: "Pure religion, and undefiled before God and the Father, is this, To visit the fatherless and the widows in their affliction, and to keep himself unspotted from the world." James i. 27.

"Cease to do evil; learn to do well; relieve the oppressed; judge the fatherless; plead for the widow. Come now, and let us reason together, saith the Lord." Isa. i. 17, 18. "If any widow have children or nephews, let them learn first to show piety at home, and to requite their parents; for this is good and acceptable before God." 1 Tim. v. 4.

Cruelty, oppression, and even neglect of the widow and fatherless, are severely censured. In the description of the wicked it is said, "They drive away the ass of the fatherless, and take the widow's ox for a pledge; they do not good to the widow." Job xxiv. 3, 21. It is given as a mark of the grossest hypocrisy, "which devour widows' houses, and for a pretence make long prayers." Mark xii. 40. There is an awful curse against " him that perverteth the judgment of the stranger, fatherless, and widow; and all the people shall say, Amen." Deut. xxvii. 19. "And I will come near to you in judgment, and I will be a swift witness against those that oppress the hireling in his wages, the widow and the fatherless, and that turn away the stranger from his right, and fear not me, saith the Lord of hosts." Mal. iii. 5.

Widows are repeatedly mentioned with honor. "Honor widows that are widows indeed. Now she that is a widow indeed, and desolate, trusteth in God, and continueth in supplications and prayers night and day." 1 Tim. v. 3, 5.

Such a widow was the prophetess Anna, which departed not from the temple, but served God with fastings and prayers night and day; and was there favored with a sight of the infant Saviour. Luke ii. 37.

The poor widow's offering of two mites for the service of the sanctuary, was graciously accepted and acknowledged above all the costly gifts of the rich and proud. Mark xii. 42.

It is very probable, though not certain, that the active and benevolent Dorcas was a widow, who cheered her own solitude by laboring for the good of others. Acts ix. 36—41.

We have also, in scripture, some remarkable appearances of Providence on behalf of widows. The prophet Elijah was sent to the widow of Zarephath, not only for his own sustenance during the famine, but also to multiply her scanty store for the sufficient supply of her household. He was also permitted to raise her only son to life. 1 Kings xvii.

The prophet Elisha was permitted to multiply the widow's oil, so as to supply her with the means of honorably discharging her husband's debt and supporting her children. 2 Kings iv. 1—7.

The widow weeping over the bier of her only son, experienced the compassion and sympathy of the Son of God. He said unto her, "Weep not;" and restored the young man to life. Luke vii. 11—15.

When expiring on the cross, our Lord provided for his

widowed and destitute mother an asylum in the house of his beloved disciple, John xix. 26, 27; and, to the present day, many widows and fatherless children can attest their experience of the compassion, faithfulness, and care of Him, who will be known as the Father of the fatherless and the God of the widow.

CHAP. LVI.

CHRISTIAN CONTENTMENT AND CHEERFULNESS.

WE had in our village two old women, who lived next door to each other, and whose outward circumstances were in every respect as similar as possible; but their tempers and dispositions as complete a contrast. Jenny Moore was always complaining; Amy Scott was always contented and grateful. A kind lady was in the habit of looking in upon them occasionally. One conversation with each would serve as a picture of their general habit and temper.

Lady.—"Good morning, Mrs. Moore; I hope you are well this fine day."

Jenny.—"It is a fine day, to be sure; but 'tis piercing cold, and I am not well; very poorly, indeed, ma'am; hardly able to get about. I am always bad with the rheumatism."

Lady.—"That is a trying pain. I suppose you are using means to remove it."

Jenny.—"No, not I; poor folks must bear their pains. It is not like the rich, who can have proper advice, and things to make them comfortable."

Lady.—"Shall I give you a turn for the dispensary? You might then have medicines and attendance free of expense."

Jenny.—"Why, for the matter of that, I have got a turn; the rector gave me one last week; but I don't see that doctor's stuff does much good. Besides, the doctor hardly ever calls on me, because I am a poor woman. He has been but once this week, though I have seen him go by twice a day to Mrs. Burroughs. But then she's a lady, and there's something to be got by going to her."

Lady.—" Mrs. Burroughs is ill of a fever, and requires constant attention, which a rheumatic complaint does not require. However, if you feel yourself neglected, I will call and speak to the doctor. He is a kind, humane man, and, I am sure, will be willing to pay you every proper attention, and do all in his power to relieve your pains."

Jenny.—" Thank you, ma'am; but it is of no use to speak to him; all he says is, I must persevere with the stuff he gave me, and wear plenty of flannel; but what's the use of telling poor folks that?"

Lady.—" Have you no flannel, then?"

Jenny.—" Yes, I have got a piece of coarse flannel that was given me at the hall; but I have not had time to make it into a petticoat."

Lady.—" And did you not receive a blanket, and some coals?"

Jenny.—" Yes, I got a few coals, and a small blanket; the large ones were given to those that have families, and I am sure they did not want them so bad as I did."

Lady.—" I should think, where three or four persons have but one bed, they must want a larger blanket to cover them than you, who sleep alone. Besides, those who give have a right to give as they think for the best; and you should be thankful for what you receive, instead of being discontented that it is no more. Think how much worse off you might have been, if you had not received the blanket, and the flannel, and the coals, and the turn for the doctor. For all this you are indebted to the kindness of friends. I really think you have great cause of gratitude instead of complaint. Pray what is your income?"

Jenny.—" I have but three shillings a week to help myself, and the parish grumble at allowing me that."

Lady.—" But you are able to earn a trifle at spinning and knitting?"

Jenny.—" 'Tis a trifle, indeed! Women's work is always a dead penny; and now they've got these new-fangled machines, as I say, they have taken the bread out of poor people's mouths."

Lady.—" No doubt, it must affect the poor in some respects; but then it is a general good, and even you share the benefit. You can get a gown, shift, petticoat, and pair of stockings, for as little money now as you would have paid formerly for a gown alone, before machinery came into such general use."

Jenny.—" Ah! it is seldom I have money to lay out in clothing; so it is little odds to me whether cheap or dear. 'Tis a hard matter to get a bit of bread to put in one's mouth; and as to butcher's meat, I scarcely ever buy any."

Lady.—" I have often been pleased to see your son's little girl bringing you a plateful at dinner-time."

Jenny.—" Yes, he sends me a bit now and then; but he has a large family, and it is not always that they have got it themselves."

Lady.—" It is pleasing to find that they have the disposition to help you. You have also a steady, respectable daughter in service: I hope she is kind to you."

Jenny.—" Why, she pays my rent, to be sure; that is some help to me."

Lady.—" A very great help, indeed! and you have a convenient, comfortable cottage."

Jenny.—" 'Tis a miserable cold place, and smokes sadly when the wind sets one way."

Lady.—" Your garden, too, must help you a little. I suppose you grow a few potatoes and cabbages for your own use, and have something to sell beside."

Jenny.—" I don't know how it is, but my crops generally fail, and the birds get at my fruit. What with one thing and another, I don't know that I am a bit better off than if I had no garden at all."

Lady.—" You have got a nice Bible here. What a blessed companion is that in our deepest solitude! Do you recol-

CHRISTIAN CONTENTMENT AND CHEERFULNESS. 267

lect the fourth chapter of St. Paul's Epistle to the Philippians?"

Jenny.—" I can't say that I do,—my eyes are bad,—I don't read much."

Lady.—" Your little grand-daughter, who attends the Sunday school, reads nicely, and would feel a pleasure in reading you a chapter or two every day."

Jenny.—" Yes, I dare say she would. She often offers to read, but it is not always that it suits me."

Lady.—"I think you would find pleasure and profit in a constant perusal of the sacred volume. There is enough good news there, if we do but take it home to ourselves, to make us rich and happy, whatever our outward circumstances may be. Let me read you a few verses; think them over, and pray that God may give you a contented spirit, and teach you, like his servant of old, in whatsoever state you are, therewith to be content."

The lady felt almost disposed to leave this grumbling old woman, without any other memorial of her visit; but recollecting, "our Father in heaven, who is kind to the evil and the unthankful," she presented her a trifle, and, taking her leave, called on Amy Scott, at the next door, when the following conversation took place :—

Lady.—" Well, Amy, how are you? I am sorry to see you tied up with the face-ache.

Amy.—" Thank you, ma'am; my face is much better than it has been; and it is a great mercy to be able to get about at all; last week I really was not able to work."

Lady.—" Why did you not let me know? I should have been glad to send you any thing you might be in want of."

Amy.—" Thank you, ma'am; I did not like to be troublesome; besides, I really have not wanted for any thing. A friend was so kind as to give me a turn for the doctor, and he gave me some stuff that has done me a deal of good."

Lady.—" Was the doctor kind and attentive to you?"

Amy.—" O yes, ma'am; he could not have been more so if I had been a lady. While I could not get about, he called on me every day; and, since I have been better, he told me to fetch more medicine as long as I wanted it, and to let him know if I was not so well again. And he spoke for me to the ladies at the hall, and got me such a nice gift, —a good piece of flannel to make me a petticoat, and a beautiful warm blanket,—only look at it, ma'am; it is fit for the greatest lady in the land to sleep under. And I have a hundred of coal every week, while the cold weather lasts, which, you know, is a very great help to a poor body. In short, I want for nothing but a more contented and grateful heart."

Lady.—" Pray what is your weekly income?"

Amy.—" I have three shillings a week; and that is more than many a poor creature has to live upon. Besides, my children are very good to me. They generally contrive to make up my rent among them; and would stint themselves to give me a bit if they knew I was in want; and one and another is very kind. I often get a few bones to boil down, and make me a drop of broth, or a little skim-milk at the farmer's; and you know every little helps. Besides, though I am not so strong as I used to be, I can still earn a little myself; and my garden helps me out nicely; I have always greens and potatoes for my own use, besides onions and potherbs, and a little fruit and flowers to sell. Take one thing with another, I think hardly any one in the parish is better off than I am."

Lady.—" Don't you find your house very cold?"

Amy.—" It was cold till my son nailed some list round the door to keep out the draft; and now it is as snug and comfortable as need be. The worst of it is, it is rather apt to smoke; but the wind does not always set one way, and then, perhaps, it does not smoke for a month together."

Lady.—" It is a great matter to have a disposition to look at the best side of every thing. I rejoice to see you so contented and cheerful."

Amy.—" I think it would be a great sin to be otherwise; besides, what have I to make me discontented? Where one is better off, a hundred are worse. I often think the lines have fallen to me in pleasant places. I have a goodly heritage. The Bible only promises bread and water, and I have generally better fare than that; and, then, let my fare be what it will, I have the precious Bible to comfort and refresh me. I often think of what it says in Proverbs,—'When thou goest, it shall lead thee; when thou sleepest, it shall keep thee; and when thou awakest, it shall talk with thee.' While I have my Bible, I don't know what it is to be dull."

Lady.—" Is your eye-sight pretty good ? "

Amy.—" Not so good as it has been; but our minister was so kind as to give me a pair of spectacles, which help me wonderfully. I have heard of a minister,* who was preaching to a large congregation, and was a long time wiping his glasses before he could read the text; the people looked up to see if any thing was the matter, and he said, 'You that can read your Bible without glasses, bless God for it,—I bless Him that I can read it with them.' And I desire to say the same. Besides, my children and grand-children often come in and read a chapter to me; and then, in course of time, one gets a great deal of scripture treasured up in the mind; and that serves to go to in darkness and dim-sightedness."

Lady.—" Well, is there nothing I can do for your comfort? You seem to be more independent than many people who possess thousands."

Amy.—" Thank you, ma'am. If you will please to read me a chapter, that is my greatest comfort; and it always sounds better if it is read by a good scholar, that knows just how to speak the words properly."

Lady.—" I think I must read the fourth chapter of the Epistle to the Philippians; and I feel very thankful that you are enabled to understand and relish it."

The verses to which she particularly alluded are these:

*Rev. J. Berridge.

—" Let your moderation be known unto all men : the Lord is at hand. Be careful for nothing; but in every thing, by prayer and supplication, with thanksgiving, let your requests be made known unto God. And the peace of God, which passeth all understanding, shall keep your heart and mind through Christ Jesus," (ver. 5—7.) " Not that I speak in respect of want; for I have learned, in whatsoever state I am, therewith to be content. I know both how to be abased, and I know how to abound : every where, and in all things, I am instructed, both to be full and to be hungry, both to abound and to suffer need. I can do all things through Christ, which strengtheneth me," (ver. 11—13.) " My God shall supply all your need, according to his riches in glory, by Christ Jesus," (ver. 19.)

Lady.—" Well, I must now bid you farewell ; and, though you seem to want nothing, I hope you will find a use for this trifle, which I wish to leave with you as an expression of my Christian regard."

Amy.—" O, thank you, ma'am, a thousand times. This will just make up enough, with what I have saved, to buy me a new pair of shoes, which I really am in want of."

Lady.—" If you should at any time be unwell, or in want, I hope you will not hesitate to let me know, that I may have the pleasure of ministering to your necessities and comforts."

Amy.—" Thank you, ma'am ; I will make bold to send if I should be in need ; and I pray the Lord to reward you for your goodness, and to make me truly sensible of his great goodness to me in thus spreading my table, and causing my cup to run over. 'Surely, goodness and mercy have followed me, and shall follow me all the days of my life, and I will dwell in the house of the Lord forever.' "

To these contrasted characters, I will add a few maxims and sayings, which I have, at different times, gathered on Christian contentment and cheerfulness :—

" Having food and raiment, let us be therewith content."

" Godliness with contentment is great gain."

"A contented mind is a continual feast."

"A cheerful countenance doeth good like medicine."

"Let not thine heart envy sinners, but be thou in the fear of the Lord all the day long."

"Better bring down thy mind to thy condition, than have thy condition brought up to thy mind."

"Bless God for what you have, and trust God for what you want."

"We must obey the revealed will of God, and then be resigned to his providential will; committing our souls to his keeping, and submitting ourselves to his disposal."

"Neither content nor discontent arises from the outward condition, but from the inward disposition. If a man is not content in the state in which he is, he would not be content in any state in which he would wish to be."

"Humility is the mother of contentment; think lowly of your deservings, and then you will think highly of your receivings. They that deserve nothing should be content with any thing. The deeper our self-abhorrence, the easier will be our self-resignation. He has the sweetest enjoyment of God's mercies, who feels himself unworthy of the least of them."

Isaac Walton, himself a man of a very cheerful, contented spirit, relates the following anecdote: "I knew a man that had health and riches, and several houses, all beautiful and well furnished, and would be often troubling himself and his family to remove from one of them to another. On being asked by a friend why he removed so often from one house to another, he replied, 'It was in order to find content in some of them.' But his friend, knowing his temper, told him, if he would find content in any of his houses, he must leave *himself* behind, for *content can never dwell but with a meek and quiet soul.*"

The following reasons may be assigned, why a Christian should be content with little.

1. Nature wants but little. A little simple food, and plain raiment, and homely shelter, and all for a little while; this

is all that man really needs; and all that he possesses beyond it, is but the beholding of it with his eyes. King George the Third, walking out early one morning, met a lad at the stable-door, and asked him, "Well, boy, what do you do? What do they pay you?" "I help in the stable," replied the lad, "but I have nothing but victuals and clothes." "Be content," replied the king; "I have no more." All that the richest possess beyond food, raiment, and habitation, they have but the keeping, or the disposing, not the present enjoyment of. A ploughboy who thinks and feels correctly has enough to make him contented; and, if a king have a discontented spirit, he will find some plea for indulging it. Nature is content with little, and grace with less; but luxury is seldom, and lust never satisfied.

2. Outward possessions are insufficient: a man's life consists not in the abundance of the things that he possesses. A good man is satisfied in himself, and a wicked man cannot be satisfied at all; his breast is like the troubled sea, which cannot rest, whose waves cast up mire and dirt. There is no peace, saith my God, to the wicked. Outward things can neither make a man happy or miserable. Ahab was discontented on a throne; Paul and Silas were happy in a dungeon.

3. Our own unworthiness should make us contented with what we possess. Wherefore should a living man complain? A sinner has no right, and a saint has no reason.

4. A Christian has enough in possession and in prospect of spiritual blessings to make him contented and happy, whatever be his outward circumstances. He is a son of God; an heir of glory; and he is going home; a mean lodging or a rough road need not greatly discompose him.

5. The providence of God orders all things for him, and has engaged to order all in the very best manner. He need not fear being neglected, for his God is attentive even to the falling of a sparrow. He need not be anxious about food and raiment, for his Father knows that he has need of these things, and has promised that bread shall be given him, and

his water shall be sure, and that all things shall work together for his good.

6. If we have but little in this world, we may content ourselves with the reflection that it is safer to have little than much. Many have been ruined by prosperity. Many have gone to hell in state; wearing purple and fine linen, and faring sumptuously every day: and "how hardly shall they that have riches enter into the kingdom of God!" Very wise was the prayer of Agur, "Give me neither poverty nor riches; feed me with food convenient for me."

7. Christians should be content, because time is short; and if time is short, trouble cannot be long. Weeping may endure for a night, but joy cometh in the morning. These *light* afflictions are but for a *moment,* and then comes an *eternal weight* of glory.

Christians should not merely be contented, but cheerful. It is a disgrace to their profession that they should go mourning from day to day, and hang down their heads like a bulrush. If they would honor religion, they should sing in the ways of the Lord, and let the world know that

> " Religion never was design'd
> To make our pleasures less."

"In all our conversation we should be lively, but not light; solid, but not sad."

"When first New England was planted, the settlers met with many difficulties and hardships, as is necessarily the case when a civilized people attempt to establish themselves in a wilderness-country. Being piously disposed, they sought relief from Heaven, by laying their wants and distresses before the Lord in frequent set days of fasting and prayer. Constant meditation, and discourse on the subject of their difficulties, kept their minds gloomy and discontented; and, like the children of Israel, there were many disposed even to return to that Egypt which persecution had determined them to abandon.

"At length, when it was proposed in the assembly to proclaim another fast, a farmer, of plain sense, rose and remarked, that the inconveniences they suffered, and concerning which they had so often wearied Heaven with their complaints, were not so great as might have been expected, and were diminishing every day as the colony strengthened; that the earth began to reward their labors, and to furnish liberally for their sustenance; that the seas and rivers were full of fish, the air sweet, the climate wholesome; above all, they were in the full enjoyment of liberty, civil and religious. He therefore thought, that reflecting and conversing on these subjects would be more comfortable, as tending to make them more contented with their situation; and that it would be more becoming the gratitude they owed to the Divine Being, if, instead of a fast, they should proclaim a thanksgiving. His advice was taken; and from that day to this, they have in every year observed circumstances of public happiness sufficient to furnish employment for a thanksgiving-day, which is therefore constantly ordered and religiously observed."

Most objects have two sides: generally one is pleasanter than the other. It is a great happiness to have a disposition to look at the bright, rather than the gloomy side of things; indeed, this disposition, founded on Christian principles, is the true secret of finding happiness in a miserable world. In the worst circumstances, a Christian has reason for contentment and cheerfulness; and it is a libel on his profession to be gloomy and discontented. Does he possess but little of this world's goods? It is all more than he deserves. Are some of his comforts taken away? He has reason to be thankful that some are left. Is he in pain and sickness? He enjoys the sympathy of Christian friends, and the sympathy and succor of a faithful High-priest. If circumstances are ever so bad, they might have been worse; and, what is more, they will be better. The Christian is passing a rough and dirty piece of road; but he is going home, and he has a good home to go to.

CHAP. LVII.

HINTS FOR YOUNG PERSONS.

I HAVE frequently referred, and have reason to do it with thankfulness, to the kind solicitude discovered by some of my friends in behalf of the young. Many of their sayings are deeply impressed on my mind, and much excellent advice on the subject I have written from books which they have either lent me or read in my presence. I most earnestly pray that, through the influences of the Holy Spirit, they may be deeply impressed on the minds of every one of my children.

"Remember, now, thy Creator in the days of thy youth." —The present is certainly the best time, and may be the *only* time. Remember God in your youth, and He will not forget, or forsake, or cast you off in the time of old age.

If you wish to be certain of finding God, seek Him in youth; for He loves those that love Him, and those that seek Him early shall find Him.

If you wish to be truly honorable, be truly religious; for riches and honor are with her; yea, durable riches and righteousness.

If you wish to have a good portion on earth, seek first the kingdom of God and his righteousness, and then all other things (good and needful) will be added thereunto.

If you wish to be eminent in piety, be early pious. Obadiah feared the Lord *from his youth*, and he feared him *greatly*. He that would reap the honor of being an *old disciple*, must sow the seed in being a *young disciple*. The youngest of Christ's apostles was the *beloved* apostle.

If you wish to make your parents happy, live betimes in the fear of God, for the father of the righteous shall greatly rejoice; and he that begetteth a wise son shall have joy of him. Thy father and thy mother shall be glad, and she that bare thee shall rejoice. My son, if thine heart be wise, my heart shall rejoice, even mine; but a foolish son is a grief to his father, and bitterness to her that bare him.

If you wish to escape the snares and pollutions of evil society, be religious betimes. Cultivate those principles which will give you a distaste for the society of the ungodly, and which will deter them from soliciting yours.

Some holy persons, brought to a knowledge of God in later years, have, through the remainder of life, bitterly regretted that their youth was spent in the society of the thoughtless and ungodly; for though that society was forsaken, it left recollections that polluted and harassed the mind, and stuck to it like the stains to the walls of a leprous house. The only way to avoid this, is, to grow up in happy ignorance of the words and ways of evil society. It is a great thing to be enabled to resist when sinners entice; but it is still more for the peace of the soul never to have been near the path of the wicked and the way of evil men; but to have been a companion of those only who fear the Lord and keep his commandments.

If you wish to possess that which will wisely guide you in all your future engagements and connections, and fit you to be useful as you pass through life, be early religious. "The fear of God is the beginning of wisdom; a good understanding have all they that do his commandments. Then shalt thou walk in the way safely, and thy foot shall not stumble."

If you wish to have a friend that may be depended upon, seek the friendship of God—the only Friend who *never* forsakes, who *never* dies, who is *never* unable or unwilling to befriend to the full extent of our need. There is a Friend that loveth at all times; that sticketh closer than a brother; that is the same yesterday, to-day, and forever; and able to do for you exceeding abundantly, above all that you can ask or think. Secure his friendship in early life.

If you wish always to have something at hand that can comfort and support you in time of trouble, this is it—early piety; the love of God shed abroad in your heart by the power of the Holy Ghost; a good hope, through grace, of an heavenly inheritance, and a firm conviction that all present things work together for good.

If you wish to be ready for death, come when it may, be early religious. Grace in the heart is oil in the lamp, that will light us through the valley of the shadow of death. The severest blasts and storms cannot put it out; but the great concern is, to have the lamp filled and lighted in good time; not to be running about to seek it when the call is upon us to go forth.

If you wish to have large capacities for the enjoyment of heaven, be early pious. All who are admitted to heaven will be happy; but we are led to conclude there will be different capacities for happiness, and, therefore, different degrees. Growth in grace on earth is growth in capacity for heavenly enjoyment. Then he whose heart is earliest opened for the reception of divine grace, and continues most expanding, is likely to be a large partaker of the bliss of heaven.

The following suggestions ought to be deeply impressed on the minds of youth:—

1. Choose God for your portion. God alone can make you happy; but all the world cannot make you happy without God.

2. Consider that by nature you are dead in trespasses and sins; a child of wrath, a stranger, and an enemy to God. Labor to be sensible of this, and let the sinfulness of your nature be your greatest burden.

3. Remember that Christ Jesus is your way to God. Justification, pardon, and acceptance with God, are by faith in him. Sanctification and a new nature are by the power of his Spirit. Let Christ, therefore, be precious to your souls. Labor for true faith in him. Take him for your Lord and Saviour. Submit to his commands in all things, and rest your soul upon him for reconciliation and peace with God. Open your heart to the motions of his Holy Spirit. Welcome that principle of a holy and divine life; improve his motions, follow his drawings, and by no means grieve him.

4. Be speedy in your repentance, and diligent in your en-

deavors after holiness. Know the time of God's gracious visitation. Consider that life is short and altogether uncertain. To defer one day may be your everlasting undoing.

5. Endeavor to be truly and thoroughly religious, and be not discouraged at the difficulties of it. God's grace shall be sufficient for your help. His promises shall be your sweet encouragement. Peace of conscience, and communion with God, shall be your ever-present cordial. The troubles and pains of religion shall be but short, and your reward shall be glorious and eternal.

6. Devote your young and blooming years to the love and service of your God and Saviour. The first-fruits are the most acceptable :—

> "A flower, when offer'd in the bud,
> Is no vain sacrifice."

Grudge not that the vain delights and sinful pleasures of youth should be lost. They shall be exchanged for spiritual delights, which are more excellent, inward, and lasting.

7. Remember you must give an account to God of your youth as well as your age. It will be no excuse, if you be found in your sins, to say, "I was but young." He that is old enough to sin, is old enough for hell. You cannot make sure of God's love, an interest in Christ, and the salvation of your soul, too soon. It may be too late, but can never be too early.

8. Let those who have been piously instructed remember, that they cannot have that pleasure in sin which others may. They know better. They sin against light and conviction. Conscience will mix gall with their honey. When they go to prayer in the evening, or (if they neglect that) when upon their bed, alone, retired, in the dark, or in a thunder-storm, conscience will read sad lectures to them, and make them review all the pleasures of sin with bitterness.

9. Repentance and conversion are easiest in youth. Sin is not so deeply rooted; Satan not so strongly fortified; grace

not so much slighted; the Spirit not so much grieved; the conscience not so much hardened.

10. Early conversion, as it is most easy, so it is also least questionable. It is little for a man to renounce the world when he is just forced to leave it; or to forsake the pleasures of sin when he has no longer the ability to pursue them. But when the bloom and strength of youth are given to God, when the world is full before it, it then appears plain that God is loved for himself; that Christ is preferred above the flesh, and grace, above the sweetest delights in the world.

CHAP. LVIII.

RULES FOR DAILY CONDUCT.

For the government of the conduct, the following rules are important:—

1. Make the word of God the rule of all you do.

2. Whatever you do, do it in the strength of Christ. Without Christ, you can do nothing. Of yourself, you cannot even think a good thought; but you may do all things, through Christ strengthening you. Nature is a dry root of goodness; no gracious actions spring from it. Grace depends on continual supplies from Christ, as of sap from the root, or heat from the sun. Be strong in the Lord, and in the power of his might, and then nothing shall be too hard for you. Mountains shall melt to plains, and valleys be filled up. All things are possible to him that believes and relies upon the power, to which nothing is impossible.

3. As we are to act by the power of Christ, so we are to present our services for acceptance in the name of Christ. The best we can do, needs his intercession, blood, and merits, to render it acceptable to God. In the Lord, have we righteousness and strength.

4. Whatever you do, do all to the glory of God. Selfish-

ness is the natural idolatry of the human heart. The design and tendency of religion is to take it off and set it upon God. That duty which does not begin and end with God is no part of godliness. Self must be entirely cast down, and God alone exalted.

By these points let every action be examined :—By whose *rule* have I acted? In whose *strength* have I acted? In whose *name* have I acted? For whose *glory* have I acted? What faith, humility, self-denial, love to God and Christ, have there been in my actions?

5. To spend every day well, let your waking thoughts be with God; let your fervent prayers ascend in the name of Christ; let the word of God be the man of your counsel; let the fear of God be always before your eyes. In all your actions, let integrity and uprightness preserve you, as those who wait on God. Set a watch over your lips, and a guard upon your spirit, that you be not provoked to wrath, nor speak unadvisedly with your lips.

At night, review the actions of the day. Give to God the glory of what has been good; take shame to yourself for what has been evil. Review the dispensations of God's providences, and consider their special meaning and application. Acknowledge the mercies of God received through the day. Submit to the afflictions laid upon you. Desire a fresh application to your conscience of the blood of sprinkling; and commit yourselves afresh to the mercy and protection of God, through Jesus Christ; that you may be preserved through the slumbers of the night, and be permitted to wake in peace, whether it be in earth or heaven.*

* Mason's Select Remains.

CHAP. LIX.

BROTHERS AND SISTERS.

It is a common remark, that large families agree better, and often prosper better, than those consisting of but two or three children. I do not exactly see how or why this should be—but common remarks are seldom altogether without foundation. Perhaps it may be traced to some mismanagement during the period of childhood, by which the selfish passions have been fostered. This supposition is founded on two principles; first, that selfishness is the great cause of disagreements, whether in families, neighborhoods, or nations; and, secondly, that the character is generally formed during the years of childhood: I do not mean to say unchangeably formed; for divine grace, in many happy instances, has given a new bias to the affections, and consequently a new aspect to the character—the man has become a new creature in Christ Jesus. Circumstances, too, may, in after life, develope traits of character which had altogether passed unobserved in childhood; so that it is often said of a man or woman, "He (or she) is not a bit like himself (or herself) in youth; the character and disposition seem completely changed" From this remark I beg to differ, and say,—the disposition was there, only circumstances were required to bring it into active and palpable operation. The character at fourteen is so far formed, that the *good man* will, through life, have more or less to struggle with the errors and evil propensities of that date; or, in the *bad man*, they will go on to their odious maturity, as naturally, as the bud and blossom will advance to the fruit or seed. At that age a great majority of young persons quit the parental roof, and the intercourse of brothers and sisters is afterwards but occasional. The principles and habits already acquired will, however, be found to give a color to that intercourse through future life. The meetings may be so infrequent and transient as hardly to afford time for rubbing off the restraints of politeness; but should any thing like the intimacy of domestic life occur, and especially should any thing like a collision of interests arise, the adult brother and sister will discover the very same dispositions as those which marked their childish intercourse; and the surviving parent will be reminded, perhaps pleasingly, perhaps painfully, of the instructions, the developements and the discipline of the nursery.

There is a probability that the children in small families are more indulged, and engross a more exclusive and injurious attention. If attention be *well directed*, it is scarcely possible to bestow too much on children. By well-directed attention, I mean attention to their real wants and interests; for I am sure it is no small advantage to children to be brought up by those who have no time to attend to their caprices; and that they should learn, at a very early age, that they will get nothing by being capricious, troublesome, and tale-bearing. I have seen a mother worn out by two or three teazing children, each bent on having its own way, to the annoyance of the rest; and I have thought, "What would she do, if there were eight or ten of them? it would be enough to drive her distracted!" And then it has occurred to me that, perhaps, larger families are more harmonious in after-life, because in childhood they have almost necessarily been more accustomed to greater degrees of mutual forbearance and self-denial. The subject, at all events, is highly important, and may suggest some useful hints both to parents and children.

Jealousies among children are often excited in the most foolish manner possible. In two families, nearly related, a second child was born about the same time. To the eldest child, in one family, a silly nurse was allowed to say, "Here, Master Alfred, here's a baby come; your nose will be put out of joint. Mamma must nurse the baby now." A spirit of rivalry was thus immediately excited. The little hero of two years old felt himself called on to vindicate his rights, and frequently attempted to pinch, or strike the babe, or to drag it from his mother's lap. It was in vain *then* to say,

"Pretty baby! you must not hurt the baby!" or even to advance to the threat, "If you hurt the baby, you shall certainly be whipped." The mind of the child had already sustained an irreparable injury. As the children became playfellows, jealousy, oppression, and resentment, marked their intercourse; and the parents were perpetually called upon to take part with one against the other in their childish brawls. In the course of a few years, the constitution of the elder child was considerably affected by a succession of the ordinary diseases of childhood; the younger child passed through them much more favorably; and henceforward, notwithstanding the disparity of age and sex, the balance of strength was on her side. Many a sturdy battle was now fought between the little champions, and many a sly and spiteful trick was performed, when opportunity offered, on the brother's kite, or on the sister's doll. Separation at school was a temporary cessation of hostilities, rather than an interruption of affectionate intercourse; and the holydays, instead of affording a welcome renewal of cheerful tenderness in a united family at home, were distinguished by ingenious contrivances of the young people to vex and torment each other. A present from the parents, or any mark of attention or indulgence, was invariably perverted into a subject of jealousy and contention. Every benefit conferred on one child was regarded as an injury inflicted on the other; and the parents, instead of being gratified by promoting the happiness of their children, were mortified by hearing perpetual altercations as to the comparative value of Alfred's case of mathematical instruments and Louisa's drawing box, Alfred's watch and Louisa's necklace.

In course of time the parents died; and the contentions which had hitherto been employed on trinkets and trifles were transferred to legacies and possessions. Though an ample sufficiency was left for both, each party seemed determined to contend for every trifle with the other. Several boisterous meetings occurred, and several angry letters passed, full of invective, reproach, and recrimination; and then several hundred pounds, perhaps thousands, were wasted on each side on lawsuits, at the close of which each party sat down, not to enjoy, but to hold the wreck of their property,—just as two quarrelsome dogs, after fighting for that which they might as well have shared amicably, each guards his respective bone, and growls envy and spite at the other.

Alfred and Louisa have lived several years in the same town without speaking to each other. The children of one family are not allowed to take the same walks, or to frequent the same school, as those of the other; the same tradesmen must not be employed, nor the same society frequented, by both families; and whoever may desire the friendship or countenance of the one, must obtain it at the expense of the enmity and persecution of the other.

It is pleasing to turn to the other family alluded to; in which the first and second children were of the same ages as Alfred and Louisa. The introduction of little Henry to his infant sister was managed so as from the first to excite benevolent feelings towards the little stranger. "See, my dear little Henry," said the father, "here is a sweet, lovely babe, which the Lord has graciously given to us. Look at its little hands and feet; how pretty and how soft! But it is tender and helpless: it cannot do any thing for itself. We must beg dear mamma to be so kind as to feed it, and nurse it, and take care of it for us, as she did of Henry; and then we hope it will grow strong, and be able to run about, and speak."

Thus the elder child, instead of being taught to regard the babe as an intruder, received it as a delightful acquisition, and as one in whose protection, welfare, and improvement, he was to cherish a lively interest. The effect was immediately visible. He would frequently run to his mother, and say, "The 'tender babe' cries; pray take it up and feed it;" or to the servants, "Pray don't make a noise; the 'tender babe' is asleep." Whatever was given him, he was sure to inquire whether the 'tender babe' might have part of it; and rapturous and benevolent was his delight when the babe began to caper and crow at the sound of his drum or whistle. For an hour together, he would amuse the little one on the carpet, and, by degrees, entice it to crawl, and then to run after his ball, at the same time carefully pushing aside whatever might injure it.

The kindly feeling was reciprocal. The earliest associations of the infant girl connected the idea of her brother with those of protection and pleasure. Illness, when it occurred, proved a new occasion of tenderness and sympathy; and restoration to health, of new cheerfulness and enjoyment. As childhood advanced, the indications of abiding affection continued to develope themselves. It was from Henry that the little Ellen first learned the form, sound, and use of letters. It was the hope of being able to make Henry's shirts that stimulated the little sempstress to acquire the use of the needle. The value of a parent's present was enhanced, as affording not solitary but mutual gratification; and the earliest appropriation of pocket-money was to purchase a little present from one child to the other.

Separation, for the objects of education and business, was felt as a real trial; yet soothed by frequent and affectionate interchange of letters, and by the delightful anticipation of meeting again. The vacations were indeed seasons of parental, filial, and fraternal delight and mutual improvement; and this lovely family often drew forth from observers the exclamation,—" Behold how good and how pleasant it is for brethren to dwell together in unity!"

In early life, Henry and Ellen became, through divine grace, genuine possessors of that religion, the principles of which had been carefully instilled into their infant minds by their pious and affectionate parents. Thus their intercourse assumed a still more sacred character; they became helpers of each other's faith, hope, and steadfastness. Nor have the subsequent vicissitudes of life in any degree weakened the delightful bond of union, so early and so successfully twined. No jealousies, no jarring interests, have interrupted the delightful harmony, but each fully participates in the happiness of the other; and, in time of affliction, each is secure of receiving from the other the tenderest sympathy and most cheerful aid.

In closing this sketch, it may be well to drop a few hints, tending to promote and secure family harmony through life. Let the sentiment be inwrought in the minds of children, that the interest and happiness of each is identified with the interest and happiness of all. As much as possible, preserve children from entertaining an idea of *selfish gratification*.

Jealousy is oftener excited than prevented, by the scrupulous care of some parents to give every child exactly alike. Let the same affection be cherished towards all, and the same principles regulate the general conduct towards all; and then occasional varieties in the detail may be rather advantageous than injurious. The minds of the children, being settled on the great points of the parent's affection and wisdom, will not be easily shaken by any trifling variations that circumstances may dictate.

Early justice should be steadily maintained and enforced. If a child has any little possession of his own, his property ought to be respected, and not alienated by the parents, or infringed on by the other children. A child should never be *compelled* to give up his toy, or to share his cake, because another child wishes for it. At the same time, early kindness should be inculcated and encouraged. In a well-regulated family, this will be done so insensibly, and at so early a period, that a child shall never remember a time when he *could* have eaten his morsel alone; having always experienced the highest pleasure of possessing any thing to result from being able to share and impart gratification to those most dear.

Mutual confidence among the members of a family should be promoted by the parents, and encouraged among the children. It is most natural, that a child should tell his little troubles at his own home; and there, rather than elsewhere, seek sympathy, counsel, and assistance. There is no friendship so safe and so delightful as that which is grafted upon natural affection. This will prepare also for that most pleasant, and yet most rare attainment, free religious intercourse among the nearest and dearest connections; and piety will ever prove the sweetest and most delightful cement and sanctifier of friendship and affection.

It may be urged upon young persons to strive together for the comfort of the parents. This common object, kept constantly in view, and diligently sought by all, will delightfully endear them to each other. They should be guarded against jealousy of parental assistance, either during the period of education, at first setting out in life, or in any subsequent season of trial; also against a selfish, encroaching spirit, which would seek to engross as much advantage as possible. It cannot be too often repeated, that selfishness is the bane of affection and happiness.

Let them guard also against coolness, through long separation. There is danger of affectionate concern, about the absent branches of a family, gradually becoming less and less vivid, until at last it sinks almost into indifference. It is therefore highly desirable that frequent intercourse should be kept up, and, if possible, little tokens of affection exchanged. A little book, presented as a memorial of affection from an absent brother or sister, has often been made a blessing in more senses than one, as keeping alive affectionate recollections during absence, and as winning the attention to truths of everlasting moment.

It will be found necessary to guard against alienation, from the formation of new connections. There have been instances in which, when entire dependence for domestic comforts has been severed from the parental home, a painful indifference has been manifested towards the earliest relations in life. There have been instances, too, in which the influence of a married partner has operated to the disparagement of former connections, and produced alienation bordering on enmity. These, perhaps, are extreme cases; but it will be found desirable to guard against the most distant approach to so unhappy a state of things. For this end, in forming new connections, it is of no small importance to select such as are likely to blend harmoniously with those already in existence;

and then, by mutual good offices, to keep alive the friendly and affectionate feeling.

In some families it may be necessary to guard against jealousies, on account of being in the same line of business. Here, again, we must come to the old remedy, Christian integrity and benevolence. Let every man look not on his own things exclusively, but also, with feelings of good-will and kindness, to the things of others, especially those so near and dear. And, finally, that brotherly love may continue, not only through time but through eternity, let it be impelled, and regulated, and sanctified by religion; let brethren and sisters be allied, not only by the ties of nature, but by the more sacred and indissoluble bonds of Christian union; let each be sharers of each other's pious cares, and sorrows, and joys, and all anticipate the day when, through divine grace, they hope to meet "a family unbroken in the skies."

CHAP. LX.

DECISION IN RELIGION.

THERE are many persons who seem well inclined towards religion, but who linger at the threshold, and cannot quite make up their minds to renounce the world, and to take up with the "one thing needful."

They frequent the house of God, and seem to listen with devout attention and interest; but *now and then* their place is empty. On some *particular occasion* they receive a Sunday party, or go on a Sunday excursion; they do one thing which their conscience disapproves to oblige a good customer, and another rather than give offence to a rich relation, and another in compliance with the urgent request of some gay companion. This is a truly miserable and dangerous state, in which to be found. Such people have just enough religion to embitter the pleasures of sin, but not enough to strengthen and cheer them in abandoning those pleasures—enough to make life restless and apprehensive, but not enough to render death safe and easy. "How long halt ye between two opinions?" If religion is any thing, it is every thing. Either settle in your own mind that you have something more valuable than religion, or else resolve to part with whatever is necessary to secure the possession of that pearl of great price. Either satisfy yourself that you can be safe and happy without yielding to the restraints of religion, or else go into it with all your heart. Turn your back upon the world, and go determinately and steadily on in the ways of religion; then, and then only, will you find them to be ways of pleasantness and paths of peace.

Without decision of character in religion, there can be neither stability nor security. How many pleasing, hopeful, promising, well-inclined young persons, have been altogether drawn aside from the ways of religion into the paths of sin, for want of *making up their minds* on the right side of the question! A hesitating, lingering character, is sure to be marked by the seducer and destroyer of men, and is almost sure to become his prey. He who is *almost* persuaded to be a Christian, is in the greatest danger of perishing for want of being *altogether* so. In the time of Noah, we may conclude that many lingered near the ark, and looked at it, and resolved to ask admission into it; but while they hesitated, the door was shut, and the flood came and destroyed them all.

Those who would secure the advantages of religion, and partake its solid enjoyments, must enter into it with all their heart and soul; then every duty will be easy, and every sacrifice light. There will be real peace and satisfaction of mind, in a conscious possession of that which is worth all the world, and which the world can neither give nor take away.

CHAP. LXI.

CONSISTENCY WITH RELIGIOUS PROFESSION.

"WHAT do ye more than others?" is a question which both the church and the world will feel themselves at liberty, often, to propose to every one, who makes a profession of religion; and it is a question which every professor ought frequently and impartially to propose to himself.

He who professes religion, says, that he acts upon higher principles, and is impelled by nobler motives, and sustained by higher strength, and cheered by sweeter enjoyments, and animated by brighter prospects, than persons in general. Then, surely, it is to be expected that his conduct should be more blameless, upright, and exemplary than those who make no such profession.

Well do I remember the endeavors of some of my friends to awaken the young to a serious concern about their souls' best interests; and well also do I recollect, when such interest was excited, when any began to take delight in reading the scriptures, in attending public worship, and in engaging in Sunday-school teaching or missionary collecting, how they used to urge upon them the necessity of consistency and circumspection in all their deportment.

To some young ones, brought to an acquaintance with religion, of which their parents, as yet, remained ignorant, they would say, "Now, if your parents won't read Christianity in the Bible, nor hear it from the pulpit, they must see it in your life and conduct. There must be a marked difference in your behavior now, from what it was before you professed religion. You are not accused of being disobedient, unkind, or ill-behaved; but there must now be a refinement, a delicacy, a tenderness in your obedience, worthy of those who do it as unto the Lord, and not unto men. Your conduct must be such as to constrain those around you to say, 'It is not whim, or perverseness, or mere outside show, that makes them forsake the company and the ways of the world, and choose those of religion,—no; they certainly are *sincere* in what they profess; and surely it cannot be a bad religion that makes them so much better than they used to be before they professed it.' "

One of our poor neighbors, a sharp-tempered woman, who led her husband a weary life, and violently used her poor children, in a long illness, received great attention from our kind friends. There instructions were blessed in awakening her concern and softening her heart. As she recovered from her illness, great was their anxiety that her future conduct might be such as to adorn religion. They spoke to her in this manner:—" Well, Martha, we hope you begin to love prayer, and find the sweetness of communion with God. It will be your desire in future to devote time to the exercises of religion; but, remember, this time must be *redeemed* by industry, good management, and self-denial, not *robbed* from your duties to your family. Your husband must find his home more cleanly and comfortable than ever, his wishes and comforts more promptly and kindly attended to, his children kept in better order. Be sure you never forget to pray for the ornament of a meek and quiet spirit: there is nothing that more adorns religion in the eyes of those who have not embraced it. There must be no more bitter words with your husband; no more violence with your children. If your husband is vexatious, or unreasonable, or unkind, you must always have ready a soft answer, which turns away wrath. With your children, you must be at once firm and mild, and then they will mind you ten times more than when you beat or scolded them. It is thus that, by your good conversation, you will recommend the religion you profess. Your temper will be often rising, and you will have hard work to keep it down; but if you constantly seek strength from God, his strength will be made perfect in your weakness; and the power of religion will be displayed in the conquest, it enables you to maintain over your easily besetting sin."

To one of my brothers, then an apprentice, who had recently indulged the hope that he was reconciled to God, a pious friend said, "Now, young man, you profess to be a partaker of the grace of God, which bringeth salvation; and it must teach you not only to deny ungodliness, but also worldly lusts, and to live soberly, righteously, and godly in the present world. Young men under its influence must learn to be sober-minded. I hope you will no longer have an inclination for the society or the pleasures of those who fear not God. I hope and believe that the light song, the public-house jest, the impure word or action, would be odious in your esteem: but this is not all; you must be more than ever diligent and devoted to your master's interests,—no eye-servant, but one who acts as if the master were always present. There must be no pert, sullen, or grudging answer, but with good-will you must do service as unto the Lord."

There was a very industrious, saving couple, who lived in a cottage belonging to Farmer West. They were religious people, very constant in attending on the means of grace, and brought up their children in a sober, orderly manner. It need hardly be said, that they were reputed very honest people,—for there cannot be a religious person who is not honest,—but there was a sort of self-love and covetousness indulged, which, though it might not be exactly called dishonesty, yet went far enough to sully the brightness of their religious profession, and gave occasion to their master and fellow-servants to remark that, "religious people generally take pretty good care of themselves." Such sneers ought not to be brought against religion: if they are false, great is the guilt of those who utter them: but if religious people, in any degree, give occasion for them, they are guilty, in a degree, of religious inconsistency; for they profess to be governed not only by the first great commandment, but by the second, which is like unto it, "Thou shalt love thy neighbor as thyself," and "Whatsoever ye would that men should do unto you, do ye even so unto them."

To the cottage inhabited by these people there was a large garden attached, half of which they cultivated for their master, and half for themselves. They had also the care of the poultry for their master, and kept poultry of their own. Now, it was observed that the fattest chickens and the largest eggs were carried to market on their own account, and the smallest sent for the use of their master's family; and that the finest cabbage, broccoli, and onions, were on their side of the garden. There was not *much* difference in the general appearance of the garden, but enough to convince a keen observer, that there was *rather* more labor bestowed on one half than the other, that the ground was *rather* better manured, and that the best of the plants and flowers found their way to that side. Now, who could say this was direct dishonesty? and yet, who could help feeling that it was *selfishness*, very unworthy of the professors of religion?

Then, again, the man in question was paid by his master regular day-wages. It is not said that he did not go to work *pretty nearly* at the appointed time; but then he had first been laboring two or three hours for himself; and every allotted hour of refreshment he was again toiling away at his own concerns; and surely industry and early rising are highly commendable; yet even these may be carried so far as to involve a species of dishonesty. If a man's time is paid for, he is bound not merely to spend the stipulated hours on his master's ground, but to allow himself sufficient repose to bring his full vigor to the task; and, unless employed and paid at task-work, it can hardly be reckoned just that he should spend the best part of his strength on his own business, and go to his master's work half wearied and exhausted.

What little things mark the character! and what improper views are formed of religion, under the impression that it sanctions all the conduct of its professors! Another laborer of Farmer West's made no profession of religion; yet there was more frankness, strict integrity, and cheerful good-will in his services: and it is greatly to be feared that the farmer was hardened in his indifference to religion, and almost led to conclude that a man is better without it than with it, by observing in the professor of religion, those little meannesses, of which an honest, generous man, who made no such profession, would have been utterly ashamed. Another fact, which led him to this false and dangerous conclusion, was, the detection of his dairy-maid in regularly handing out cream at the dairy window for the washerwoman's tea, without her mistress's knowledge. The girl who was guilty of this, and several other sly, dishonest tricks, made a great pretence of being religious, and was very clamorous for liberty to enjoy her religious privileges, even to a degree incompatible with the discharge of her ordinary duties. "Well," said the farmer, "I am sick to death of religious servants; and, if I can have my will, there shall never come another into my service." In consequence of this prejudice, several deserving persons were kept out of the farmer's employ, solely because they were known to be religious: and what is still worse, the honest farmer and his honest man flattered themselves that they should do exceedingly well without religion, and went on in the self-satisfying delusion to the end of their days.

Very different was the effect produced by the conduct of a truly consistent apprentice. This youth was awakened to deep concern about the interests of his immortal soul; and a striking change was manifested in his general conduct. His parents regarded this change as a heavy calamity, fully expecting that, by thus taking to serious religion, their son would be unfitted for common duties, and would neglect his worldly interests. In the hope of preventing these evils, they determined to remove him from the society and connections which had thus (in their esteem) ruined him, and to place him apprentice in another town. The lad willingly complied with the wishes of his parents, and declared his readiness to obey his master and mistress, and to serve their interests to the utmost of his power; but that he must stipulate for liberty to serve God according to the dictates of his conscience on the Sabbath. His parents, thinking that opposition in this particular might defeat the whole scheme, begged that for the present he might be indulged; observing, that when once the indentures were signed, the master might oppose his folly, if he were not wholly cured of it. "Nay," said the master, "if he minds my business, I shall not interfere with his religion, provided he does not bring it home to turn the heads of my family."

At this time, the master and mistress, and their family, lived in total ignorance of God, and neglect of his worship. They had some confused idea that it was a very bad thing to have too much religion; and as this was alleged to be the failing of their new apprentice, they expected to find him proud, morose, and insolent. Nothing, however, could be farther from the truth: a more diligent, faithful, civil, obliging lad they had never seen, and withal so cheerful and contented, that it was a pleasure to do any thing for him, or to have any thing done by him. The master and mistress, notwithstanding their prejudices, could not help approving and loving him; and the little children, too young to share the prejudice, clung fondly round his knee, or climbed his chair in the evening, to hear a pretty story or to enjoy a merry jump.

At the time appointed, his father came over to bind him, if approved. All parties expressed themselves satisfied and willing.

"And how is it," asked the father, "about his religion?"

"O," replied the master and mistress, "we have not seen any thing at all of that. He is always minding his business, and always cheerful and happy." True enough, they had not seen his religion, which, like the roots of a tree, lay hid in his heart; and it had not yet occurred to them that all this good conduct, and cheerful, pleasant temper, were the natural results of it, just as much as the leaves, and blossoms, and fruits of the tree.

Several months elapsed. The youth continued steady, faithful, and diligent in business; but, at the same time, fervent in spirit, serving the Lord. He never neglected his duty to his master; but he delighted to redeem time for the service of his God; and on the Sabbath, especially, it was observed that no proposal of pleasure could seduce him from the house of his God, or the sacred retirement of his chamber.

At length the mistress said to her husband, "Well, I cannot imagine what there is so much amiss in John's religion. I am determined some day to go and hear for myself." She did accordingly. She was impressed with the solemnity of the worship, and the sacred truths she heard enforced; and she went again and again, first taking one child with her and then another: and all seemed pleasingly surprised at what was so new to them. At length she ventured to propose to her husband to have a cold dinner on the Sundays, that she might be enabled to attend public worship in the morning. This proposal aroused his suspicion and anger.

"No," said he; "I work hard all the week; it is hard indeed if I can't enjoy myself on a Sunday. If this is what your religion comes to, I will soon put a stop to it." He declared she should attend public worship no more; but was at last won over by the gentle persuasion of his wife and his apprentice, first to go once—just once—and hear for himself. He went, and from that time, so far from attempting to hinder others, he became himself a constant attendant in the house of prayer,—a diligent inquirer after salvation. The aspect of the whole family became changed. Family worship was established; family order maintained; children trained up in the way they should go; and servants instructed to keep the commands of the Lord: and all these blessed effects might be traced, under God, to the steady, unobtrusive, consistent piety of an apprentice boy, who adorned the doctrine of God his Saviour in all things Nor was he left without hope that his prayers were heard, and his endeavors succeeded on behalf of those still nearer and dearer to himself. The opposition of his parents was in time subdued. They often took sweet counsel with the child they had so bitterly censured, and walked to the house of God in company, entertaining the delightful hope of a happy meeting at last in the house eternal in the heavens.

Let all who profess piety be thus humble, consistent, modest, uniform, and exemplary. Let their religion be rather seen and felt than heard. If heard, let it rather be in the gentle expostulation of love, than in angry reproach and clamorous disputation. True religion will regulate the whole deportment and temper; it will teach its subjects to walk in wisdom and in kindness; and it will lodge a testimony in the bosoms of observers, that there is such a thing as true religion; that it is a blessed thing; and that those they observe really possess it. Thus will they be constrained, by your good works which they behold, to glorify your Father which is in heaven.

CHAP. LXII.

ADVICE FOR CHILDREN.

I HAVE many things which I wish to say to children. Some things, perhaps, will amuse them; and I hope they will feel interested in what I write. But, more than all, I hope they will remember and profit by what may be related; for it is for their improvement and good that I write.

In these days almost all children have the opportunity to attend Sabbath schools, and some of the richest religious privileges, which they enjoy, come through this institution. Children, however, we fear, do not sufficiently feel their responsibility for these privileges.

I recently met, somewhere, with the following description of the members of a class, written by their teacher. My young readers may perhaps learn a useful lesson by perusing it.

"A. has been with me nearly three years. In that time she has been absent only twice, morning and afternoon. I cannot speak decidedly as to her piety; but there is a love to the school shown by her that is highly gratifying; while diligence in learning, readiness in answering questions, attention to her teacher, and respectful behavior, mark her character. A. does not stay till the clock *has* struck, but is generally seated, with a smiling face, before her teacher's arrival. You will perhaps say she is a favorite; true, but then I have several.

B., sister of the above, but younger, strives to imitate her sister in regularity and punctuality, but is not her equal in ability. There is great difficulty in drawing an answer from her; and sometimes there is an appearance of something like sullenness. She has more trouble in getting her task than the others; but no excuses are made, and the timid little girl, with a pale cheek, who is occupied all the week in nursing an infant, stands up to repeat her lessons with her more gifted sister.

C. has been several years in the school; and she once occasioned her teacher much pain by her trifling conduct; but there is a marked change in her behavior, and the blush that overspreads her face, and the tears which glisten in her eyes, if she is reproved, argue a degree of feeling that is quite encouraging. Her parents are extremely poor, and, though young, she has to work for her bread; but the delight shown in her countenance when she enters the school, after being absent but once, is very pleasing. She is quick in understanding, and often surprises me by the correctness of her answers. I do hope this school will prove a blessing to this little girl.

D. is a little giddy gossip, whom I have much difficulty in restraining; but when I see her sparkling eyes, after her long walk, and as early as any, I confess I am pleased. She is very shrewd, and has little difficulty in learning correctly. As far as I can judge, this child has very few advantages at home: her parents are continually changing their residence, seldom remaining a month in one place.

E. is the only child of her mother, who is a widow. She is a very interesting little girl, of gentle, pleasing manners, and an intelligent countenance; she takes great pleasure in reading the books from the library, which are also read by the mother. I trust the *one thing* which is wanting, will be supplied by Him from whom all good things proceed; and that will be a sure preservative against what I grieve to witness—the unwise fondness of the mother, displayed in the fine dress of the child.

F. has the misfortune to possess parents, who, with a large family, care little for their children's real welfare. Destitute of religion, and lovers of pleasure themselves, their children are greatly to be pitied; and while F.'s behavior at school leads me to trust that her attendance will be useful to her, I cannot but hope that the books obtained from the library, which are read at home, may have a beneficial tendency on the family, as well as on her.

G. is a girl of considerable ability; but conscious of this, she displays a degree of conceit painful to witness. She possesses advantages over the others in point of circumstances, and I often observe her contrasting her own dress with the plainer clothes of the others. My ardent prayer for her is, that she may be clothed with humility, and have the ornament of a meek and quiet spirit.

H. is quite a contrast to the last. She has been with me but a short time, but bids fair to be my best scholar—early in attendance, diligent in learning, neat and becoming in her dress, respectful in her behavior, humble and teachable in disposition. I hope for solid, lasting fruit from such hopeful appearances.

But the flower of my class is K. Young in years, her manners and appearances would proclaim her much older than she is. Her modest, unassuming conduct, her willingness to learn, her meek and quiet spirit, render her quite a pattern. I trust there is indeed some good thing in K., though her reserve has not permitted her to communicate her thoughts and feelings on religious subjects at present.

Little L., the youngest in the class, and sister of the above, displays abilities far before her years. This little girl loves her teacher, and I am sure you would be as pleased as I am, to see her eyes glisten with delight when she enters her class. I am afraid I love this child too well; but I believe I do not show it to the others. K. and L. possess pious parents; and this in some measure accounts for their superiority.

And now, having faintly sketched the character of my youthful charge, I confess the feeling of responsibility presses heavily upon me, and the inquiry escapes, "Who is sufficient for these things?" When I reflect on the fact so forcibly stated by Mr. James in the "Teacher's Guide," that "Every child who passes the threshold of our school on a Sunday, brings to our care, and confides to our ability, a *soul*, compared with whose worth and duration the sun is a bawble, and time itself but as the twinkling of an eye;" I deeply feel the solemn engagement of a teacher. When I remember that the character of these young ones is now forming, I pray earnestly, that He who loves little children may be their guide and friend forever, and that he would make me "apt to teach."

Children should be diligent and attentive in all their studies, as well as in those of the Sabbath school. In fact, success in any pursuit depends far more upon the habits of attention and perseverance that are formed, than upon genius or any extraordinary endowments of nature.

A friend of mine has a little girl, whom I shall call Maria, whose character well illustrates what I mean. She is a persevering child: by this I mean, that she is not soon frightened with difficulties; that she endeavors to overcome all obstacles, and to give satisfaction to her friends. Maria has not very great abilities, and is not naturally so quick and sharp as many of her companions; but she has a strong desire to improve, and this carries her above them all. When she finds her lessons hard, she is so much the more desirous of mastering them and of giving greater diligence. She is not only persevering in lessons, but in all that she undertakes. She is a poor girl; and if her mother tells her to scrub and clean any thing, she *will* make it look well, or she is not satisfied. If she sits down to needle-work, that must be done well also, or she does not feel pleased. Her motto always seems to be, "Persevere;" and you know there is an old saying, "Patience and perseverance will accomplish all things."

Thus I have drawn Maria's character; and so far as it is praiseworthy and suited to us, I hope we shall follow it. But there is such a thing, you know, as perseverance in evil and iniquity. I need not tell you that I do not recommend this. Persevere in all that is right; but we should set our faces as a flint against sin. We have some lovely examples of perseverance in the Holy Scriptures, and those scriptures contain many exhortations to this duty. Christ Jesus has said that "men ought always to pray, and not to faint;" with respect to increasing in knowledge, we are told, "get wisdom, get understanding, forget it not," and we are commanded to "press toward the mark for the prize of our high calling;" and sure I am, my dear little reader, that you will never be a clever child, or a good child, or a kind child, or, what is far above all, a *pious* child, unless you are persevering. You must not give up as soon as any thing goes wrong; you must try all the harder for that; for, believe me, you will never get any more forward by sitting down and crying over your trouble. But, above all, suffer me to entreat you to persevere in the path of holiness. You are young, and exposed to Satan's temptations: "he goeth about as a roaring lion, seeking whom he may devour." Be earnest in praying for God's strength; and may the Redeemer bless your soul, give you ability for your proper employments, preserve you from all evil, and lead you at last to a happy home above.

I am always pleased when I see children careful of their little property; especially I like to see them keep their own little books neat and clean; yet I am persuaded many do not understand what it is to take proper care of their Bibles, and other good books, such as hymn-books or prayer-books. A lady had lent some linen to a laborer's wife when her youngest child was born, and in the box was a Bible for her use while she was confined to the house. When the lady called to see the poor woman, she remarked to her, "I am glad to see you getting so well, and it pleases me to see you reading the Bible." "Why, ma'am," said she, "I was very glad to find it among your things; I have read in it a great deal, and must try to buy myself one, for I have not one of my own."—"The Bible always goes with the box," said the lady, "and therefore it was sent to you; otherwise, I should have thought it unnecessary; and I am surprised to hear you say you have no Bible. I thought you had received several at the church." "O yes, ma'am, and so we have; my three boys have each obtained one for saying their catechism well; but then they belong to the children, and they will not allow any one to *read* in them. They keep them locked up in their own boxes."

"When they go out to service, or in any way to live from home," said the lady, "it will be quite right that each boy should have his own Bible with him."—"To be sure," said the woman, "it is a good thing to have it in a house."—"It is indeed," replied her visitor; "but only good when used. Bread is a good thing when used; but what good would it do you to lock the loaf in your cupboard, and never suffer it to be cut or tasted?"—"Not much, to be sure," replied the laborer's wife.—"None at all," said the lady; "you might be starved with bread in your house: so a Bible must not be looked upon as a charm that every body ought to possess in the house. It should be our constant support, like daily bread; and though you should not deprive your children of their own books, given them as rewards for diligence in learning, yet, till you have one of your own, I think you ought to read theirs, which you may do without injuring them."

She has now a large one of her own, with very clear print, for which she subscribed to the Bible society.

Now, do any children who read this possess a Bible, whose parents are destitute of one? and do they, like these boys, lock them up from their relatives? I hope they will see their mistake, and help to get one for their parents by subscribing, or some other way; and till they have one of their own, lend them theirs, if they can read, or read it to them if they cannot. They worked hard to get you bread; and where would you have been if they had locked it up from you before you were old enough to labor? Some children do help their parents in many ways. Now, consider, I pray you, how you can help yours: it is God's command you should do so.

I have something to say upon a subject which *you*, perhaps, may think of very little consequence; but which I think a very important one—it is that of dress. I have often been much grieved to see many children at church and Sabbath schools dressed in a very improper and unbecoming manner; that is, with very gay gowns and ribands, and a great deal of trimming on their bonnets. Now, I dare say, those little girls who wear such things are quite proud and delighted to be dressed so much like fine ladies, and fancy that all the teachers and scholars, and every body, will think them more worthy of notice than children who are more plain and neat, or even badly clothed. How much surprised and mortified they would be, if they could hear the remarks upon them, and see how much they are ridiculed for that very dress they are so fond of, and how much *less* they are really thought of by every sensible person! I have often heard ladies remark, "What a pity it is that little girl is dressed so! Poor thing, she would be quite a nice-looking girl if she were dressed in a plain, neat, colored frock, and without all that trimming on her bonnet; but now she looks quite awkward."

My dear children, you know the Bible tells us to be "clothed with humility:" now, though this text is generally very properly understood to mean that we are to be humble in mind and heart, yet I think it may also mean, that we are to be dressed according to our station in life; for it would be equally improper for a young person, whose parents are fully able to afford it, to be dressed like a poor person's child, as it is for them to attempt to appear like young ladies; for according as God has placed us in this life, so ought we to appear; if servants, let us be servants; if masters, as masters; for both are admonished and directed in the Bible, and should be faithful in their appropriate duties. Now, you know, on the Sabbath day, we ought to try and forget the world as much as possible, because God has set apart this day for his worship, and to prepare us for a future state after death, and has given us the means of learning our duty towards him, and the way to heaven, on this day, by attending at school, and going to his house. Now, let me ask those children who are always so much smarter on that day than any other, if they are not generally thinking more about their fine clothes than any thing else. I can always see that they are, for we can judge of people's thoughts by their actions; and when I see girls taking up their *white* frocks for fear the bench should soil them, tying and untying their bonnets, putting their sashes in order, and every now and then taking their eyes from their books, to look at their fine clothes, I am quite sure they must be thinking about their dress, rather than what their teacher or minister is saying. And do you not know, my dear children, that God will bring us to account for every opportunity of worshipping Him, and learning our duty, which we have neglected? And while you are thus thinking of your dress, how can you worship God, and learn your duty?

Now, how different it is with an attentive girl who is dressed becomingly; she has not this temptation to be inattentive; and I generally find that those who are neatly and plainly dressed are the best scholars. But do not mistake me; I dislike a slovenly dress, as much as a fine one; I like always to see you in clean frocks, and hands and face, on the Sabbath, for it is more a disgrace to be dirty or untidy on this day more especially than any other, though it is a disgrace on any day. Perhaps some of you will say, "I cannot help wearing my fine frocks, because my father and mother buy them, and bid me put them on. I know that this is the case; but when they do, it is very often in order to please you; but if they saw you unwilling to wear them, and you were always better pleased with neat, plain clothes, I am sure they would never go to the expense (for it is a great one) of finer ones; therefore you have it greatly in your power to prevent it.

Should any parents read this, I would advise them, as they regard the welfare of their children, to keep them from the love of fine clothes. This has been the first step to the ruin of many a poor girl, and the pride of human nature should be checked, not encouraged. But while you guard against the *outward* appearance of vanity and pride, remember that the heart must be changed by divine grace, or it will never be truly humble. Let all, then, both parents and children, pray, "Create in me a clean heart, O God, and renew a right spirit within me." Such a heart will always be humble, and the outward appearance will agree with it.

Mary Merton was one of the prettiest little girls that ever was seen; her eyes were blue and bright; her lips and cheeks were red as a ripe cherry; and oh! if you had seen her flaxen hair hang around her neck and forehead!

She sometimes dressed more showy than a Sunday school girl ought to dress; for neatness and cleanliness are much more creditable than fine clothes; but her mother used to indulge her in many things.

Strange it is that we should pride ourselves in adorning this sinful body, which will so soon moulder in the grave; and neglect the soul, which Jesus Christ died to save, and which must live forever!

This Mary Merton went to the same Sunday school that Sally Gardner attended; and many a time have I seen them trotting along the green fields with a little bag of books in their hands, to be in time for the opening of the school.

Sally Gardner was very different in body and in mind from Mary Merton. She was rather short, of a pale complexion, and her hair did not curl at all: in short, I never heard any one say that Sally was pretty.

There is no gift useless that God has given; and fine eyes, and fair faces, and beautiful hair, are gifts not to be despised, when united to an humble heart, and a spirit that feareth God; but when possessed by the vain and proud, and those who scoff at God's holy word and commandments, they become sad snares. Though beauty is not given by God in vain, nothing can be more foolish than to value ourselves for possessing it; because it is a thing that may in a moment be destroyed, and never can be expected to last long.

> E'en as the frost, in hapless hour,
> Will nip and blast the freshest flower,
> So grief and pain will soon displace
> The roses from the fairest face.

Oftentimes did the squire's lady observe Mary Merton and Sarah Gardner, as they returned from the Sunday school; and as often did she exclaim, looking at Mary Merton, "What a *lovely girl!*" But the squire's lady knew nothing of the dispositions and conduct of the two girls.

Now, it happened that one of the maid-servants at the squire's house became ill and unable to work; and the squire's lady sent to the Sunday school to know whether the little girl with the flaxen hair would come to her house until her servant was better.

The mother of Mary Merton was glad to hear that such notice had been taken of her daughter; so little Mary prepared to go to the great house in the park. Had Lady Rose known the temper of Mary Merton, she never would have chosen her to be in her house. Whether it was that Mary had been praised for her beauty, or whether her mother indulged her too much, I cannot say; but surely there never was a more proud, passionate, obstinate, and idle girl. There was no girl in the school half so untractable; and had it not been for Sarah Gardner's kindness in getting her to school, and in persuading her to amend her conduct, she never could have remained so long at the Sunday school. Sarah Gardner, though not pretty, was just what a Sunday school girl should be. Whether at home, or at her class, she was always diligent, respectful to her superiors, and kind to her equals. She loved her teachers, and her young heart was devoted to Christ. She was not very wise, but she had been taught that the first step towards wisdom is "the fear of the Lord." She did not know a great deal, but she knew that she was a sinner, and that "Jesus Christ came into the world to save sinners." The advantages of pious parents, kind teachers, and a godly minister, had been blessed to her; so that in very deed her soul "magnified the Lord," and her "spirit rejoiced in God her Saviour."

When Sarah knew that Mary was going to Squire Rose's, she gave her very good advice, and earnestly besought her to pray to God, for Jesus Christ's sake, to control her passions, and to enable her to be a faithful servant; but Mary paid very little attention to the advice of her friend.

Though Lady Rose was delighted when Mary Merton made her appearance at the hall, dressed in her best gown, with her fine flaxen hair curling around her brow, yet it was not the same with the servants of the house; for they saw that Mary prided herself upon her beauty, and were determined to mortify her as much as possible. "What a *lovely girl!*" said Lady Rose, as Mary walked from the parlor where they had been talking together. Mary heard the words, and was silly enough to hold up her head higher than before: this was immediately noticed by the servants.

The troubles of poor Mary now came thick upon her: it was a part of her duty to wait on the sick servant; but this she did so carelessly, and showed so many airs, and flew into such passions, that complaints were made of her continually: every fault she committed was made the most of; for she found no friend, neither, indeed, did she deserve one.

Lady Rose found, at last, that though Mary was a *lovely girl* in her looks, she was lovely in nothing else; and as she had something to do besides admiring her, so Mary Merton was sent home in disgrace, and application made at the school for a girl who was more likely to suit the situation. Sarah Gardner was sent directly; and though Lady Rose did not call her a *lovely girl*, she soon found the difference between a pretty, vain, passionate, idle girl, and one who was humble, meek and diligent, though with a plain set of features.

THE FAMILY AT HOME.

I dare say, that you have often remarked, however pretty a face may be, that, if there be a bad temper in the heart, the face has been far from pleasing; while, on the contrary, a good temper, a cheerful spirit, and a contented, grateful heart, have made a plain face very agreeable.

While Sarah Gardner was gaining the good opinion of all around her, Mary Merton was visited with affliction. She was taken ill with the small-pox, and her face was covered all over with frightful blotches. Mary had no patience, and could not control herself, but picked her face so much, that, when she recovered, instead of being pretty, she was as plain a girl as I ever saw. During her illness, Sarah Gardner visited her frequently, and comforted her. On these occasions, she never forgot kindly to tell Mary of her faults, pointing them out not as trifling errors, but as great sins; and directing her, in simple language, to "the Lamb of God that taketh away the sin of the world." When Mary Merton was well, her mother was silly enough to tell her that, though she had not so pretty a face as she once had, yet she had the finest head of hair of any one in the parish; and Mary became as proud as ever. But poor Mary's troubles were not ended, for in this world we cannot sin without sorrowing; "God is of too pure eyes to behold iniquity," and he is too good to look to his creatures to allow them to sin without chastising them.

> Thus when a flock has gone astray,
> And wolves are watching for their prey,
> The shepherd still, his flock to hold,
> Will fright them back into his fold.

Mary Merton was asked out to a party of young people, at a distance; and though it rained very hard, she obstinately persisted in going there, with light clothing and thin shoes. Mary's principal reason for going was to show off her fine flaxen hair. She got wet, took a cold, which was followed by a fever, and all her beautiful hair fell from her head. Deprived of the gift she had made so poor a use of, she became fretful and repining, tormented her silly mother by her bad passions, and was as well known for her ill temper as Sarah Gardner was for the sweetness of her disposition.

Remember, my dear young readers, that we were to try to improve this year; learn, then, from this account, how much more valuable is the mind adorned with Christian graces, than the body adorned with fleeting beauty. Like Sarah Gardner, be diligent in every duty you perform; but, above all, seek the grace of God; for had not Sarah Gardner done this, she had never shown so many Christian graces as she discovered in her life. A life of faith in the Saviour will probably be followed by a peaceful death, and is sure to be succeeded by an eternal life of peace and joy. Remember how closely the present life is connected with that which is to come, and give your young hearts to the Lord your God, for his power is great; his truth extendeth from one generation to another; and his mercy " endureth forever."

Sarah Gardner remained at the hall respected by every one; for she continued to be not only a faithful servant to Lady Rose, but also a servant of the Most High. One day, as Lady Rose looked out of her drawing room window, she saw Sarah Gardner walking down one side of the shrubbery with Mary Merton, who had called at the hall. "Ay," said Lady Rose to herself, "if I had known as much of these two girls when they were at the Sunday school together, as I do now, I should not have called Mary Merton a *lovely girl*, but Sarah Gardner."

CHAP. LXIII.

REMARKS ON RELIGIOUS EDUCATION.

In a call I once made on a lady well known as an humble Christian, and much devoted to the care and religious instruction of her children, the conversation turned upon this interesting and important part of a mother's duty. Her children seemed early ripening for heaven; and she could calmly view the approach of sickness and death, which had taken two of her lovely children from this world; for she knew they had only " gone before " to a happy inheritance.

I inquired how she thus early obtained such an influence over her children, and interested them so strongly in their duty, and in religious instruction. She replied that she had always supposed it of the first importance that mothers should have the entire confidence of their children; that into all their little troubles, as well as pleasures, a mother should enter with ready sympathy. She made a point of devoting a few minutes to them as soon as possible after she returned from a walk, a meeting, or a visit, and endeavored to relate something which should interest all, even the youngest. This habit also improved her own powers of observation and attention. Her mind was on the alert; no little incident passed unnoticed, which might be made to convey some moral or religious lesson. She never attempted to give religious instruction to a child *merely* because she herself happened to be in a frame for it; but if the circumstances were such as to render the opportunity favorable, she endeavored not to let it pass by unimproved. If any act of kindness or benevolence attracted their notice, she would give it its due commendation, and bring to their minds the greater benevolence and kindness of God to them and all his creatures. If they witnessed or heard of a scene of suffering or distress, she would hear their story, and then lead their awakened feelings to the scene of Christ's sufferings and death; and I believe the opportunities thus watched and improved were blessed, in an uncommon degree, in calling up their attention, and impressing their minds with the importance of the subject.

If a child committed a fault, she would gently explain to it that it had done wrong; but she would endeavor, if it was one which exhibited unkindness, ill humor, or impatience, to convince it that the greatest sin in conducting thus was committed against God; and he only could bestow that forgiveness which would give them peace and happiness. In such a case, she would, if possible, pray with them, or, if circumstances were such as to make it proper, the elder child would pray with the younger.

If a child, through carelessness or accident, did any mischief or injury to any thing, she thought that in many cases immediate punishment would give the impression that it was the injury done, far more than the habit of inattention or carelessness, that was noticed; and great caution should be used in such cases. If the child had been previously *forbidden* to touch or play with the injured article, and the case was one of *decided* disobedience, she inflicted punishment for that, and not for the harm done; if an act of forgetfulness had occurred, or an instance of the want of care, the child in fault was deprived afterwards of some pleasure or indulgence which it valued, and, by calmly explaining the reason, the lesson was more strongly impressed. The following is an example.

"May I have on my hat and go with Jane?" said a little boy of four years old.

"No," said the mother; "I want you to go up stairs with me, while Jane is out."

After they were alone, the mother says, "Charles, you like to walk with Jane very much, and see all the things in the street. I like to have you go out and be happy; but yesterday you were disobedient. I let you go in the court to play, for you promised me you would not go out of it; and you disobeyed, and went into the street."

"I forgot it, mamma."

"I know you did; but you must learn to remember; and so to-day you must not go out, but stay in my room while Jane takes her walk. I am now going to be busy. Here is a little book which has some pretty pictures in it; now you may sit down here, and be still till I am ready to go down stairs."

With regard to very early religious instruction, my friend made some remarks which pleased me much.

She said it seemed to her, that, in attempting to begin to

store the minds of young children with religious truth, there was one great and irreparable mistake. As soon as a child begins to speak, it is taught hymns, or short texts of scripture, or even a simple prayer, in which the name of God is introduced; and these he is allowed to repeat in a light and careless air, entirely inconsistent with the words he uses. "Every parent knows," continued my friend, "with what interest the first lispings of childhood are watched, repeated, and made a subject of amusement. Children are continually brought forward to tell a visitor what they have learned from the Bible or hymn-book. This kind of display is wrong where even the sentiment uttered is one, at which we may innocently smile, and is understood by the little prattler; but it is far more injurious when solemn and serious words, taught to a child at this early age, are repeated in such a way. As it grows older, can you expect any exhortations of seriousness to produce the desired effect? You talk to the child of God. He is told, perhaps, that God sees him when he is naughty; that he is displeased with him for disobedience or ill humor. All this is felt by the mother, and is said with a seriousness which the solemnity of the truth would naturally produce; but if the words employed have before been often used in a light and playful manner, which has called forth many a half-smothered laugh or suppressed smile, they will not easily afterwards make any serious impression. If a child learns words only to express ideas, or, rather, only as fast as they can be explained to him, and the first religious truths be simply conveyed, in a serious manner, and when he is not engaged in play, how much greater is the probability that they will sink into his heart, and hereafter bring forth the desired fruit!"

Let all who have any thing to do with children remember how important is every step. It is no easy thing to eradicate ideas once given; and every parent should be doubly watchful lest, in endeavoring to bring her child to God, she does not, either by precept or example, do away the effect which she intends to produce.

In my frequent visits to different families, I have, with interest, watched the various methods and ways of giving children religious instruction, or leading them to their duty, which have been very useful; and I shall give some anecdotes which will interest and instruct some of my readers, who have the important charge of immortal souls, not merely to train and instruct for duty in life, but for eternity.

A young mother once pursued the following course with a child of less than three years old, who had not been good during her absence of a few hours.

"Mamma, where have you been?" said she, when her mother entered.

"I have been to walk, and have had a very pleasant time. Shall I tell you what I saw?"

"O yes; tell me."

"Well, first tell me if you have been a good girl?"

"Sometimes I have; but I cried, and I tore that little book you gave me."

"I am sorry you tore it. When I gave it to you, you promised me you would be careful, and not tear it."

"If you will give it to me now, I shan't tear it."

"I cannot, for I can't trust you. I can't believe you."

"Believe me?"

"Yes, I am afraid you will not keep your promise."

"But I shall keep my promise;" looking up sorrowfully. "Will you give me the book again?"

"If I was to give you the book, and you were to say, 'Mamma, I wont tear it,' and then I was to go out, and you were to tear it while I was gone, that would be breaking your promise. I should be very sorry to have you do that; for it would displease God, and make us unhappy. You cannot have the book now; so do not ask me again for it."

The child had been, a few days before, told distinctly the nature and guilt of breaking her word; and this was the first time it had been referred to.

The conversation ended here. At night, when she knelt

down to say her prayer, she, as usual, inquired, "What have I done that is naughty to-day?"

"You must think," replied her mother.

The child then repeated her usual prayer, closing with, "I pray God would forgive me always,—and when I tore the book,—and that I may not do so any more;"—and looking up, she added, "I am very sorry; I won't do so again."

More than a year after this, the child saw the torn book, and recollected her fault.

I recollect hearing a mother one day telling a child of about two years and a half old, in a very simple manner, the story of the disobedience of Adam and Eve.

"Must I eat apples?" said the child.

"Not if you are told not to, for that is disobedient. It is naughty to take any thing you have been told not to touch," replied the mother.

"Will God be displeased with me?"

"God is always displeased when children are disobedient."

"Does God love me now?"

"God loves you when you are good, and obey your father and mother quick and pleasantly."

The child seemed for a minute studying this truth; and as soon as her mother desired her to get down and go away while she was busy, she directly and cheerfully obeyed, and found her own amusement in another part of the room.

Lucy was just six years old. One day she was sitting on a little stool by the side of her mother's chair, and reading the last chapter of St. John's Gospel. "Mamma," said Lucy, "what did Christ mean when he told St. Peter to feed his lambs?"

Mamma.—My dear, do you not recollect reading some time ago, that Christ said he was the Good Shepherd, and that his people were the sheep?

Lucy.—O yes, mamma, I recollect reading that: but I forget where it is.

REMARKS ON RELIGIOUS EDUCATION.   315

M.—It is in the 10th chapter of St. John.

L.—Stop, mamma; please let me find it. O here it is, the 14th verse—"I am the Good Shepherd." I suppose Jesus said so.

M.—Yes: and it is also said in the Bible, "He shall feed his flock like a shepherd; he shall gather the lambs in his arms, and carry them in his bosom."

L.—But, mamma, I do not quite understand this. Christ is not now upon earth; and when he was here, he did not keep sheep.

M.—No, my dear; but it is to make us understand that our Lord takes care of his people, as the shepherd takes care of his sheep; and he does not forget children, as the shepherd does not forget his lambs.

L.—But who are his lambs?

M.—You, my dear Lucy, are one, if you love him and believe in him as your Saviour, and seek to do his will in all things, and are willing to follow his word.

L.—O, mamma, I should like to be one. How happy and quiet the lamb seemed to be, that we saw the shepherd carrying in his arms the other day!

M.—Well, then, my dear love, pray to the Saviour. He said, "Suffer little children to come to me, and forbid them not." Pray to him that he may give you a new heart, which will be happy in loving him, and obeying his word, through the power of the Holy Spirit, which he has promised to give to all that ask it; and try to be a good girl, and to subdue all naughty and unkind tempers.

Lucy again thanked her mamma; and as she had finished her lesson, she went and put her book away in its place. This story will have little readers. I hope they will remember this, for it is very untidy to leave books, littering about, upon chairs or the floor. She then took her work, and went and sat down by the window, and began to sew very busily.

Just as she had begun, her little brother Samuel came into the room. He went up to her, and said, "Lucy, dear, if you please, will you cut out this paper stag for me? I have drawn its legs very nicely, as you see; but I am afraid I shall not be able to cut them out properly, they are so very slender; and I want to put them on papa's table, before he comes home, to surprise him."

I am sorry to say, that instead of doing this directly, and in a kind manner, Lucy frowned, and said, in a short, sharp tone, "How troublesome you are! You are always teasing me. I have just sat down to work, and I am too busy; go and do it yourself."

Little Samuel was a good boy; and, instead of returning a sharp answer to her sharp speech, he said, "Lucy, please do cut it out, you will do it so much better than I can; and it will not take you a minute." Lucy put down her work, and took up her scissors; but when people set about a thing in an ill humor, they never do it properly; and this was the case with Lucy. Her brother had taken a great deal of pains to draw the stag very nicely; but she cut it out very carelessly: and presently poor Samuel saw that one of its legs was cut quite off.

"There," said he, "there, my poor stag; it is quite spoiled: you have cut its leg off."

"Finish it yourself," said Lucy, throwing the stag one way and the scissors another. "It is all your fault: you ought to have let me go on quietly with my work, and not come to interrupt me, as you always do."

Poor Samuel looked quite surprised: he was sorry to see his nice stag spoiled, but he was still more sorry to see Lucy so out of humor; and he could not think it was his fault. Indeed I have generally found that when people are very ready to blame others, the fault has commonly been their own, after all.

"Lucy," said her mother, "is this like one of the little lambs we were talking about? Remember, my child, God sees you; and do you think he is pleased that you should speak in such a manner to your brother? Is that following the example of Christ?"

Lucy felt that she was wrong, and burst into tears. Her

mother took her upon her knee, and said, "Lucy, now you see it is necessary to pray to the Saviour, to give you a new heart, and to enable you to subdue all naughty and unkind tempers, and that you should try to do so. Do you feel happy because you were so cross and out of humor?"

Lucy was now really convinced that she had done wrong; and that, if she had behaved to Samuel as a sister should act to a brother, she would neither have spoiled his stag, nor have done what was a great deal worse. I mean, she would not have given way to a naughty temper, quite contrary to what the Bible tells us—"Be kindly affectioned one to another, with brotherly love." "O, mamma," said she, "I do feel very sorry, and I will pray to the Saviour."

"That you may be one of his lambs," said her mother, "do this really from your heart, and then you will feel more happy. For God is very kind to us, and we ought to try to be the same to others. Remember Christ said, "All things whatsoever ye would that men should do to you, do you even so to them; for this is the law and the prophets."

Lucy kissed her mother, and went to her little desk. She then took out a very pretty drawing of a basket of fruit, and gave it to Samuel, saying, "Here, Sammy, pray take this instead of your stag that I spoiled, and this besides:" she then gave him a kiss: he gave her another, and then away he ran, quite consoled for his loss."

"Not far from our village lived Susan Woodward. No mother could be more kind; her children loved and feared her, and she taught them betimes, to the best of her knowledge and ability, the love and fear of God. She kept her little family from evil company, of which there was a great deal in the village; and though she knew herself but little of the explanation of religious truth, yet one thing she knew, and that she carefully taught her children: it was the great truth, "that Jesus Christ, the Son of God, came down from heaven, to lay down his life upon the cross to save sinners." It would have gladdened your heart to see this poor, simple-hearted woman getting all her children around her, and talking to them of this Saviour, and trying to gain their attention.

All her children treated what she said with great respect; but upon *one* it made a yet deeper impression.

He was only five years old, and was particularly interested in what his mother said about Jesus. The history of his coming into the world to save sinners, deeply affected his little heart, and brought tears into his eyes: he anxiously inquired how that could be, and how Jesus's people were to be saved by Jesus. Susan had not much knowledge or clear views, but she simply told him it was by repentance, and gave one of her own illustrations. "God," she said, "writes your sins in a book: suppose, then, 'a little boy told a lie;' but then if he is sorry, God writes ' but he repented of it;' and so,'" said she, "it is forgiven."

CHAP. LXIV.

RICH AND POOR.

Riches and poverty are relative terms, and often very mistakenly applied. That the titled possessor of a splendid mansion and spacious park can fail of being a *rich* man, would no more enter the mind of a superficial observer, than that the tenant of a low cottage on the side of the moor, with one room on the ground-floor and two above, can be any thing else than a *poor* man; but the acute observer of human life will probably find reason in each instance to adopt a very different conclusion. The very same amount of income, that, in one man's esteem, would be reckoned abundance, to another would appear as destitution; besides, the outside show that excites the admiration and envy of the vulgar, is often purchased at the expense of comfort and independence. The word *riches* is derived from one signifying *a kingdom,* or *to rule,* because *riches* and *power* are intimately connected; and it is supposed that he who has abundance of money can command whatever he wishes, to gratify his desires or to please his fancy. *Poverty* is that state in which a person is abridged of the conveniences of life. Taking along with us these two definitions, we shall peep at the interior of several family residences; and it is probable the scales may vibrate, if not completely turn in our judgment of rich and poor.

Yonder tasteful cottage is the property of A——, a tradesman in the bustling part of the city. By industry and frugality he rose from very small beginnings. His wife was active and managing. In busy times she sometimes lent a hand in the operative part of the business, and was often seen behind the counter. Trade flourished; and A. congratulated himself on being able to enlarge and new-front the shop, to extend his connections, and increase his establishment. At this time the family usually took their meals in the kitchen; and Mrs. A. sat at work in a small back parlor, where she could overlook the shop. The first floor was divided into three comfortable bed-rooms; over them were three attics of equal size, occupied by the apprentices and maid-servant. But when the shop was new fronted, two or three of the neighbors, who before had regarded Mrs. A. as a mean, drudging person, quite beneath their notice, now condescended to speak, if they met her in the street, and at length went so far as to invite her to one of their tea-parties. Mrs. A. was mightily pleased with the distinction thus conferred upon her; but when she thought of proposing the honor of this visit being returned, she was greatly perplexed at the idea of having no other room in which to entertain her guests than the little back parlor, with a window peeping into the shop. For a year or two this was a source of vexation to Mrs. A.; and now and then it gave rise to altercation with her husband, who very justly remarked, that he could not extend the ground on which their house was built, and that if he could, he should much rather add to the shop or the bakehouse than to the parlor:

"besides," added he, "if you had a larger parlor, you would want more furniture, which I'm sure we can't afford to buy; and if your parlor was any where else than it is, how would you be able to attend to the business?" This was all very sound reasoning; but the truth was, Mrs. A. had imbibed from her new acquaintance an idea that it was vulgar for her to assist in the business, and her mind was often ruminating on some plan for gradually releasing herself from the confinement, and also of obtaining a room more worthy of the accommodation of her friends. These projects, however, she was obliged to defer, having just wheedled her husband into compliance with her assertion, that her two girls ought to be allowed to add to their *accomplishments* those of music, French, and drawing. Poor A. looked very long-faced when he saw the addition of these items in the school-bill, but was pacified, or at least silenced, by his wife's observation, that not only were these things very genteel and desirable acquirements, if her daughters, as she hoped, should be brought into society as young ladies, but they were quite essential to qualify them for taking situations as governesses or teachers, which would be the only genteel way of getting their own living. This difficulty surmounted, the next grand object was to get the two front bed-rooms converted into a smart drawing-room. A. pleaded the expense and inconvenience that must attend this project; but Mrs. A. endeavored to convince him that the expense would be but trifling, and that they could do very well without those bed-rooms. They could remove to the back room which their little girls had hitherto occupied, and there was plenty of room to put up their bed in the garret beside that of the maid-servant; and even the accommodation of a friend might be arranged for by means of a sofa-bed in the drawing-room. Mrs. A. congratulated herself on her excellent contrivances, and poor A. was at last won over to comply. After several weeks of confusion, by reason of workmen in the house, Mrs. A. beheld with delight her tasty drawing-room, and for the first time felt not ashamed of receiving her tea-party. Her guests were quite as loud as she could desire in their admiration of the improvements; but a few qualifying expressions of comparison left a vague but mortifying conviction on her mind, that the carpet, and the looking-glass, and the sofa, &c., were not quite so handsome as those of Mrs. B. and Mrs. C., or as she had at first imagined them; beside, there was one grand deficiency, which rendered the drawing-room very incomplete, and Mrs. A.'s satisfaction at least equally so : there was no piano-forte. This next became the grand object of ambition; and many a solitary musing had Mrs. A. on the practicability of obtaining this desideratum. She had once or twice ventured to hint the matter to her husband, and hoped it might be brought round in time; but the bills for alterations and furniture proved so far beyond the previous calculations, and occasioned so much dissatisfaction, as convinced her the project must be deferred. Besides, the expenses for dress and housekeeping had so much increased since Mrs. A. had been in the habit of visiting and receiving visits, that, instead of frequently depositing a few pounds in the bureau, (a resource which had often enabled A. to take advantage of a favorable turn in the markets,) almost all the ready money of the shop was consumed as fast as received. Often a pound or two went secretly to the milliner or the mercer, and some bills were left unpaid, which, however, Mrs. A. flattered herself she should soon be able to surmount, when she had just accomplished the one additional expense of getting the piano, and when her husband's angry feelings about the late alterations had subsided.

About this time, a distant relation left the A—s a legacy of a few hundred pounds, with an expression of his approbation of their industry and frugality, and his desire to assist them in enlarging their business and bringing up their family. The will had been made two years or more, and it was generally supposed that, since the alterations in A.'s house and manner of living, with which the old gentleman was greatly disgusted, he had intended to make some alteration in the manner of his bequest. However that might be, a sudden illness precluded the fulfilment of any such intention; and, to the great joy of Mrs. A., they found themselves in the unshackled possession of the legacy, which came, as she observed, most opportunely, just as her eldest girl was about leaving school, and when they could not possibly do any longer without a piano. It was not without a gaze of wonder and a sigh of regret, that A. saw so large a dip into one of the hundreds bestowed on what appeared to him of very little use; but as his wife had set her mind upon it, and the money came from her relation, he submitted without a murmur. It is not always that persons are richer for an accession of property. Not unfrequently, common report magnifies hundreds into thousands, (it is only adding a cipher,) and a correspondent enlargement of expenditure is expected from them. If people are weak enough to regard such expectations, nothing is more likely than that they should be plunged into embarrassments, instead of finding themselves more at ease. Poor A. found this to his sorrow. His wife now considered it quite out of character for her to be seen in the shop; and fresh expenses were continually represented by her friends as absolutely necessary to people in their circumstances. At the year's end, so far from finding the interest of the legacy adequate to the increased expenses, it was found necessary to infringe still further on the principal. Besides the expense of an additional journeyman to assist in the bakehouse and serve in the shop, as Mrs. A. had formerly done, it was found that the flour, and other ingredients, did not go nearly so far as when the mistress was not above superintending affairs; nor was the till found so productive since she had deserted the little back parlor. Frequent suspicions arose, which, however, could not attach to any individual servant; and things went on with the mortifying conviction that the family was daily impoverished and defrauded by imperceptible means; and poor A. sometimes felt an apprehension that, instead of keeping his carriage, according to the prediction of some of his neighbors, his name would one day appear in the *Gazette*. But all this while he bore the reputation of being a rising, flourishing tradesman,—a supposition fully supported, in the opinion of superficial observers, by the dashing appearance of his wife and daughters, and always most fondly cherished by themselves. If ever A. hinted to them his apprehensions, or expressed a wish for greater industry and frugality on their part, he was always talked down with assertions that he must be very nervous to think of such things; and that they *must* be going on well, considering how much the business had increased, and especially considering their cousin's legacy, of which Mrs. A. declared she had *only* used one hundred for her own gratification, while many people would have insisted on spending the whole in making a better appearance. As to assisting in the business, Mrs. A. was from day to day more and more persuaded that it was quite out of the question, as neither herself nor her daughters enjoyed good health, and as she was fully determined that her girls should not stoop to any thing so vulgar. Poor woman! she would not admit the repeated testimony of a skilful medical man, that health was sacrificed to irregular hours, and to sleeping in close and crowded apartments; she could not be induced to recollect how robust and cheerful she was herself, when stirring about in her shop and kitchen, and while taking frugal meals and seasonable rest; nor would she admit the idea that her girls imbibed far more vulgarity from the conversation of the servant, who was their regular associate and confident, than they would have done in employments of real utility. Indeed, whatever notions of gentility the young ladies or their mamma might entertain, a real judge could discern no superiority in their conversation and manners; the only distinction between them and the maid-servant consisted in gayer dress and whiter hands, as exercised only in thrumming the piano, instead of the useful employment of washing the linen and scrubbing the house.

Extravagance, and a desire to make an appearance beyond circumstances, are usually attended by meanness. It was so in the family of A. Formerly, their servants had found a comfortable home, and a liberal, though frugal, supply of all their wants; and the circumstances of the neighboring poor had often been met there with kind consideration; but display dried up the springs of liberality. Mrs. A. had no longer time to attend to the cases of the poor, nor any thing to spare for their relief; and whenever her husband appeared dissatisfied at the frequent demands for money, it produced a few days' altercation in the house about the extravagance of the servants and apprentices, and the stinginess of the mistress. Her own little monthly and quarterly contributions to designs of civil and sacred benevolence were first deferred, and gradually dropped; and the annual contributions, which poor A. had long with grateful pleasure produced, were now suffered to be called for again and again, until the collectors were weary and discouraged; yet all this time the general impression was maintained, that the A—s were getting up in the world very rapidly. This impression was confirmed by the purchase, a few years after, of a cottage a mile out of the town, which, together with repairs, alterations, and furnishing, somewhat more than exhausted the remainder of the legacy. It occasioned many a pinch; but Mrs. A. was sure it would prove a saving in the end, for she began to think that her health suffered from living in a confined part of the town, and it would be much cheaper to have a country house near at hand, than to make annual journeys to watering places. Many persons, when they have a favorite object in view, make all their calculations on one side of the question. Thus Mrs. A. almost overlooked the increased expenditure of two establishments, and the additional degree in which the business must necessarily be intrusted to servants, with a long list of other expenses and inconveniences, too numerous to be inserted in a scheme for obtaining the point at all events. Suffice it to say, the point was gained, and in due time the family removed to the country house. Hitherto the charge of extravagance had rested principally with the female part of the family, and its head was chiefly to blame for want of firmness in resisting the encroachments of imprudence; but at length, A. began to yield to the conviction, that he ought to set up for a gentleman. He accordingly invited parties to visit him at his cottage; and it need scarcely be said, that the wine parties of the gentlemen were fully as expensive as the tea-parties of the ladies. Another feature of A.'s gentlemanship was keeping an expensive horse and two or three dogs; and disinclination for business kept growing apace with the relish for company and amusements. The consequence may be easily imagined;—the investigation of affairs became less and less inviting,—A. less and less prompt and punctual in fulfilling his engagements,—and those with whom he had been accustomed to do business less and less inclined to trust him.

On one occasion, whisperings and surmisings ran pretty high against A.'s stability; but a friend came forward to his assistance—the cottage was mortgaged—and things went on apparently straight again. Some faint attempts at retrenchment were made, with a view to recover unshackled possession of the little estate; but they proved very short-lived. Mrs. A. was fully determined that whatever retrenchments were made, should be out of sight, where they could excite no suspicion among her gay friends of the existing necessity; and her servants, both in word and deed, protested against any curtailment of their allowance. In a very few weeks, expenditure had arisen to its old standard, and Mrs. A., finding herself surrounded with the same accommodations as before, seemed to forget that they were not held upon the same tenure, but that an annual sum must be raised for interest on the mortgage, to say nothing of the desirableness of gradually clearing off the principal. With the most thoughtless vanity, prudence, principle and real comfort were continually sacrificed to appearance; and many a pound was wantonly alienated from its legitimate object, lest people should suspect they had it not to spare. Indeed, to meet Mrs. A. and her daughters in the street, or to glance at the furniture of their dwelling, or the provisions of their table, no one could entertain such a suspicion; but the servants of the family, and those connected in the way of trade, received very different impressions. Several years passed on, of struggles between meanness and extravagance—between the displays of vanity and the secret shifts of embarrassed circumstances. The deceptive bill system, from which honest A. once shrunk with abhorrence, was now eagerly adopted. And he who had long acted on the principle of making no bargain except when he had resources in the bureau to meet it, and who seldom had to turn aside from an advantageous offer, was now driven to deal where he could obtain the longest credit, though he should be furnished with inferior articles, and on less advantageous terms. Old and respectable connections in trade were gradually breaking up—business neglected, and customers displeased. Outward appearance, however, was still maintained; and though a few, who knew and lamented the real state of affairs, anticipated the downfall of these victims of display, the unthinking many still regarded A. as a rich and flourishing tradesman, and his wife and daughters among the first ladies of the place. But truth will come out—the interest on the mortgage had not been paid for several years, and the mortgagee, irritated by repeated promises, made only to be broken, called it in. This brought affairs to a crisis—and the *tasty cottage* has the auctioneer's bills sticking on the windows, announcing the sale of the house, together with the *elegant modern furniture*, upright grand piano-forte, beautiful bay horse, &c. &c. Mrs. A. and her genteel daughters, where will they find a shelter? Are they to be reckoned *rich* or *poor*? They, no doubt, feel themselves in circumstances of deplorable destitution; and yet even now their circumstances are not hopeless, could they but be roused to exert the old-fashioned virtues of humility, industry, self-denial and content. Time will prove whether troubles have a salutary effect, and whether or not, five years hence, they may be the richer for their present poverty.

Who has not visited a stately mansion and extensive park, the whole of which bears the aspect of splendid poverty? Who has not been told that the noble owner, in early life, gambled away all his then present possessions and future reversions—that he is restricted now to an income of a few thousands a year, and often reduced to the most mortifying privations and retraints—and that there is not an industrious peasant in the neighborhood but feels himself a richer and more independent man than his lordship?

Another affecting example of the change of these relative terms, is in the following authentic and well-known anecdote:—A respectable widow lady, with a very small income, which she was obliged to eke out by the produce of her own industry and ingenuity, was remarkable for her generous liberality, especially in contributing to the cause of religion. When any work of pious benevolence was going forward, her minister hesitated to call on her, lest her liberal spirit should prompt her to contribute beyond her ability; but she was always sure to find out what was in hand, and voluntarily to offer a donation equal to those of persons in comparative affluence, accompanied by a gentle rebuke to her minister for having passed her by. In process of time, this lady came into the possession of an ample fortune, greatly to the joy of all who knew her willing liberality. But it was with no small degree of regret that her minister observed she no longer came forward unsolicited to contribute towards the good cause, and that, when applied to, she yielded her aid but coldly and grudgingly, and sometimes excused herself from giving at all. On one occasion, she presented a *shilling* to the same cause to which she had formerly given a *guinea*, when in a state of comparative poverty. The minister felt it his duty to expostulate with her, and remind her of her former generosity when her means were so circumscribed. "Ah! sir," she affectingly replied, "then, I had the *shilling* means, but the *guinea* heart; now, I have the *guinea* means, but only the *shilling* heart. Then, I received from my Heavenly Father's hand, day by day, my daily bread, and I had enough and to spare; now, I have to look to my ample income; but I live in constant apprehension that I may come to want!" Can any reader be at a loss to decide which was the time of her *poverty* and which of her *riches?*

In yonder neat, modest dwelling reside B. and his family. I know not the amount of their income—but they may fairly be reckoned rich. Their house, though small, is convenient, and always in good repair. Their furniture is plain, but sufficient, and adapted to its use. Their table is well spread, though with simple and frugal fare, and surrounded by those who enjoy a healthy and unsophisticated appetite. They keep no servant; but the industrious and judicious mother has brought up her girls to the management of domestic affairs. Each has a general knowledge of household economy; but, at the same time, each has a regular department assigned her, according to her peculiar turn. Thus the whole business is performed with order, ease, and regularity. One manages the pantry, and another the bed-rooms; one is an adept in making the clothes of the family; another superintends the laundry; and one excels in the management of the younger children, and in attendance in the sick room. One of the sons cultivates the garden, and another manages the brewery and the home-made wines. The dress of this family is of a piece with all the rest. The materials chosen are good of their kind, and durable, and they are made up in a neat and becoming manner. A foolish fashion is never servilely followed, nor a decent fashion designedly opposed. In whatever engagement a member of this family is found, the apparel worn is suited to the occasion. By the way, this gives one an idea of their being well supplied; whereas, if a person is seen about domestic work, dressed in finery, (perhaps dirty finery,) it gives one the idea that they have nothing else to put on. It must be added, that when any deserving case presents itself, whether for the relief of distress, the diffusion of knowledge, or the promotion of religion, B. and his family are never backward in lending their aid; and their contributions, on the average, double those of their more showy but less substantial neighbors. Though the B—s are thus domestic in their habits, their minds are not uncultivated. Their library is select and valuable, and they possess intellect and taste sufficient for enjoying and improving it. It is generally supposed that B. has a little store in reserve for placing out his children in life, and as a provision for old age; and whatever be the contents of his purse, industry has furnished it, and frugality has found the strings. Perhaps it would be no easy matter to find a richer family than this, in the true sense of the word.

From a lower rank in society some pleasing instances may be selected. A laborer, in a stone quarry, with a large family, is justly reckoned one of the richest men in the parish, which, it should be observed, contains but few inhabitants, and most of them wretchedly poor, though possessing means of competence at least equal to their neighbor. How can this be accounted for? C. is an industrious and sober man: he neither idles his time nor squanders his money: besides this, his wife and children, instead of being a burden to him, are really a source of income. It is a great thing for poor people to have a bit of land; that is, if they are inclined to turn it to account; if not, it might as well be on the common. Now C.'s cottage, though in other respects a poor place, had this advantage. It was situated on the sheltered side of a high hill (I say *was*, for the old cottage is not standing now). The floors and walls were of mud, the roof roughly thatched, and a ladder was the only way of access to the upper room. Many people wondered that such a decent young couple as C. and his wife should take such a poor place; but it had several recommendations in their esteem. The rent was low, only twenty-six shillings a year. Mrs. C.'s aged parents dwelt in the cottage adjoining, and by settling so near, she was enabled to minister to their comforts; moreover there was a slip of waste land which C. thought he might obtain leave to cultivate. A good character for honesty, industry, and sobriety, generally proves a sufficient passport to the esteem and good will of discerning neighbors in the higher classes of society; and most country gentlemen would much rather encourage and accommodate a spirited man in his endeavors to support a family in honest independence, than contribute to the relief of the poor in the degraded character of parish paupers. The lord of the manor, who was also C.'s landlord, readily granted the desired permission to him. He worked early and late to get the land in good condition, and succeeded in raising an abundant crop of potatoes and cabbage for the supply of both the families. The cottager's next step in the scale of comfort, is to keep a pig. By working hard and living frugally, this industrious couple soon saved enough money to purchase a pig, and, with merely the expense of contrivance and labor, reared a place for its reception. It is probable that at first they calculated nothing from the land beyond raising vegetables for the supply of their own family; but the idea soon suggested itself to them, that it might be made yet more profitable. In order to this, it was desirable to get it on a tenure more secure than mere sufferance, which might do very well while the same lord of the manor lived, but which might prove very insufficient under his successor. With considerable hesitation C. mentioned the matter to his generous patron, who most readily granted him a lease for seven years, without any increase of rent on account of the garden, and, moreover, offered him, if, in the course of that time, he could raise thirty pounds, to make free to him the two cottages, and the land he had taken into cultivation, the whole comprehending nearly an acre. The worthy couple joyfully set to work, securely to enclose their little estate, and spared no pains to render it productive and profitable, stimulated by the hope that they should one day possess it as their own, and leave it for an inheritance to their children's children. They had now a family rising round them, and at a very early age the children were accustomed to contribute something to the general support. The little ones were often seen with their wholesome, ruddy faces, and neatly-mended clothes, collecting manure on the common, or weeding a bed in the garden, or carrying vegetables to the town. From the situation of the garden, it was favorable to early production, being sheltered by the hill from the north and east winds, yet airy and open to the sun. Hence they had cabbage, lettuce, broccoli and radishes to dispose of while they would obtain a good price, as well as abundant crops of later productions. Each year this garden became more profitable, as the fruit-trees, which they planted mere twigs, came into full bearing, and the asparagus beds became productive. It will be concluded that such success was not the result of industry alone, but of industry, frugality and perseverance combined, and acting under the direction of sound judgment. Without a plan, great exertions may be made to little purpose. The plan of these industrious people was, as soon as possible, to obtain entire possession of the estate, and, meanwhile, not to alienate from that grand object any part of their savings for mere self-indulgence; but, at the same time, not, in over eagerness to complete that purchase, to withhold what was necessary for the real advantage of the land. On this system they were content still to mount the ladder staircase, and to inhabit the rough-floored apartment, though they hesitated not to purchase convenient tools for the garden, manure for the cucumber-bed, and seeds and plants of the best kind, to begin with, trusting to their own care and attention to procure a good succession for the future. Though the principal part of the garden was devoted to vegetables, flowers were not neglected. A few flowers are easily collected : by getting a few seeds or slips as opportunity offers, a good variety may soon be obtained. Mrs. C.'s first flower-bed was nearly stocked by the children picking up the sweepings which were cast out at the back gate by the squire's gardener, to which additions were made, from time to time, by one friend or other. The situation being favorable, and proper attention being paid, C. and his wife soon became famous for their success in raising flowers of all the common kinds. A few nosegays were sent to market every week through the first season, which, to say the least, cleared a few weekly pence ; and, what with the produce of the garden, and of the bee-hives, (a source of profit not to be overlooked in so favorable a situation,) together with the sale of a porker, when C. paid the first of his seven years' rent, he had the pleasure of handing to his landlord five pounds towards the grand purchase, beside having maintained his family through the year in decency and comfort far beyond that of the neighbors in general. The next year the garden was considerably advanced in value, and a larger sum was paid; and the third year completed twenty pounds out of the thirty.

It is possible that the good people set their hearts too much on the attainment of their favorite object; for, in this imperfect state, there is no attachment or pursuit, however virtuous in itself, but may be carried to excess, and so become an occasion of sin. When this is the case, a check is often mercifully sent, in the all-wise dispensations of Providence, to remind us that prosperity is not the result of our own exertions merely, and that there are concerns of vastly higher importance than even the supplies and comforts of this life. During the fourth year, C. and his family were visited with sickness. First the eldest boy fell ill, who used to carry the flowers and vegetables to market; then the mother was seized with the fever, and her life hung in doubt for several weeks. The younger children all had it slightly; and, last of all, the father was laid aside. During this time, it will be supposed that the garden was much neglected, and great expense was necessarily incurred. When the family recovered, they exerted themselves to the utmost to get things in order again; but at Michaelmas they found it impossible to carry to their landlord any more than the few shillings of rent. "Well," said Mrs. C., "let us be thankful that we are ready with that, and that we have been enabled to reduce the rent to such a little compass."—"True," replied her husband, "and let us be thankful that, in our affliction, friends have been kind to help us, and that we had a trifle in the house to help ourselves, and so we have been brought hitherto without troubling the parish; and, most of all, if we may hope the affliction was sent in mercy to wean our hearts from this world, and set them more upon a better."

Poor C.'s heart almost failed him when he knocked at the squire's door with only a few shillings in his bag, instead of five or seven pounds; but he comforted himself with the thought, that it was not through idleness or extravagance, but through affliction. His landlord received him most kindly, and, to his great astonishment, desired him to put the silver in his pocket again, for any little comfort that might yet be required, and, together with a receipt for the year's rent, gave him a discharge for two pounds, on account of the purchase, adding, "This is a smaller sum than the proportion I have paid, in the shape of poor-rates, for other families visited with the like affliction; and I feel the highest pleasure, in assisting those, who so nobly struggle to maintain an honest independence." The poor man hastened home with a full heart, and, having informed his wife and family of their landlord's kindness, read to them that beautiful Psalm, "Bless the Lord, O my soul, and forget not all his benefits," &c. Psalm ciii.

During the next winter, Mrs. C.'s aged father died. He had struggled hard to lay by a trifle, which, in case of the sickness either of himself or his wife, might serve to keep them, without applying to the parish. Sickness to him was not expensive, for he died suddenly; but his little hoard provided decently for his funeral; and, henceforth, the widow took up her abode in the family of her daughter. The additional room of her cottage, with its little furniture, contributed greatly to the comfort of an increasing family, and, together with her assistance in looking after the children, was considered a full equivalent for her board. Her kind and motherly domestic aid left her daughter more than ever at liberty to attend to the garden and market. The season was favorable, the crops productive, and at Michaelmas the striving family had the happiness of paying off the remainder of the purchase money, and receiving from the worthy landlord a regular investment of the little estate as freehold property. C. was now regarded as a substantial man among the neighbors. Some wondered, and some even envied his *good luck*, as they called it, who were not disposed to imitate his industry and frugality, which, under Providence, were the real sources of his success. It is pleasant, however, to know that this worthy example has not been without effect in stimulating other families to bestir themselves, to endeavor to better their condition.

It will not be supposed that so enterprising a spirit had exhausted itself on the attainment of one object. A donkey, to carry the vegetables to market, was soon obtained. The next object was to improve the comfort of the dwelling-house. By persevering diligence and frugality, and by going the most economical way to work, both with materials and labor, the two old shattered tenements were taken down, and a neat stone cottage erected soon after the expiration of the seven years originally proposed for the purchase. Since that time, the wealth and comfort of the family have been successively increased by the possession of two cows and a horse, and by renting an additional acre of ground. Notwithstanding his success in life, C. still continues to work at the quarry, in which he is promoted as an overseer among the rest of the men. The garden and farm are chiefly managed by Mrs. C., with the assistance of the two boys. She has now for several years driven to market her own cart, well loaded with butter, eggs, and poultry—the finest vegetables, fruit and flowers of all kinds in season, besides plants, seeds, roots, and young trees, for all of which she finds a ready sale. Thus this family, by the blessing of God on their own industry and forethought, is well lodged, well fed, well clothed, well taught—has the means of supporting an aged parent in comfort—something laid up for a rainy day, and always something to spare to help forward any good cause—and if this is not a *rich* family, we may look far before we find one!

D. once possessed a place under government, and with his wife and family lived in the first style of elegance. A splendid house, a numerous establishment of servants, costly entertainments at home, and fashionable amusements abroad, kept full pace with his large and flattering income, and left no reserve in store for any unforeseen change of circumstances. After several years of prosperity and luxury, D. and his family experienced a sudden reverse. A change took place in public affairs, the party from which D. received his appointment was suddenly thrown into the shade, and D., like his employers, must give way to successors. This vicissitude brought in full view the real state of his circumstances. His expensive style of living had exceeded his large income, and it was only by selling his beautiful country house that he could close accounts with his creditors. He had the good sense and principle to take this honorable step, and at the close of affairs found himself possessed of a sufficient sum for the purchase of a small farm, where he immediately settled with his family, and only one man-servant and one maid. The change of situation and circumstances was at first keenly felt by the female part of the family; but by degrees they became habituated to their new duties, and felt a growing interest and pleasure in them. At the close of the first year they congratulated themselves on the accession produced to their health, cheerfulness, and independent enjoyments. They contrasted the grandeur, the beauty, the harmony of nature, with the splendor of the crowded ball-room; and the heart-sickening insipidity and insincerity of fashionable circles, with the pure pleasures of domestic life; and they mutually confessed, that they felt themselves unspeakably richer and happier on their little farm of three hundred a year, than on their former courtly income of several thousands. So true it is, that "a man's life (that is, enjoyment of life) consisteth not in the abundance of the things which he possesses."

We read in Roman history of a celebrated epicure, named Apicius, who spent immense sums of money on the indulgence of his luxurious appetite. At length, having reduced his finances to *two hundred and fifty thousand crowns*, he poisoned himself for *fear of starving—poor* miserable wretch! Contrast his scale of poverty and riches with that of a poor pious woman with four small children, who thus expressed herself:—" My husband earns seven shillings a week in ordinary times; at haymaking and harvest, eighteen pence or two shillings more. When I can get field work, I can earn sixpence a day, four days in the week; but I pay threepence a day for having my children looked after. So we have but a *moderate income;* but the Lord makes us very comfortable with it. No poor people can be happier than we are. It makes a great difference since we knew the Lord." Another poor, old, crippled man in a workhouse declared he lived like a prince, and wanted for nothing; and on a friend presenting him with a half-crown, he burst into tears, and exclaimed, " It is too much—I am afraid the Lord will put me off with my portion in this life."

How lively is the picture given us in scripture of one who was elevated to the highest rank by his sovereign's favor, possessing abundance of wealth, a numerous family, and success attending all his enterprises and designs, yet rendered miserable by the workings of a malignant passion within! He told of the glory of his riches, and the multitude of his children, and all the things wherein the king had promoted him, and how he had advanced him above all the princes and servants of the king, and how he alone was invited to a banquet with the king and queen. But he added, " Yet all this availeth me nothing, so long as I see Mordecai the Jew sitting at the king's gate." Esther v. 9—13. Was Haman a *rich* man?

Another affecting instance is given of one whose grounds brought forth plentifully, and who was perplexed within himself, not how he should provide for his daily bread, or for the wants of a growing family, but " because he had no room where to bestow his fruits and his goods." At length he resolved to pull down his barns and build greater, and then to solace himself with his possessions. " Soul, thou hast much goods laid up for many years. Take thine ease, eat, drink, and be merry. But God said unto him, Thou fool! this night thy soul shall be required of thee: then whose shall those things be which thou hast provided? So is every one that layeth up treasure for himself, and *is not rich* towards God." Luke xii. 15—21.

In closing this sketch, which the writer hopes may have suggested some useful hints of industry, prudence, moderation, contentment, and liberality, it is especially desirable to lodge in the mind of the reader a conviction that the following particulars are essential to true riches; that our possessions, be they more or less, should be acquired by lawful means; that they be used with moderation and constant reference to God —with feelings of gratitude to Him as the author and giver of all—with humble prayer for his blessing upon all—with a habitual sense of our responsibility to Him for the improvement of all his gifts—with pious resignation of all to His disposal, either to continue or remove—and, finally, the possession of a portion which death cannot sever from our grasp, nor the fire of the last day destroy.

CHAP. LXV.

MY OWN WAY.

There was one little cottage, near Cotman Deen, that attracted my attention: it had not the outward marks of any thing like expense, nor even those little indulgences which the poor can often with propriety afford themselves. But a little garden in front was neatly cultivated; the pink and carnation bloomed green on its borders; thyme, daisies, and southernwood, were to be seen; and roses, that scented the evening air with their perfumes, shaded the rustic portico. An aged female sat spinning beneath it.

Tired with my ramble, and delighted with the decent look of the place, I lifted the latch of the little gate that led into the garden, and going towards the seat at the door, asked the old woman if she would allow me to sit down, and rest a few minutes. She readily agreed, and we began to converse.

" You have a comfortable, quiet little abode, in which to

spend your old age," said I. She expressed her gratitude to God for it, and added, " It is more than I deserve, for I have been a rebellious child to that God who has led me, these many years, in the wilderness."

" How old are you?" I asked.

" How old am I ?—ah, Miss! I have arrived at the end of our time here ; my strength is labor and sorrow, as the wise man said, for I am fourscore years old."

" And can you not say that goodness and mercy have followed you all the days of your life ?"

" Yes ; they have followed me, gone before me, restrained, encouraged and brought me to this last stage. I was young once, and, like most, *I loved my own way;* but God, in mercy, generally imbittered it to me ; and if I persisted in following it after the sad consequences had been felt, he brought me back with weeping and supplication.

" My good old father and mother often told me, that I must learn to submit my will to the providence of God ; but I heeded not their counsel as I ought : I loved the world and its gayeties, and never felt so well pleased as when finely dressed, and in the midst of light and thoughtless young people like myself. The wake, the fair, and every opportunity of village dissipation, I eagerly embraced.

" Once—I remember it was on a fine summer's day—my poor old father had gone to his work, and my mother was spinning as I may be now : it was fair-day, and I was going there. I came down our little stooping staircase, very smartly attired for the holyday. My mother looked at me from head to foot; I thought she seemed not quite pleased with my purpose, and yet felt a mother's exultation in the appearance of her child.

" ' Now you'll mind where you go, and with whom,' said she, ' and be sure you are home before dusk.'

" I met my companions, and in the fair, a young man joined our party, who knew some amongst us. He was very attentive to me, and before I quitted the company, I had become, perhaps, a little interested in him.

"In a few months after this we were married; but this step was taken against the advice of my parents, the voice of conscience, and the dictates of common prudence. My husband was in the habit of getting intoxicated; but since our courtship, and for a little time after our marriage, he gave up the alehouse. Then he made such fair promises, and laid such pleasant schemes, that I believed him, rather than my parents, who judged from the past, and dissuaded me gently and kindly from the step. But I trimmed my new hat with ribands, and bought my new gown, and went to church to promise to honor and obey a man, whom certainly I loved as far as passion goes, but whom I could neither respect nor take for my guide through life.

"My poor old father and mother went home with us to a little cottage which my husband had decently furnished, and left us not till God's blessing had been implored.

"I thought now I should be quite happy, and that for once my mother would find *my own way* to be right. Things went on well at first; my husband brought me home his wages regularly, and as I laid them out as carefully as I knew how to do, we lived comfortably, and put by a part. I added a little poultry; I sold my eggs, and reared chickens. I also prepared my husband's meals with neatness and comfort, when he returned home from work.

"But still I loved *my own way*, and when it happened to interfere with his wishes, I carried my point against all reason. At last my husband used to give up; but I thought he did not seem to love his house so well as before; he was always engaged to play at bowls, or quoits, with his shopmates, which at last I found was nothing but an excuse for going to the public-house. I felt discouraged, and asked why he again gave way to sins he had so faithfully promised to avoid. He said he would mend; but continued to promise and relapse. I had indulged in many purchases of a useless and showy nature in my furniture and dress, that I never saw at home; but the approaching birth of my first infant led me to be more careful; for my husband's earnings, I found, were not all brought home to me, as formerly. I felt joy in the prospect of becoming a mother; and a certainty that his babe would so take his attention, that my husband would be a changed character. The hour of my trial approached. My babe was a lovely little creature, and my husband also loved it; he was very proud of it, and liked to stand with it in his arms, and hear folks say, ' What a lovely child it is!'

"The wages were again brought in punctually, and then I felt sure that *my own way* was right.

"But in a few months 'my little son!' was an old story, and again the alehouse was the centre of attraction. About this time my baby was very ill; I had given up my poultry, and had therefore no store of my own to apply to. I wanted medicine for the child, which was expensive, and little preparations that were needful on such occasions: and now came the first pinch. I saw my babe languishing with heavy eye and feverish skin, and had not money to procure for him the little comforts I thought would do him good. I flew into a passion with his father, and told him his conduct would kill his child and break my heart. He told me I might have had what I wanted but for my idleness in giving up my poultry-yard. This exasperated me, and a burst of tears was my only relief. I sat watching my infant through the night, and, solitary as I was, could not help acknowledging to myself that this was the sad effect of having *my own way*.

"But little Charles looked better at the glad return of morning—his eye was less heavy, his dimple and smile again sweetly cheered my anxious heart. I gave him his scanty breakfast of coarse fare, and he dozed off gently to sleep again.

"My gloom dispersed, I thought I should not care for any thing if he but lived. My wish was granted, and God spared the child of an ungrateful parent; and I once again saw him run to meet the return of his poor, unhappy father.

"It was now with difficulty I could provide our table with food, and keep the remainder of our clothes tidy and whole.

But the reflections I had, during my Charles's illness, led me not to upbraid my husband so violently as I might have done had I not seen that all was caused by my having *my own way*.

"The birth of a second child was to put my economy and contrivance to the test. I again strove to provide things comfortable; but it was no such easy matter—very little was brought me by my husband, and I found, that, besides his drunkenness, he was in the habit of gambling. I had, as long as I could, from pride, kept all from my mother; I knew my parents had but very little, and I could not take from them. But now, worn out with fatigue and sorrow, I went to pour out my grief into my mother's bosom. I found her in her neat kitchen, all tidy, though poor. She was reading, 'O that my people had hearkened unto me, and Israel had walked in my ways; I should soon have subdued their enemies. He should have fed them with the finest of the wheat.' I sobbed out the tale of my wo; and I confessed to my mother that I felt my sorrows arose from my obstinacy in having *my own way*. I asked her if God would forgive me, and lead me in his own right way, if I sought him.

"'Alas, my child!' she said, with tears in her eyes, 'you have indeed forsaken the fountain, and hewed out to yourself broken cisterns that can hold no water. But yet return to God: he may, he will have mercy upon you. He will seek after and restore the wandering sheep, and has but imbittered your own way, that you may return unto him: "I will hedge up her way with thorns, that she shall not find her paths."

"I told my mother how ill I was: she soothed and advised me. I told her how I was grieved to see my husband's conduct, and that I feared his inveterate habits would eventually wear him out, for I saw disease already taking hold upon him. I told her I was poor, and had not needful supplies for my situation—she promised to help me, and she kept her word. Above all, I told her I feared God would call me to judgment at my approaching hour of trial. I felt I was a sinner, and should perish, and leave behind me, perhaps, two dear little helpless children.

"I returned home to my cottage, comforted by my good old mother's conversation. I put my child to sleep, and sat down to work, and when my husband returned, drunk as usual, I made the best of my desolate situation, and tried to recollect the scriptures my mother had read to me. As my trial approached, I begged that God would spare my life for the sake of my family, and determined that I would exert myself to support them in some way, that we might not wholly depend on their father for bread. But after the birth of my infant, I continued so ill that I could not put my plan into execution, and I thought God was going to call me to give an account of my actions—I dreaded the thought.

"Day after day, as I lay weak and languishing, did I meditate on the self-will and folly that had brought me to all this. The little nourishment I took was provided from the scanty means of my poor parents. It was a wretched house; for in it drunkenness and swearing abounded, and want was pressing hard upon us. Slowly I began to mend, and thankful was I to find myself once more seated in our little room below. But it was not what I had made it when we married. My gay carpet had been sold for bread; four of my chairs were gone; and the whole appearance was now bare and comfortless.

"I had now two children to provide for; my husband's health was sinking under excess, and oh, how heart-breaking was the prospect before me! With the little money he brought me I endeavored to manage, till my recovery was completed; and then I knew not what step to take for bettering our condition. I had no money; my baby prevented my going out to seek employment; and I began to sink into despair. At last I bethought me of my mother's remedy—prayer. I determined to beg of God to help me to some relief, and to give me strength to bear up under all my trials. It was evening. I had nursed my infant to sleep, and, as she lay quietly by me, I kneeled down, but I uttered not a word;

I could only sigh and weep forth the burden of my heart. The night was tempestuous; the wind, in gusts, shook our little abode, and the rain was pelting violently against the casement. I looked out to see if my husband was returning; but, unable to discover any thing, I sat down supperless, to wait his arrival. In the dead of night I thought I heard a deep groan near the door-way, and, looking out, discovered my husband in a state of insensibility; I ran to a neighbor, and obtained assistance to lift him in doors; but was shocked beyond measure to find, on seeing his face by the light, that the ghastly hue of death was spread over it. In his dying moments he had uttered the groan that had roused my attention. My mind was all distraction—I had loved my husband even in the midst of his profligacy, and this, with the distressing uncertainty as to his future state, nearly overcame my reason; moreover I was a widow, and my children orphans. Oh, when I saw the coffin carried from my wretched door, when I found myself alone in abject poverty, then I saw the folly of *my own way!*

"My poor father's cottage received me again, not what I had left it, a blooming, gay, thoughtless girl, but a widow, a mother in distress. As I used to sit nursing my baby on the old garden seat, where the playdays of my childhood were spent, many a bitter tear has fallen, many a heavy sigh escaped me. To this period, however, I look back with grateful feeling, as one in which I learned much that was good; and while I acknowledged the folly of having *my own way*, the Almighty turned the curse into a blessing, and led me, in the midst of my distress, to seek refuge in Him. I was gradually enabled to see that in Christ alone solid happiness was to be found; and seeking eagerly from the lips of my mother that instruction I had so often despised, I tasted some of the enjoyments of true religion; but alas I was not yet brought simply to the foot of the cross.

"While I was toiling to assist in our support, my little Charles was growing a fine, tall, healthy boy, turbulent in disposition, and often I found it difficult to manage his temper. My father and mother often told me that I was suffering my children to get the better of me, and that one day or other I should repent it; but I thought they were only like all children, and like what I once was. I loved them so dearly that I made a thousand excuses for them. If they troubled me, I gave them a slap, and talked loudly to them of what I would do; but I never took the trouble to administer proper correction; indeed, my system partook more of idleness than of a wise concern for their welfare. Charles's headstrong temper often made his grandfather sigh, and give some wise counsel to me; but I loved *my own way* still. I thought time would do what I indolently neglected, and that as he grew older he would behave better. His conduct at divine worship disturbed the congregation; in the neighborhood he was mischievous; and to me he was very often tiresome; yet there was nothing about the boy but what, under the divine blessing, timely chastisement might have subdued, and brought into good order.

"My Susan, a lovely little girl, seemed to give fair promise of being my chief comfort. I denied her nothing, whether resonable or unreasonable; and when she threw her little arms round my neck and kissed me, all the mother's feelings rose tumultuously in my breast; I longed to bring her up to a higher station, and make her more than her mother had ever been; but my means were few and contracted. I now labored for them, and I hoped to rise and lift them with me into a higher station. I could read, write, and work well, and by the advice of my parents and friends, I opened a school for the village children. Unfit as I was for the charge, I got forward; I had an increase in a few months of so many, that I could afford to place Charles daily with a respectable person, to learn to read, write, and cast accounts, while my little Susan sat by me, and learned, or was idle, as it happened to suit her inclination.

"My father gradually sunk in the vale of years, and infirmity after infirmity crept upon him, till at last, without any positive complaint, he sunk into the sleep of death. His last hours, like his whole life, were consistent; he had no new religion to seek, but the firm foundation on which he had rested his hope supported him in a dying day. He found consolation in the Saviour; the hope which had cheered his life supported him in his dying hour.

"The day after the funeral, which my numerous though humble school enabled me to see decently conducted,—I shall never forget it,—the clergyman stepped in as we were just sitting down to our tea. 'What an interesting sight!' said he; 'how in the appearance of this cottage circle is the pattern of life portrayed! Here,' pointing to Susan, 'is the dawn of life, knowing no real ill, and sporting on the very verge of a scene of trial, soon to be entered upon, unthinkingly. There,' said he, pointing to me, 'is the traveller in the burden and heat of the day, often overpowered by the toil of the journey, anxious to provide for and rear the offspring God has given. There,' pointing to the corner in which my dear aged mother sat, 'is one who has passed the sultry hours; a few steps farther, and her toils are ended. And there,' pointing to the empty arm-chair, the old stick, and the hat that hung upon the wall, 'there are the staff and sandals laid aside.' May each follow close in the steps of this aged Christian, and arrive as he did at the Christian's end. My children, love and fear your aged parents' God: my young friend, walk in the steps of your holy father, and beware of having *your own way*. To you, my venerable friend, what shall I say? Look forward and rejoice that there is a rest awaiting you; and to the happy spirit, were it possible, I would waft the congratulations of a sincere heart.'

"My mother now gave up her labors entirely, and attended only to my little household concerns. I shall here pass over several years of my short, chequered pilgrimage: Charles was eighteen, Susan was seventeen, and not quite so affectionate to her mother as when, a laughing child, she used to clasp me to her with delight. I had allowed her to *love her own way*, when it was only a trifling inconvenience to me; but this temper had grown with her growth and ripened with her years, and now she formed an attachment to a young fellow, which I saw, with anguish, would lead her through the same scene her wretched mother had passed. But Charles was wringing my heart with more bitter anguish—still froward in childhood, he had become ungovernable in youth. A desirable situation, procured for him by our clergyman, was thrown away in a fit of mad folly to go to sea. Oh, when I went with him to the vessel, saw him step upon its deck, and when he bade me adieu with a tear struggling in his eye, as if half inclined to repent, how did I bear it! It was of him I was so proud; for him I had offered my first prayer; for him I had labored many a weary day; his whims I had indulged, his folly in childhood and wickedness in youth I had failed to correct; and now he could blaspheme, and was plunging headlong into ruin.

"I turned away from the scene, sick at heart with sorrow excited to the extreme. It was at the close of the day, in the latter end of autumn; I passed several windows, where the fires were blazing cheerfully, and the happy family parties collecting round the tea-table; but no cheerful fireside was waiting my return. My mother was sleeping silently by my father's side, in the church-yard; my boy was going to dare the dangers of the deep, with all his sins upon his head; and my girl, my lovely, blooming girl, was going wilfully to unite herself to a fascinating, but deceitful man, who, I saw, would bring her to poverty and disgrace. 'And this,' said I, ' is *having my own way*. I was warned, but I would not see, or correct the faults of my children; I brought them up with no consistency; I refused to check their foibles, till they grew into sins, and were past my ability to control. O that I had taken advice, that I had attended to the law of God, rather than to my own way! O that I had taught them to honor me in childhood! I should not now have to weep over their ingratitude, and live to see their ruin.'

"I returned to my solitary abode—it was dark and dreary. My daughter was pleasure-taking with some idle acquaintance; I kindled a little fire to give something like cheerfulness to the dismal room—dismal, not for want of outward comforts, but from my own mental agony; and I sat ruminating upon my desolate situation; and bitter and cutting was my self-reproach, for I knew that having *my own way* had brought all this upon me. As I caught a glimpse of myself in an old glass that hung opposite, I could not help comparing it with the bright, blooming, gay girl that used to appear in its face, and the declining, grief-worn widow I saw there. But my mind felt a keener agony when I recalled my neglected duties and self-will.

"Susan, in spite of me, married her wretched admirer, who in less than three months treated her cruelly; and for two years I used to sit, after I had sent away my little flock of children, brooding on her distress, and on the hardships and dangers my boy was contending with. No letter from him arrived, and I began to conclude that God had called him to his awful bar. Susan, pining away from poverty and ill-treatment, was led to her mother's sad acknowledgment, that she had been wrong in having *her own way*. But I saw her struggle against the tide of afflictions; I saw her, with subdued temper, bow at the foot of the cross, and maintain before one, who met her but to abuse and ill-treat her, a line of conduct becoming the principles that now guided her—she lingered long in a decline, and I laid her at last beside the two green hillocks in the church-yard. I had *my own way* with her in childhood, and it ruined her happiness; but while I repented of having *my own way*, I thanked God, who had overruled my misconduct, and had converted her by his grace, and then taken her to himself.

"But, ah! my poor boy—seven years passed, and I neither saw nor heard from him; I had given up all hope of ever meeting him again. I had just sent away my young charge one summer's evening, and was sitting down to my table, my Bible open before me, my coarse loaf and my tea prepared —a slight-made figure appeared at the door. Hectic was the flush on his cheek, and disease had set its mark upon him; but it was my boy—yes! I knew my Charles—years of foreign imprisonment, hunger, poverty, disease itself, could not obliterate that look by which I knew him. And while I wept at the tale of his woes, and charged myself with his sorrows, by allowing him *his own way*, I had to rejoice that he was taken from me, to be taught by a stranger's tongue, in a distant land, the error of his way, and *the way of eternal life*.

"Eight months he lay upon a sick bed, sighing over his past follies, yet looking to the Lord Jesus Christ for mercy. He lies with my Susan, my father, and my mother, in yon church-yard. One little corner still remains for me; and as the last ebbing sand runs out, I would tell to all around, the wisdom and goodness of God, and THE FOLLY OF MY OWN WAY!"

CHAP. LXVI.

ONLY FOR ONCE.

This is an expression of every day occurrence; we must not say *use*, for it generally proves the reverse of useful. It is never applied in reference to an action clearly right, but very often as a palliation, or excuse for something very questionable, if not decidedly wrong or foolish. But until there is no sin or danger in doing a wrong thing *only once*, nothing can be more foolish than the attempt thus to justify it. The fact is, that what it would be wrong to do often it is wrong to do at all. Very serious mischief results sometimes from only one foolish action. Besides, *only for once* generally opens the door, and paves the way for the frequent repetition of what is wrong.

This silly phrase is a perpetual source of mischief in

families. A few real examples both of a more trivial and a more serious nature will be presented in this sketch, and, it is hoped, will not prove either uninteresting or useless.

A young domestic, on entering a new place, received from her mistress particular directions as to the manner of doing many things to which she had been unaccustomed. Among other things, she was taught how to clean a handsome French lamp, and especially charged always to dust the glasses, and leave them in the place where they then stood, while she carried the lamp down stairs, to trim or fill it. Not very long after she came, just as the evening was drawing in, she met her mistress on the landing place where the lamp stood, and with some agitation said, "Ma'am, are you going to light the lamp?" "Yes." "Because, ma'am, it is broken." "What is broken?" "The great outside bell-glass." "How did that happen?" "When I was down stairs a cleaning of it, I let the scissors fall and broke it." "But why did you take it down stairs? I desired you never to do so." "I never did before, ma'am; but I forgot to bring up a duster, and I thought it would not hurt to take it down *only for once*, and then I just happened to break it—it was so unlucky." "No, it was careless, not unlucky; you also neglected my commands: you now remember that neglecting and disobeying orders may lose you a good place. It will cost me twelve shillings to replace the glass, and though I am sorry for the loss, I am more so when I see any want of attention in a girl to faithfully obey the orders given her." Does any young servant think it was not worth while to say so much about a lamp glass? She should be reminded that, by such acts of destruction and waste in servants, their employers find their means of doing good very much circumscribed. Twelve shillings would have afforded very acceptable relief to six poor families; perhaps her own family has known the time, if it is not so at present, when two shillings' worth of bread, or meat, or coals, would have been no trifling present. Besides, it is not the one accident and expense that is the extent of the mischief, but the many evils arising from the habit against which it is our object to guard them.

Another servant, a nursemaid, was sent out to walk with two children, one in arms, the other between two and three years old. She had been most strictly charged never to enter into any house, or join any person in conversation, when she had the children with her. Perhaps some one may say, " Why should her master and mistress be so very particular ? Why may not a servant speak to her acquaintance as well as another person? What harm could it do if she went into a decent person's house?" It may be replied, that a servant is bound in all lawful things to obey the orders of her employers, without asking questions; and that there is no particular in which implicit obedience is more required than in the care of children. All good parents make it their study to adopt the best plans for managing their children; and they have a just right to expect that those employed by them, in this important business, should not thwart their designs, but conscientiously endeavor to promote them. If, however, any further reason is required, take the following :—As the nursemaid in question went along the street with the children, a woman with whom she was acquainted was leaning over the hatch of her door, and Mary stopped a few minutes to chat with her. She might have known she was doing wrong, by the confused, anxious manner in which she looked up street and down, to see that none of the family were coming; but she did not yield to this admonition of conscience. On the contrary, recollecting that her mistress was confined up stairs, and her master was gone to his farm, out of town, she stood several minutes at the door, and at last was persuaded, *only for once,* to step in and look at a very beautiful dress, which Mrs. J.'s daughter had been making for a lady. Meanwhile the little boy stood at the door, and presently said, " *Pa's moo cows.*" " Yes, my dear," answered Mrs. J., " pretty moo cows ;" and continued her gossip. Several minutes more elapsed, and Mary began to think of pursuing her walk; but to her great consternation, the little boy was no where to be found.

She ran hither and thither, but could gain no tidings of him. At last she was compelled to return home, trembling for the consequences of her misconduct, yet fully hoping to find him there; but he had not been seen since he left home, in her charge, nearly an hour before. The poor girl's agony was extreme, and the alarm spread rapidly. It was with difficulty restrained from reaching the ears of the mother, to whom, in her circumstances, it might have proved fatal. The alarm was greatly increased by the proximity of the river, which the child had often attempted to approach. More than an hour of dreadful suspense and anxiety was endured by the relatives of the dear little wanderer; and the dusk of evening was drawing on, when the father appeared gallopping home with the little boy before him. The joy of his arrival may be better imagined than described. It proved that he had followed the cows which he supposed to be his father's, expecting that they were going to the farm; but they belonged to another person, and the poor child, having lost sight of them, wandered on, he knew not whither, and had nearly reached the entrance of an extensive wood, when he was providentially met by an intelligent lad, who addressed him kindly, won his confidence, and conveyed him to his father at the farm.* Poor Mary, though properly reprimanded, was forgiven, and allowed to retain her place; but she could not forgive herself. She felt that she had proved herself unworthy of confidence, and she fancied that she no longer received it. She became gloomy and discontented. Nor was this all; the conversation and the display at Mrs. J.'s awakened in her a love of finery, which she had never before discovered. One showy article and another were secretly purchased, and secretly made up, and secretly worn. (How very silly! What pleasure could it afford?) Then her wages were found insufficient, and she threw herself out of a good situation, in hope of a bet-

---

* It is desirable, as soon as children can speak, to accustom them to speak distinctly their own name and place of abode. In this instance it was the means of the child being so soon restored to his anxious friends.

ter, which, however, she never obtained. This was the consequence of disobedience " *only for once,*" for up to that time Mary was a willing, obedient and contented servant.

A little boy, of very delicate health, lived with his grandmother, who kept him constantly under her own immediate care, and paid the closest attention to his welfare—fondly hoping that, under the blessing of God, all her care would be rewarded in seeing him grow up a good and useful man. It happened that some very particular circumstance called the lady from home for a few hours; and the little boy, having taken medicine, was prevented from accompanying her. She left very strict injunctions with the servants to be particularly attentive to him, and directed every thing that was to be given him to eat. But the maids indulged themselves with some hot bread for tea, and wishing the child to partake their enjoyment, ventured to give him some, thinking it could not hurt him "*just for once.*" The child had never tasted any thing of the kind before, and ate heartily of it, little thinking the price he was to pay for the indulgence. At the usual hour he was put to bed, and, on his grandmother's return, her first concern was to inquire after her dear child's welfare, and to visit his chamber. She was informed that he was quite cheerful and well, and had eaten a hearty meal; but the moment she approached his bed, she was shocked to find him groaning with pain, and insensible. The best medical aid was instantly called in; but in the course of the night the poor child expired; and it was fully proved that his death was occasioned by the indigestible food that had been given to him—food at all times unfit for a delicate stomach, and especially so when under the influence of powerful medicine. The distress of the agonized parent, at the disappointment of her fondest hopes, scarcely exceeded that of the servants, whose injudicious indulgence had been the unthinking cause of so melancholy a catastrophe. Many similar instances might be adduced to prove the folly of tampering with duty *only for once.*

Let us observe also that *souls* are susceptible of evil and danger, as well as natural life and worldly interests. It was *only for once* that a Sunday scholar broke the Sabbath, and spent it, in vain, ungodly mirth, at the cherry feast.* And another, *only for once*, went skaiting instead of attending the house of God. Both met their death in Sabbath-breaking—and—what became of their immortal souls? It was *only for once* that a youth was tempted to borrow a few shillings from his master's till, intending to repay it in a few days; but instead of that he borrowed again and again, till he was detected and disgraced. From one step of vice, he proceeded to another, till at length he committed forgery, and was hanged.

Helen was piously educated. She had been accustomed from her infancy to reverence the Sabbath, and to frequent the sanctuary, and had been taught to discern between good and evil. She was placed at a school where religious advantages were enjoyed in a very high degree, and she left it apparently with a high sense of their value. She attended the house of God regularly, and discovered a great and hopeful interest in the things she heard. It was observed with pleasure that she frequently brought with her a young relative, and it was fondly hoped that her own early promise would ripen into mature excellence, and that she might be eminently useful in extending the influence of the religion she adorned. About this time she received an invitation to visit some relatives at a distance. It was not a pious family, nor could it be expected that the society to which this young person would be introduced, would be of the most profitable kind. But many pleasant circumstances concurred in the invitation—and " it was *only for once*—no *great harm* could result. Beside, it would afford Helen an

---

* In some parts of the country where cherries are very abundant, it is usual for the proprietors of trees, which stand out of any enclosure, to give one or more cherry feasts in the height of the season; that is, on one appointed SUNDAY all the lads in the neighborhood are permitted to climb the trees and eat what they please there, but not carry any away. The poor lad alluded to, ate so freely as to occasion his death in a very few hours.

opportunity of judging for herself, and it might be hoped she would return home more than ever attached to those privileges and those habits from which she had for a while been separated." Such were the reasonings which led Helen and her parents to comply with the invitation. She went, fully resolved to observe the Sabbath as nearly as possible in the manner to which she had been accustomed, and to refrain from joining in such pleasures as she could not in conscience approve. A few weeks tried the strength of her resolutions. Some engagement was made for the Sabbath, in which she could not *well* refuse to join. It *only* interfered with *one* public service, and she fancied that circumstances justified her compliance *just for once*. But was that all? Was it *merely* one service that was interrupted?—*merely* one service! Oh! what would an awakened sinner on the bed of death think of even *one* religious service given up for the sake of a party of pleasure? But it was *not* all. The dissipations of the afternoon obliterated the instructions of the morning: Helen retired to rest with a mind full of worldly impressions, and with reflections and feelings any thing but suitable to the close of a Sabbath-day. From that time principle was weakened, and when a Sunday party was proposed, it was no longer considered necessary to consult Helen's religious scruples. Her compliance was taken as a matter of course. In like manner, invitations to the card-table, the theatre, the assembly-room, and other scenes, unlike her former habits, were first feebly resisted, then yielded to *only for once*, not to seem particular, and at last pursued with avidity and almost without compunction.

After some months Helen returned home; and because she herself was altered, she fancied that circumstances were altered. The quiet, sober pleasures of home no longer seemed interesting—the services of the sanctuary no longer delightful—the preacher was dull, or insipid, or severe. A very slight indisposition or trifling engagement served as an excuse for occasional absence, and a marked and growing indifference, amounting almost to dislike, was manifested towards every thing of a religious nature. At length Helen received proposals of marriage from a gay young gentleman. It could scarcely, with consistency, be made an objection against his addresses, that he was not a religious character, for it was too evident that Helen was not one herself. She, however, felt a kind of consciousness that his company was not good for her, and she never intended the acquaintance to be carried on to any thing like intimacy; yet, when invited to parties where she knew she should meet with him, she consented to go *just for once*, and then *once more*, until her affections were engaged and her honor pledged to a man who could scarcely be injured by being called an infidel and a libertine. The first few years of Helen's marriage were spent in worldly gayety, half relished, half scrupled, or loathed. A family came on. She felt conscious that her children *ought* to enjoy the privileges of her own childhood. But in whatever her husband was indulgent, he was decidedly hostile to the admission of any thing like religion in the education of his children, and Helen herself was too much engrossed in the world to make any decided and vigorous efforts for their good. They were left to the mercy of ungodly servants, and trained in the way they *should not* go. Trouble visited Helen in worldly circumstances, and sickness in her person, and she felt that she was without a refuge—of worldly friends she had indeed reason to say, "Miserable comforters are ye all!" And of religion, she pathetically said, "I know enough to make me miserable; but not enough to make me holy or happy." While her own health was in a precarious state, her husband was suddenly carried off by a brain fever, and she found herself a widow in embarrassed circumstances, surrounded by children whose education and habits left her no ground to expect from them solace or satisfaction; and destitute of such resources in herself, as would qualify her to sustain changing circumstances with composure and grace, and to derive from them solid advantage. Oh, how different might have been Helen's character and circumstances through life! How much personal stability and excellence, and how much relative usefulness and enjoyment were sacrificed in the first worldly compliance, *only for once!*

CHAP. LXVII.

INSTABILITY IN RELIGION.

"BEWARE of itching ears," is a caution which may be given to young and ardent professors of religion.

About two miles from our village, a minister preached, who was famous for saying wonderful, new, and startling things, such as proved very attractive to those who had a smattering of religion, but who were but scantily and superficially instructed in its general scope and bearings, and thus were ready to be carried about with every wind of doctrine. This minister was famous for crying down all the neighboring ministers as dry, dark, cold, and legal. He dwelt much on those matters about which the Bible says but little; laid down his assertions with great positiveness; and regarded all who questioned them as opposers of the truth. He was much more concerned to bring people up to a set round of expressions, or to high-flown notions and impressions of personal revelations and assurances, than to lead them to examine the scriptures humbly and impartially, and, as new-born babes, desire the sincere milk of the word, that they might grow thereby. This person made a great noise for a time, and had many hearers and many followers. *Some*, previously altogether unacquainted with the gospel, were drawn together by curiosity to hear some new thing. Of these, some went away to ridicule sacred things which had been set before them, clothed in rash and coarse expressions; *others* took up a hasty profession of a cheap religion,

INSTABILITY IN RELIGION. 357

which required little more than the adopting a few set phrases, eagerly following their leader through thick and thin, and bitterly denouncing all who followed not with them.

There were others who had begun to run well, but who, on listening to the instruction that causeth to err, were soon transformed from humble, modest learners, to self-conceited and censorious disputants, and such as caused their best friends to weep and to stand in doubt and dread of them.

Very few there were who had resisted—still fewer who had not been tried with the bait—"Do go and hear him, if it is only for once. You never heard such a preacher in your life. How can you know what it is if you have never heard him?"

Among others, I was pressed by two young friends to go and hear this "new light," as he was called. One of these young friends had frequently been, and was wrapped up in her teacher, and spoke with contempt of those to whom she had formerly listened with reverence, delight, and profit. The other young person had been once; she scarcely knew what to think; from some things she had heard her mind revolted; but he said many things that were very good. Her companion observed, that it would be uncandid to condemn for one hearing, or for a few expressions that she might not approve or understand. She ought to go again, and then she would be better able to judge for herself. Thus she was induced to go again and again; every time her mind becoming increasingly unsettled, and unable to profit by the more sober ministrations of her own pastor. She could no longer find spiritual enjoyment in reading the Bible, because, by the new friends with whom she had associated herself, she was taught to read it for other objects than those for which it was given; not that she might be made wise unto salvation, and use it as a light to mark the daily path of duty, but that she might learn to speculate, and dispute, and support a certain set of opinions by a few detached passages of scripture, without regard to the general bearing and practical tendency of the whole. I knew these persons many years, and I lived to see the former altogether abandon her religious profession and attendance on the means of grace. I have heard that she could even utter scoffs at religion; but I cannot bear to admit the thought. The latter was, I believe, a really conscientious woman; but I question if she ever after that period knew much real enjoyment of religion. She was like a bird that had wandered from its nest, and had forsaken her own satisfaction and comfort. She looked shy at her minister, and fancied that he looked shy upon her, or that his ordinary admonitions and cautions were intended as public reproofs of her. Then she would absent herself awhile, and try some other place of worship; or come only occasionally when a stranger preached. By and by she would be convinced that the fault was in herself. Then her mind would be harassed and distressed with apprehensions that she had never known the grace of God in truth. Her own course afforded her no satisfaction. She had too real and deep a concern about her soul to be satisfied with the bold assurance and enthusiastic impressions of which some of her acquaintance boasted, and on which they were content to risk their eternal all; yet she could rarely divest herself of all other associations, and venture, simply, as a poor, perishing sinner, on the mercy of God in Jesus Christ. To the end of her days she was tossed about with winds of doctrine and changeableness of frames. We hope she was saved, though it was "*so as by fire*" or shipwreck. She certainly did not enjoy that *abundant entrance* into the everlasting kingdom of our Lord and Saviour Jesus Christ, which is generally reserved as the especial privilege of those who have held fast the profession of their faith without wavering, and whose religion has been more eminently that of the heart and life, than that of the head and tongue.

For myself, I am thankful to say, that, on the occasion to which I have referred, I was thrown into the way of some good friends in Hawthorn-lane, and was induced to ask their judicious advice, and to abide by it.

"Mary," said one of them, "why is it that you wish to go and hear this Mr. —— ?"

"I don't know, sir, but almost every body does go; and I have been very much persuaded."

"Do those who persuade you think more highly of him than of our own minister?"

"Yes, sir, they say he is a wonderful way before him."

"Mary, I believe you read your Bible?"

"Yes, sir."

"And you pray that God will assist you to understand it?"

"Yes, sir."

"You constantly hear our minister. Do you ever hear him say any thing but what he proves from scripture?"

"O no, sir."

"When he proves any thing from one part of scripture, does it ever seem to contradict another part of scripture? For instance, when he proves that sinners are justified by faith, without works, does it lead you to suppose that it is no matter whether we perform good works or not?"

"No, sir, because he takes such pains to show how it all agrees together, and sets us examining from one part of the Bible to another, and so helps us to understand the whole."

"Is there any doctrine of scripture that you *never* hear explained?"

"No, sir; I have often minded that if any thing puzzles me, I am almost sure to hear something about it just afterwards."

"And do you find that the word you hear is suitable to the state and feelings of your heart?—I mean, when you are distressed with a sense of guilt and danger, do you find that you are directed to the way of salvation and comfort which the Bible alone reveals? And when you are in doubt and perplexity, are you directed in the path of duty?"

"Yes, sir; I have constant reason to be thankful for what I hear in both these respects. I have often come with a drooping heart, and heard that which revived and cheered me; and I have often been roused to the performance of duty in which I had been negligent, or warned of snares and dangers of which I was quite heedless and unaware."

"Then, Mary, do think again, and tell me for what object it is that you want to go elsewhere. It is not for greater edification, for you yourself readily admit that the whole counsel of God is faithfully declared and profitably explained to you. You own you are well off; then, according to the saying, do be content, and let well alone. Mere curiosity is not a worthy motive; nor ought you to be satisfied with asking what *harm* you shall get in going. This question, perhaps, is easier asked than answered. But rather ask, What real *good* am I likely to gain there, of which I am at present destitute? Else, if you forsake the solid, wholesome food with which your soul is at present nourished, there is great reason to fear that you may be left to feed on husks which will not satisfy, or to delight in luscious but unwholesome doctrines, which would tend to surfeit, intoxicate, and poison your soul."

My friend's words had great weight with me; and I resolved not to go that evening. We afterwards had much conversation upon the subject; my friends seemed to know something of the minister and his connections. Both of them said they should be exceedingly sorry to entertain an injurious thought themselves, much more to prejudice others against a good and faithful minister; but from what they knew of this gentleman's sentiments, (I believe he had printed a book or two,) and from the effects they had seen produced by his preaching, they could not but consider his doctrines as having a dangerous tendency. They hoped, however, he might be altered since they heard about him before, and wished they could receive the testimony of some judicious and impartial person. At length Mrs. —— said, "What do you think of sending our old cook and gardener? Though they are not educated persons, they both possess sound discernment; they are well established in the truths of the gospel, not likely to be unsettled themselves, or to bring an unkind report; and yet their testimony might be very useful to younger and less experienced persons." Her husband approved the proposal; accordingly the old cook was called in. "Cook," said the lady, "it is a fine afternoon: should you like to take a walk over to ——, and hear Mr. ——, the new minister? He is said to be a fine preacher." "Thank you, ma'am, if you please, I will go. I love to hear any minister who preaches the precious gospel." "Then, ask Robert, the gardener, to go with you, and take care of you. I dare say he will have no objection." "O no, ma'am; he will be glad of the opportunity. He loves to hear what is good, and will be very glad to know that good is doing to others."

When they were gone, the gentleman observed that he thought it a very different thing to trust two established, experienced Christians, like them, from what it would be to encourage the young to hear what might unsettle and injure their minds.

On their return, he inquired what was the text, and what account they could give of the sermon.

"Why, sir," said Robert, "if you want my account of the sermon, you must just let me give it in my own way. There was a great deal of it that might be very *true*, for what I know; but then, to my mind, it was not worth hearing. Then there was a great deal very *new*, but this was not true. And then there was a great deal (but not so much as there might have been, if the others had been left out) that was both *good* and *true*, but this was not new. The gentleman spoke this just as if it was something of his own finding out, or at any rate as if it had never been preached from the days of the apostles to his own; but I do assure you, sir, there was not a bit of it, but what you may find in the Bible, and what we hear every Sabbath of our lives."

"Well, cook, and what account do you give?"

"Why, really, sir, I can't give much account about it, for, try how I would to attend, it still kept coming into my mind to pray that it might not do any harm. Even when the minister brought forward texts of scripture, they somehow seemed so put in the wrong place, I was afraid people would be taking comfort when they wanted reproof: and so I still kept saying in my heart, 'Lord, grant that it may not do any harm.'"

"Then, do you wish to go again, cook? or do you think you have heard enough for a fair trial?"

"Thank you, sir, I have no desire to go again. I only wish to go to the house of God for real profit; and as to trial, I think it does not become such as I to set up for triers; but if that were all, I think I have had enough for a trial. You remember, sir, what good Mr. Newton used to say—'If a joint of tainted meat comes to table, one slice is a trial; there is no occasion to eat it through to prove that it ought to be sent away.'"

The sentiments of my older and more judicious friends prevailed over the enticements of my younger acquaintances; and from that hour to the present it has been my mercy constantly to find the house of prayer, with which I was first connected, a house of food and satisfaction to my soul; and the sentiment I then adopted I have never seen reason to retract:

> "Here would I find a settled rest,
> While others go and come;
> No more a stranger or a guest,
> But like a child at home."

The above remarks chiefly apply to the folly of following preachers for the sake of hearing something new, and with an evident danger of hearing something questionable; but even where the change is merely from one sound preacher to another, the love of novelty is in itself hazardous, and should be guarded against.

Every prudent Christian will wish to have a *home*; a society on which he has established claims, and to which he is responsible; in which he has obligations to sustain, and duties to perform. This need not be his prison; yet he will seldom feel inclined to wander from it: while cherishing every feeling of good-will towards other denominations, and other congregations, he will habitually be found at home. Though he may sometimes miss an occasional excitement, such an individual will generally be found the most steadily

INSTABILITY IN RELIGION. 363

growing, established, fruitful Christian. "As a bird that wanders from his nest, so is a man that wanders from his place;" but "those that be planted in the house of the Lord, shall flourish in the courts of our God."

In putting together these hints and observations for the use of my children, it has been my desire ever to bear in my own mind, and to impress it on theirs, that the only source of real, genuine, abiding excellence of character, is true religion in the heart,—a life of faith in the Son of God; and that, wherever this genuine principle exists, it ought, and it will, produce attention to whatsoever things are true, honest, just, pure, lovely, and of good report, in which there is any virtue and any praise.

"Let us hear the conclusion of the whole matter: Fear God and keep his commandments: for this is the whole duty of man. For God shall bring every work into judgment, and every secret thing, whether it be good or whether it be evil." "Those things which ye have both learned, and received, and heard, and seen," in the truly consistent Christian, "do; and the God of peace shall be with you." "And the peace of God, which passeth all understanding, shall keep your hearts and minds, through Christ Jesus.'

THE END.

Other Related Solid Ground Titles

In addition to the volume which you hold in your hand, Solid Ground is honored to offer many other uncovered treasure, many for the first time in more than a century:

THE MOTHER AT HOME by John S.C. Abbott

THE CHILD AT HOME by John S.C. Abbott

SMALL TALKS ON BIG QUESTIONS by Helms and Kahler

MOTHERS OF THE WISE & GOOD by Jabez Burns

THE EXCELLENT WOMAN by Anne Pratt

OLD PATHS FOR LITTLE FEET by Carol Brandt

STEPPING HEAVENWARD by Elizabeth Prentiss

SHW Study Guide by Carson Kistner

THE YOUNG LADY'S GUIDE by Harvey Newcomb

WOMAN: *Her Mission and Her Life* by Adolphe Monod

THE KING'S HIGHWAY: *10 Commandments* by Richard Newton

HEROES OF THE REFORMATION by Richard Newton

HEROES OF THE EARLY CHURCH by Richard Newton

BIBLE PROMISES: *Lectures for the Young* by Richard Newton

BIBLE WARNINGS: *Lectures for the Young* by Richard Newton

THE SAFE COMPASS: *Lectures for Young* by Richard Newton

RAYS FROM THE SUN OF RIGHTEOUSNESS by R. Newton

LIFE OF JESUS CHRIST FOR THE YOUNG by R. Newton

FEED MY LAMBS: *Lectures to Children* by John Todd

TRUTH MADE SIMPLE: *Attributes of God for Children* John Todd

CHILD'S BOOK ON THE FALL by Thomas H. Gallaudet

CHILD'S BOOK ON REPENTANCE by Thomas H. Gallaudet

CHILD'S BOOK ON THE SABBATH by Horace Hooker

Call us Toll Free at 1-877-666-9469
Send us an e-mail at sgcb@charter.net
Visit us on line at solid-ground-books.com